When Children Suffer

Published by The Westminster Press

By Andrew D. Lester
Pastoral Care with Children in Crisis
Coping with Your Anger: A Christian Guide

By Andrew D. and Judith L. Lester
Understanding Aging Parents (Christian Care Books)

Edited by Gerald L. Borchert and Andrew D. Lester
Spiritual Dimensions of Pastoral Care:
Witness to the Ministry of Wayne E. Oates

Edited by Andrew D. Lester
When Children Suffer: A Sourcebook
for Ministry with Children in Crisis

When Children Suffer

A Sourcebook for Ministry with Children in Crisis

edited by
Andrew D. Lester

The Westminster Press
Philadelphia

Unless otherwise identified, scripture quotations are from the Revised Standard Version of the Bible, copyrighted 1946, 1952, © 1971, 1973 by the Division of Christian Education of the National Council of the Churches of Christ in the U.S.A., and are used by permission.

The quotation from Proverbs in chapter 10 is from *The New English Bible.* © The Delegates of the Oxford University Press and The Syndics of the Cambridge University Press 1961, 1970. Used by permission.

The quotation from John in chapter 12 is from *Good News Bible: The Bible in Today's English Version.* Old Testament: © American Bible Society, 1976; New Testament: © American Bible Society, 1966, 1971, 1976.

Book design by Gene Harris

First edition

Published by The Westminster Press®
Philadelphia, Pennsylvania

PRINTED IN THE UNITED STATES OF AMERICA

9 8 7 6 5 4 3 2 1

Library of Congress Cataloging-in-Publication Data

When children suffer.

　Bibliography: p.
　1. Church work with children. I. Lester, Andrew D.
BV639.C4W48 1987　　　259'.22　　　87-8165
ISBN 0-664-21327-8

Contents

Contributors

Daniel O. Aleshire, Ph.D., Associate Professor of Psychology and Christian Education, The Southern Baptist Theological Seminary, Louisville, Kentucky.

Regina Andrews-Collette, M.S.W., A.C.S.W., Staff Therapist, Child and Family Outpatient Service, Hall-Mercer Community Mental Health/Mental Retardation Center, Philadelphia, Pennsylvania.

Gary Brock, M.Div., Director, Department of Pastoral Services, Vanderbilt University Medical Center, Nashville, Tennessee.

Kathryn N. Chapman, Ed.D., Associate Professor of Childhood Education, The Southern Baptist Theological Seminary, Louisville, Kentucky.

Sue H. Enoch, M.Ed., Minister of Childhood Education, Crescent Hill Baptist Church, and Elementary Program Supervisor, Kentucky School for the Blind, Louisville, Kentucky.

John L. Florell, Ph.D., Executive Director, Illinois Pastoral Services Institute, Bloomington, Illinois.

Freda A. Gardner, M.R.E., Professor of Christian Education and Director of the School of Christian Education, Princeton Theological Seminary, Princeton, New Jersey.

Allen R. Gilmore, Ph.D., Executive Director, The Pastoral Counseling and Consultation Centers of Greater Washington, Washington, D.C.

Benjamin T. Griffin, D.Min., President, United Theological Seminary of the Twin Cities, New Brighton, Minnesota.

Virginia W. Hammond, M.Ed., Director, Child and Family Mental Health Services, Hall-Mercer Community Mental Health/Mental Retardation Center, Philadelphia, Pennsylvania.

George F. Handzo, M.Div., M.A., Director of Protestant Chaplaincy and Pediatric Chaplain, Memorial Sloan-Kettering Cancer Center, New York, New York.

Charles R. Koch, M.D., Clinical Assistant Professor, Division of Child Psychiatry, School of Medicine, University of Pennsylvania, Philadelphia, and Director, Child and Family Mental Health Component, Hall-Mercer Community Mental Health/Mental Retardation Center, Philadelphia, Pennsylvania.

Andrew D. Lester, Ph.D., Professor of Psychology of Religion, The Southern Baptist Theological Seminary, Louisville, Kentucky.

Wayne E. Oates, Th.D., Professor of Psychiatry and Behavioral Sciences and Director of the Program in Ethics and Pastoral Counseling, University of Louisville School of Medicine, Louisville, Kentucky.

Barbara J. Prescott-Ezickson, M.Div., Staff Chaplain, Hospice of Louisville, Inc., Louisville, Kentucky.

Andrew C. Puckett, Jr., Ph.D., Chaplain for Pediatric Hematology/ Oncology and for the Cancer Rehabilitation and Continuing Care Program at the Medical College of Virginia, Richmond, Virginia.

J. Bill Ratliff, Ph.D., Assistant Professor, Pastoral Care and Counseling, Earlham School of Religion, Richmond, Indiana.

Virginia D. Ratliff, M.S.W., A.C.S.W., Therapist and former Coordinator of Victim Assistance Network, Washington, D.C.

Olle Jane Z. Sahler, M.D., Associate Professor, Departments of Pediatrics and Psychiatry, University of Rochester School of Medicine and Dentistry, Rochester, New York.

Carolyn W. Treadway, M.S.W., A.C.S.W., Pastoral Counselor, Illinois Pastoral Services Institute, Bloomington, Illinois.

R. Wayne Willis, B.D., M.A., Chaplain, Kosair Children's Hospital, Louisville, Kentucky.

1

Ministry with Children in Crisis
Andrew D. Lester

When I was a young boy, a picture hung on my bedroom wall depicting an artist's image of a shepherd living in the ancient Middle East. The shepherd had just rescued a lamb from the clutches of a lion and was now binding its wounds. The artist, of course, as with so many illustrations in Sunday school literature, used the shepherd motif to remind the viewer of the nature of God's love and care. The relationship of the shepherd with the sheep, which includes life-giving and lifesaving functions such as guiding, guarding, providing, caring, healing, and seeking, was characteristic of God's action as experienced in history by the ancient Hebrews. They experienced God's trustworthiness in times of crisis. God was known as protector and intervenor, an ever-present help in times of trouble. In their religious writings and worship, therefore, the Hebrews frequently used the shepherd/sheep analogy for describing God's relationship to the people of Israel.

Surely the most well known psalm is the twenty-third, which proclaims "The Lord is my shepherd, I shall not want . . ." and rejoices in the trustworthiness of God's guiding ("in paths of righteousness"), providing ("preparing a table before me in the presence of my enemies"), caring ("he leads me beside still waters"), healing ("he restores my soul"), and guarding ("I fear no evil," not even when "I walk through the valley of the shadow of death").

The shepherd analogy is also important in the New Testament. In John's Gospel, Jesus says, "I am the good shepherd." Thieves come "to steal and kill and destroy," but the Good Shepherd came that we "may have life, and have it abundantly." A hireling "sees the wolf coming and leaves the sheep and flees" because he does not care for the sheep, but

Andrew D. Lester is Professor of Psychology of Religion, The Southern Baptist Theological Seminary, Louisville, Ky.

the Good Shepherd knows and cares for them and "lays down his life for the sheep."

In both these references, and many others in both Testaments, the shepherd imagery is significantly related to human need in times of crisis. It is easy to see why the shepherd images for both God and Jesus have provided over the centuries a sense of security for many Christians, particularly children.

Despite criticism of ancient shepherding as a valid model for ministry in modern Western culture, many of us envision ourselves faithfully fulfilling these same tasks of guiding, guarding, providing, caring, healing, and seeking. Most of us still would accept the designated role and title of "undershepherd" of the flock. Most of us still see ourselves as intervenors in times of crisis and perceive this intervention to be a major responsibility in our ministry. To this extent the analogy is still significant.

I am concerned, however, that a central figure in that picture from my boyhood room, the lamb, is no longer a major recipient of our pastoral care. In ancient times the lambs were the hope of the flock. They represented continuity with the future and were, therefore, a prime responsibility of the shepherd. It is my experience that in modern times the care of children, particularly those in crisis, has been abandoned by the pastor.

My concern for ministry to children has been growing for a long time. My first experience in clinical pastoral education was at a children's hospital. I will never forget how helpless I felt in caring for those children who were in pain, frightened, lonely, and suspicious of strangers who might represent more medical attention. At a later time I served as a chaplain and supervisor of divinity students in hospital pediatric wards, where I was reminded constantly of how difficult it could be to minister to children in crisis and how many pastors dodged the opportunity.

Like other pastoral counselors, I am impressed by the number of persons who have been through significant crises in childhood without any ministry from the church or from Christian ministers. It is clear to anyone who works in depth with people that crises in childhood can cause problems for people in their teen and adult years: unresolved grief, unnecessary fears, lack of trust, loss of self-esteem, and distorted ideas about both the character of God and how God works in the world. It is also apparent that intervention by a committed, caring minister can enable children to pass through crises with a strengthened sense of self, renewed trust in their coping skills, and a firmer faith in God-who-is-love.

My interest was also sparked by another problem, the lack of resources for the minister who wishes to work with children. For these reasons I planned a sabbatical leave in 1983–84 to study and write about children in crisis. While doing this research I interviewed a number of pastors from many denominations about their ministry to children. Two major conclusions were obvious. The first was stated in the following words:

> *Few pastors give any systematic attention to pastoral relationships with children, even those in crisis.* Many pastors have never structured a pastoral conversation with a child, either in their office or in the child's home, with the specific goal of offering pastoral care during a crisis.[1]

How are we to understand this neglect of children? Why the oversight? Several reasons were obvious from that research.

1. Pastors are the victims of a cultural myth that pictures childhood only as a time of fun and happiness, conveying that children have few serious crises. Childhood is largely idealized in this culture, perceived as a time of innocence.

2. Since they communicate differently from adults, children find it harder to identify and conceptualize their crises. Children are frequently unable to share their interior world with adults, leaving us unaware of those times when they feel anxious, fearful, sad, ashamed, angry, or embarrassed.

3. Because children often express their feelings through play and have a short attention span, some pastors assume that children are unaware of the crises around them, or they perceive that because children are so adaptable pastoral care is not necessary ("She will be okay in the morning").

This lack of awareness is not the only reason why children get short-changed in our ministry of pastoral care. Even when pastors are sensitive to children within the parish who are in crisis, they may hesitate to take the initiative for several reasons.

1. They may perceive dealing with children as the parents' prerogative and feel that any initiative would be taken as interference in the parents' task.

2. They may fear, given today's media coverage of sexual abuse of children, that their concern for a child may be misinterpreted and suspicions aroused.

3. Because children make no tangible contributions to the congregation, such as giving money, providing leadership, or teaching classes, some pastors choose, either consciously or unconsciously, to spend their time and energy caring for those who make more obvious contributions.

4. Some pastors may find it difficult to give ministry to children because they have stereotyped such work as "women's work" and feel unmasculine if they focus care on the children.

The second major conclusion of the interviews with pastors about their ministry with children was the following:

> When they do attempt to provide pastoral care for children, *pastors are usually frustrated by their perception that they lack the knowledge and skills to offer such care effectively.* [2]

Because we pastors perceive ourselves to be inadequate in relating to children, some neglect of children in crisis is simply avoidance of uncomfortable situations. Most of us received little training in the pastoral care of children while we were in seminary or divinity school. Pastoral care and counseling courses, which introduced theories of personality development, therapeutic techniques, and crisis intervention, rarely applied this information to the actual care and counseling of children. Even in specialized courses like Clinical Pastoral Education, care of children was probably not discussed unless the course took place in a children's hospital. Many questions—What do I say? What should I try to accomplish? What does the child need from a minister? How do I make the child comfortable? and How do I help a child participate in pastoral conversation?—have not been explored academically or clinically by most ministers.

This lack of training may leave us without much confidence in our ability to relate creatively with children. We may be self-conscious, wondering if we know enough to be competent and fearful of making a mistake. Our experiences with children in crisis may have been negative, putting us on the spot without anything to say, which provokes anxiety. After being uncertain and uncomfortable in certain circumstances, most of us find ways to avoid such situations in the future.

Despite all the problems stated above, we pastors have a responsibility to care for children in crisis. After all, they are members of the family of God, parishioners for whom we have responsibility for proclaiming, in both word and deed, the whole gospel. They have as much right to receive pastoral care as any adult in the congregation. Jesus demonstrates the importance of ministry to children, and his identification with them, when he says to the disciples, "Whoever receives one such child in my name receives me; and whoever receives me, receives not me but him who sent me" (Mark 9:37). In fact, a case could be made that since so much of their future growth and development is dependent on the successful negotiation of their crises, they should actually be first on our list!

Pastoral Care with Children in Crisis was the result of this research with children in crisis. The book was written for several reasons. One was to discuss the history of the myths mentioned earlier in order to dispel them and heighten the pastor's awareness about the real world of children. The truth, of course, is that children also go through divorce, separations, abuse, illness, death, and accidents. Like adults, they experience guilt, shame, anger, fear, and grief. If ministers become more realistic and sensitive to what many children actually experience in life, they will be more likely to offer ministry.

A second purpose was to plead my case that children are also parishioners and deserve our best ministry. Toward that end my book describes the relationship that Jesus had with children and the place of children in the family of God called the church. It also describes how to involve parents and to protect against arousing suspicions.

The third purpose was to provide information and ministry skills for the care of children that would enable the pastor to feel more adequate and comfortable fulfilling that responsibility. The entire second half of that book was given over to a discussion of how to use art, play, storytelling, and writing in pastoral conversation with children. Activities of this sort give children more freedom to share their inner thoughts and feelings with adults. At the same time, to have a game, a story, or a drawing "in between" the minister and the child makes it easier for the minister to relax and listen attentively to the child.

The response to *Pastoral Care with Children in Crisis* was quite positive. Pastors asked the publisher if something could be written to give more specific help about the particular crises that children experience. This book, therefore, is a sequel to the first, an attempt to meet the need for more detailed information and ideas for ministry about specific crises.

Each author has been chosen because he or she has both academic knowledge and clinical skills developed through years of ministering to children. Part I includes four chapters that will introduce you to the school-age child (like the first book, "children" will refer to those in kindergarden through puberty, about five to twelve years of age). Part II includes nine chapters that deal with specific crises. The authors of these chapters have plenty of experience with children caught in a particular crisis. Each of these authors has described (1) the impact of that particular crisis on the child, (2) the faith issues raised for children experiencing that particular crisis, and (3) specific ideas for ministry in that type of situation. Part III concludes with four chapters that offer thoughts and ideas to increase the minister's proficiency as a caregiver with children.

I would like to express my appreciation to these contributors for the careful work they have created. Each spent significant time and energy writing and revising so that the whole book would have continuity. Many of them were already personal friends and professional colleagues. Others have become friends through this process.

This book is purposely designed so that each chapter stands on its own. You can quickly read a certain chapter to inform a pastoral visit you have to make today. On the other hand, each chapter has ideas, illustrations, suggestions, and principles for ministry with children that are applicable to any child's crisis. After these chapters were gathered, it became clear that there are basic characteristics of ministry with children in crisis which are the same regardless of the situation. Some of these are highlighted below.

Presence. It is difficult to minister to children without being where they are. Your physical presence is the first rule of care. Children are concrete thinkers, and what they see is what they are more likely to consider. It takes initiative, but visiting children in their homes or in places like hospitals and funeral homes or inviting them to your office communicates both your interest and God's involvement. Telephone calls and notes can also communicate your presence, particularly with older children.

Listening. When children feel free to share with you, use all your intuitive skills to understand both their words and their meanings. As many of these chapters describe, it is important to distinguish between those times when the child is asking a concrete question that needs a concrete answer and those times when the question expresses a deeper need that calls for both a specific answer and a reflective question in response. Listening actively means paying attention to both thoughts and feelings. It is a wonderful experience to be in conversation with a child who really believes you understand his or her thoughts and feelings.

Representing God. Most of the children in your congregation will have ideas about you which include that you are related to God in some unique way. Many younger children equate the pastor with God or assume that the pastor has some special knowledge of, or relationship with, God. This is an awesome responsibility but also a wonderful opportunity to address the faith issues that surface for children in crisis. Each author in this book has addressed the specific religious questions and concerns raised by children suffering from that specific crisis. It is amazing how many lifelong concepts about God are formed by children in the midst of a crisis event. We pastors have the opportunity to help them know God as One who loves and cares for them, rather than Someone who hurts or punishes.

Advocate. Children do not have many people standing clearly on their side. As the following chapters will make clear, when children are the victims of disease, accident, disability, divorce, abuse, or family conflict, few people may offer protection. As the shepherd of long ago stood to defend his sheep against those who meant them harm, so must we be social, legal, emotional, and spiritual advocates for the children.

It seems that Jesus and his disciples had a disagreement over the priority of ministry to children. Remember this famous story:

> And they were bringing children to him, that he might touch them; and the disciples rebuked them. But when Jesus saw it he was indignant, and said to them, "Let the children come to me, do not hinder them; for to such belongs the kingdom of God." (Mark 10:13–14)

Whether the disciples thought the children were insignificant, or believed that other ministries (such as healing and teaching) were more important, or were concerned about Jesus' schedule, we don't know. In any case, it was obvious that Jesus felt differently about the children. Perhaps we should remind ourselves more frequently of the example set by the Good Shepherd.

Other aspects of Jesus' ministry with children will be described in the chapters that follow. We will be reminded that Jesus invited children to spend time with him and must have enjoyed talking with them. He felt free to touch and hold them. "And he took them in his arms and blessed them, laying his hands upon them" (Mark 10:16). May this book enable you to develop numerous ways to bless the children, for such blessings are a wonderful way of conveying God's love and acceptance.

NOTES

1. Andrew D. Lester, *Pastoral Care with Children in Crisis* (Philadelphia: Westminster Press, 1985), p. 27.

2. Ibid.

PART I
Understanding
the School-age Child

2

A Developmental Understanding of the School-age Child

Daniel O. Aleshire

A hundred years ago, and for much of human history, children were treated as miniature adults. By age twelve, they were in the fields and mills and factories. They were doing adult work for child's pay. In the past fifty years, however, children in American society have been treated as people very different from adults, almost as a unique genre of the human family. Suburbs, Disney World, and Saturday-morning television have all been invented with them in mind, resulting in major adult work growing up around child's play.

The truth about school-age children is probably somewhere between these two cultural treatments. In some ways children are like adults, and in other ways they are not like adults at all. To see only the wide-eyed Disney World side of childhood is to deny the social and psychological need for the child to develop sophisticated competencies in language, social skills, and physical abilities. To see only the more "adultlike" side is to doom the child to an unimaginative and grueling experience of life. A proper developmental perspective on childhood requires looking in both directions.

Middle childhood (elementary school grades 1 to 6, ages six to twelve) mixes the adultlike and the childlike in ways that baffle parents and teachers. Just when a son has convinced his parents that he really does understand some of life's complexities, he invariably does something that proves the opposite. Just when the exasperated parents think their daughter has succumbed to a terminal Saturday-morning-television worldview, something is said or done that shows insight and understanding "beyond her years."

Many of the debates about children in current American culture deal with this mixture of child and adult. How much special treatment

Daniel O. Aleshire is Associate Professor of Psychology and Christian Education, The Southern Baptist Theological Seminary, Louisville, Ky.

should children receive in our society? How much should we assume they can handle the complex emotions associated with expectation levels for school performance and competition in everything from organized sports to organized beauty pageants to organized spelling bees? Are children being hurried needlessly into adulthood—or at least into adolescence—or does the pace of modern Western society demand accelerated development?

This chapter provides an overview of several developmental issues that emerge during the elementary school years. Since every child is a unique person, no single approach adequately describes the developmental process for all children, so several cautions are in order. First, the child is an integrated person. Cognitive, physical, and emotional development will be discussed in separate sections, but they exist as integrated and interactive aspects of the growing child. Second, what is true for children generically is not necessarily true for each child. Children cannot be lumped together into one commonality any more than adults. The thing the children who are discussed in this book have most in common is a similar chronological age. Third, children do not develop in isolation from the world or worlds in which they live. Much development is best understood in the contexts of family, community, and culture. To grow up the fourth child of Spanish-speaking migrant farm-worker parents is a very different experience from growing up the first child of Anglo parents who work in Midwestern factories. The particular contexts in which children grow interact with the individual characteristics the children bring to their environment in ways that create even more uniqueness and individuality.

Since I do not think there is one all-inclusive way to characterize the development of children,[1] this chapter presents three different developmental characterizations: (1) a brief description of school-age children in terms of their physical, emotional, and cognitive development; (2) a summary of the developmental tasks that should be accomplished during middle childhood; and (3) a summary of some developmentally influential issues in the broader culture and context in which children grow. With each characterization, attention will necessarily be paid to the relationship of developmental issues and the kinds of crises children may experience.

Physical, Emotional, and Cognitive Development

Physical, emotional, and cognitive changes together comprise the most noticeable areas of development in middle childhood. The developmental process in each of these areas is markedly different from what it was in early childhood or what it will be in adolescence and adulthood. Certain risks and stresses are always a product of change in persons, and the developmental process can both cause its own crisis in the child's life and influence the child's experiences of other life crises.

Physical Development

The pace of the child's physical development slows dramatically during elementary school years. During the period of birth to five years, a child's weight increases sevenfold, height more than doubles, and the relative proportions of head size and leg length to overall body size shift appreciably. During the seventh through eleventh years, however, no similar physical rate of growth occurs. The child's weight may double during this five-year period, and height will grow by 20 to 25 percent. These changes reflect a major decrease in the rate of growth.

The result of this much slower rate of growth is that the child has time to develop skills and competencies in the use of the body. The child develops walking and running skills during early childhood, but rapid growth affects body proportions so the youngster is always adjusting and relearning these physical skills. The school-age child's body, by contrast, is changing much more slowly. This allows children the opportunity to become quite accomplished at basic physical skills like running, jumping, catching, and throwing. Children also become skilled in fine motor tasks such as writing and coloring.

Physical growth, however, is by no means uniform. The differences that children experience in their individual rate of growth or physical abilities can have a variety of effects in a child's social world. Some children grow obese. Other children notice the obesity and may treat those children differently because of their size. Some children do not develop the physical abilities that other children do, and they are always the last to be chosen for a team in neighborhood baseball games. Still others grow faster, taller, and stronger than most children. They are frequently tapped by their peers to be leaders because of their size or ability. Adults are also more likely to treat larger, more physically mature-looking children as if they really were older.

Even though children have little control over their physical growth, it affects them in many ways. Sometimes it can create crises, as when illness withdraws a child from play and neighborhood games for prolonged periods of time. Size and physical ability sometimes become major factors in the ways others treat children. Some small children must learn to cope with ridicule and even rejection. The effect of both physical characteristics and the reactions of others to those characteristics can make children retreat from others, avoid interaction, create imaginary worlds, or wish they could be different. At other times, physical growth affects the ways children deal with crises that arise in other areas of life. A small child who already feels ostracized because of size may be even more traumatized by a parent's physical abuse.

Perhaps one of the most influential aspects of children's physical development is that they become increasingly aware of their physical appearance. Children start looking in the mirror a little more—not necessarily to make their appearance conform to adult standards, but to notice it, take account of it, and make some judgments about it. As a result of this increasing self-awareness, for example, children with physical handicaps become more aware of their differences in appearance and ability compared with other children. When handicapped children are four or five years old, adults can talk with them about being "special." But at nine or ten, these children are more likely to be aware that they are different and to know that many people in their world construe the "difference" negatively. This awareness may make them more committed to compensate for their handicap, or make them increasingly angry or despondent. Fortunately, the former case is much more frequent than the latter.

Another area of physical development of which children become readily aware is the emergence of secondary sexual differences in the later stages of middle childhood. Historically, children have not always been as physically mature at this stage of life. At the turn of the century, for example, the average age for the onset of puberty in girls was somewhere in the fourteenth year. By the latter part of this century, the average age moved to somewhere in the eleventh or twelfth year. The phenomenon of earlier onset of puberty is known as the "secular trend." Hypotheses as to why children are maturing sexually at an earlier age vary, but they generally include assumptions about better nutrition and health care. More subtle hypotheses also raise the possibility that the present cultural emphasis on sexuality may somehow be influencing the rate of physical development. Whatever the reasons, issues associated with sexual maturing have entered the elementary school. Children look older at a younger age, and some tend to adopt behavior patterns more typical of early adolescence than middle childhood.

Emotional and Psychological Development

Children have a tendency to be very comfortable with their emotions. They are capable of feeling and expressing anger as readily as they are able to experience and express love. Emotions can change quickly, and children are not as constrained to appear emotionally consistent as adults are inclined to be. The school-age child's emotional development can be portrayed in a variety of ways.

Competence and inferiority. Erik Erikson,[2] in his theory of lifelong human development, views the primary psychological agenda of this stage as the development of a sense of competency. In both academic and social settings, children need to learn to use the tools and develop the skills that allow them to live up to social expectations. The failure to achieve these basic competencies leads to a sense of failure and feelings of inferiority. As children become increasingly self-aware, the reactions of peers, parents, and teachers to their competence become a key ingredient for development. Positive reactions incite feelings of confidence that lead to the development of more and better competencies. Negative reactions lead to feelings of fear and failure, to resistance toward new tasks, and to a sense of inferiority.

Life crises frequently upset the delicate emotional balance that nudges healthy children into feelings of competence. Inferiority is not always a consequence of the child's own actions. Children who have divorcing parents, or who have been subjected to sexual abuse, or who are victimized because of their race or poverty may develop intense feelings of inferiority—even though they are capable of the skills and tasks their society requires.

Childhood emotions. Another approach to emotional development consists of assessing the emotions children bring into the school-age years, and the likely changes these emotions undergo during this period. Generally, individuals enter middle childhood with more capacity to sense and respond emotionally to their environment than to comprehend and articulate it intellectually.

The ability to love is firmly established by middle childhood. In earlier years, children may have expressed love and affection for animals and favorite objects, as well as for parents. But as they grow through middle childhood, the ability to love becomes more informed, is more discriminating, and gradually becomes more altruistic. Young children do not assume the role of another very well and cannot comprehend what it is like to be in another person's position. Elementary-school children begin to develop an ability for social role taking, and this new ability influences their experience and expression of emotions—especially love and affection.

Children have a tendency to be joyful and pragmatic. They are frequently optimistic and are eagerly adventurous. These positive emotional tendencies make them easy for adults to work with and enjoyable to be around.

Elementary-age children also experience the more negative emotions of fear and anxiety. While the fears of earlier childhood frequently dealt with imaginary forces and beings, the fears of middle childhood are more realistic. These tend to relate to children's ability or inability to perform academically and to their acceptance or rejection by their peers. Fears may also come in the form of worry about a parent's dying or divorcing. These fears are not resolved by the parent's comforting presence or reassuring words. They are the kind of fears that only positive reality can relieve. For some children, whose reality only confirms that their parents are divorcing or that other children think they are stupid, the fears will grow and influence personality development.

Self-concept. A major psychological influence in the child's life has already been referred to in the discussion of physical development: the child's increasing self-awareness. As the child continues to discover the various aspects of selfhood, a sense of identity continues to emerge. This self-identity will be challenged in adolescence and at other times in the life cycle. An awareness of identity brings with it a concept of self. The individual may have a positive self-concept ("I can do things well, I am a good person") or a negative self-concept ("I do not do things well, I am not a very likable person"). Virginia Satir[3] suggests that self-concept develops through the composite of life experience. School-age children form self-concepts through their perceptions of the way they are viewed and treated by others—parents, siblings, teachers, other adults and children—and the capabilities they see in themselves. A negative self-concept formed in childhood can have debilitating effects on later stages and tasks of development.

Crises have an impact on children's concepts of themselves. Even though the crisis may involve a terminally ill parent, divorcing parents, or the death of a grandparent, the effects sometimes manifest themselves in the child's self-concept. Many crises will tend to lower a child's self-esteem. A divorce or illness sometimes causes children to think they have done something wrong or to imagine that if they were better persons the crisis would not have happened at all. Self-concept can also be lowered when a crisis directly involves the child, as with a debilitating illness or lengthy hospitalization. Self-concept is formed, at least in part, by physical ability and skill. When these change due to illness or injury, a subtle side effect can be a decrease in the child's sense of personal value and worth.

Cognitive or Intellectual Development

The phenomenon of cognitive or intellectual development has received considerable attention in the past twenty-five years. This study has been influenced by the massively creative work of Jean Piaget.[4] A major concept in his theory is that cognitive development occurs not so much in the amount or quantity of intellectual ability as in the quality or kind of thinking the child is capable of doing. In other words, cognitive growth is not so much a matter of "getting smarter" as it is in learning to think in altogether new ways.

The school-age child differs from the younger child in the very quality of the cognitive processes. Piaget labels the kind of thinking most frequently associated with middle childhood as "concrete operational" thought. In concrete operations, the child is capable of several kinds of thinking that were not possible at age four and five. For example, most nine-year-olds can see water poured from a tall narrow glass into a short wide one. If the water fills both glasses, the child will conclude that both hold the same amount of water—even though the glasses' dimensions are different. Younger children do not have this ability to "conserve." They will center on either the tall or thick dimension and conclude that one glass holds more than the other.

The concrete operational child also develops the ability to sort and classify concepts and objects into groups and categories. As a result, the child becomes capable of learning basic mathematical concepts like additive and identity. Concrete operational children also learn the concept of reversibility. If Jack is Sara's brother, they can tell you that Sara is Jack's sister. Younger children cannot draw that conclusion, even though it seems obvious to adults or older children.

While the child develops considerable ability during this stage, it is important to note that concrete operational children still differ from adults in their thinking ability. School-age children, for example, still do not have the ability to think in abstractions. As a result, they are not very adept at considering the various possibilities of a situation. A child may associate one possible meaning for some abstract reality (like baptism) as its only possible meaning. Or a child may assume the interpretation given some story in scripture to be the only meaning the story can have.

Cognitive development also influences the way in which children identify, evaluate, and react to crises. They think about death, illness, disability, and divorce differently than from the way younger children do. They are not satisfied with the answers that five-year-olds readily accept. Middle childhood provides the cognitive ability to reflect on crises, to ask Why? and What does this mean? Adults are frequently frightened by these questions, or want to protect children from them, or want them to be satisfied with an answer more appropriate for preschool children. The quality of thought that middle childhood brings to the way children confront crises requires sensitive and appropriate adult responses.

Developmental Tasks

During the 1950s to early 1970s, Robert Havighurst[5] and his associates developed a way of assessing human development in terms of the tasks that must be negotiated at each stage of life. This task approach is aware of a variety of psychological issues but takes the perspective that the best way to understand developing persons is to identify the particular developmental jobs or tasks that need to be accomplished at each stage of life.

These developmental tasks are anchored in a particular context and culture. What may be a necessary task for an American elementary-school child may not be a task for a child of the same age growing up in African bush country. The culture, context, and life skills needs are so different in these two settings that what a child must become proficient at in one may have little to do with effective life in the other. Havighurst takes the cultural contexts quite seriously, so the summary of tasks he proposes for American school-age children applies only to them. Even more precisely, he notes that some tasks appropriate for middle-class suburban children may be different from those required of inner-city low-income children in the same metropolitan area.

A "task" is something whose successful achievement leads to happiness and to success with later tasks, while failure leads to "unhappiness in the individual, disapproval by the society, and difficulty with later tasks."[6] At certain points in life, particular tasks can be most fittingly and effectively accomplished. Problems can result either with forcing later life tasks on a child too soon or with coddling a child and encouraging the delay of appropriate tasks to some later time.

Havighurst identified nine developmental tasks for the elementary-school years, including such areas as physical skills, wholesome attitudes, social skills, gender roles, academic skills, and moral values. Our discussion will necessarily mention only a few tasks as illustrative.

Social skills. One task area, for example, relates to social development: the child needs to learn to get along with peers. Social life requires a give-and-take, an understanding of reasonable expectations, and sensitivity to social commitments. To fail to learn these skills and sensitivities will negatively influence the child's ability to get along with others and to develop meaningful relationships later in youth and adult years.

Moral values. Another task faced in middle childhood is the need to develop a sense of conscience and moral values. By the later elementary-school years, children are expected not only to know right from wrong—at least in the expressions of those categories that children are most likely to confront—but also to be able to control their behavior in ways that conform to these standards. The issues of moral and spiritual development are complex and have attracted a host of theoretical evaluation. Developmental task theory is less concerned with how the development of morality and conscience occurs than it is with the importance of children learning both a system of morality and how to allow that morality to influence their behavior.

Viewing children's development in terms of the tasks they must negotiate has its disadvantages and limitations. But it does have the strength of focusing the more abstract psychological descriptions of development into observable behavior and goals. It provides a way of evaluating a child's development.

Development in the Child's Culture and World

The first section of this chapter dealt with those developmental issues that can be located most accurately within the child. Physical development is most easily traced to some genetic plan or predisposition. Emotional development is less reliably traced to an internal world of influence, but even in this area, theorists like Erikson consider genetic endowment an important part of psychological development. The discussion of Havighurst's developmental tasks in the second section turned the focus more to forces and influences which are external to the child, but which contribute significantly to the child's development. These influences include cultural values, responses and expectations of other people, and culturally defined skills and abilities. In this final section, I want to discuss some contemporary influences on the development of school-age children in American society in the last decades of this century. These are issues that influence growing up at a particular time, in a particular location, at the crossroads of particular forces and trends. However unique and transitory these influences may be, they will be affecting the developmental experiences of many children in the next fifteen years.

Changing Ethnicity

One of the dramatic influences in American society is the rapidly changing ethnicity of American children. An increasing number of American children are black, Hispanic, or Asian. The population of these three groups is growing at a faster rate than the population of Anglo children. For example, from 1980 to 1983 the average birth rate among blacks was 22 per thousand, while for whites it was 15 per thousand.[7] American black and ethnic children will comprise a larger percentage of the total population of school-age children than adults of these same groups will of the total adult population. In the 1980 census, non-Anglo groups comprised 19.5 percent of the population of adults aged twenty to thirty-nine, while non-Anglo children comprised 26 percent of the total population of children aged five to nine.[8] This ethnic shift means that the cultural influences to which children are sensitive will be far less uniform than has been true for immediate past generations. A second-grade Hispanic child, for example, may need to be proficient in Spanish at home and English away from home, learn both the broader cultural values of American society and the particular values of family and ethnic heritage, and learn to do things children are expected to do in more than one way (a generic American cultural way and a particular family, ethnic way). The developmental process obviously becomes more complicated. With more complexity, there is a greater chance that problems can emerge.

Of course, there has always been a generation of American children who have grown up biculturally. These children, like most children, have been very durable and adaptable human beings. Many have done quite well. The difference in the present generation is in the sheer proportions of the ethnicity of American children. A much larger percentage of American children will be growing up in the more complex social systems of bicultural experience and expectation.

American Family

Another major developmental influence is the shifting pattern of the American family. At any one time, approximately 10 percent of American children are living in single-parent homes. In some low-income black communities, this percentage may increase to 50 percent. Some studies of children in single-parent families suggest that these parents make fewer demands on their children, show less affection, and are more inconsistent in administering discipline.

The impact of the single-parent home is further influenced by the tendency of many Americans to live away from the communities where grandparents, aunts, and uncles live. These factors combine to increase the stress on school-age children in the household.

The effects of divorce and single-parent households on children are difficult to identify. However, the percentage of children growing through middle childhood who experience the conflict which leads their parents to divorce, or who live in single-parent homes, or who have to make the adjustments required as they become part of blended families is so significant that these issues must be considered as part of the culturally dictated influences on development.

Hurried Children

Another major cultural influence on development, documented by David Elkind,[9] is the phenomenon of "hurrying." Elementary-age children, Elkind contends, are being hurried by parents, school systems, and the media. The hurrying may take the form of parents pushing their children to achieve socially or athletically, schools pushing for more scholastic achievement at earlier grade levels, or the media pushing ten-year-olds into the consumer wants and expectations of early adolescence. The result of the hurrying is that children experience a harmful amount of stress, which affects healthy development. Children respond to the stress by antisocial behavior, by academic burn-out, and by a free-floating anxiety that makes them fearful of and resistant to the normal demands of growing and living.

Elkind's concern about hurrying children brings back the observation at the beginning of this chapter. Some adultlike qualities in children can emerge and develop during elementary years. They are obvious enough that adults may see these qualities, ignore the more childlike ones, and hurry the children. This may happen as much by necessity as by choice. A divorced parent, living with the stress of working for income, keeping house, and parenting, may see these adultlike qualities and take the child into a world of adult confidences and expectations.

Other adults limit their vision of children to only their more obvious childlike qualities and indulge them. Indulgence can delay appropriate development and contribute to the child's becoming self-centered, irresponsible, and demanding.

Healthy development is a process in which children slowly surrender their childish qualities as more appropriate adultlike qualities emerge. It does not help children to arrest them in some child's world where they are never encouraged to develop the skills, perceptions, and abilities they will need to function effectively as adolescents and adults. It is as destructive to sentimentalize childhood and constrict children to terminal childishness as it is to hurry them into an emotionally stressed adult world.

Children face enough unavoidable crises. Hurrying and indulging are crises children do not have to face. Child-rearing advice in the United States has become as plentiful as advice on dieting, and much of it is of the same quality. Crash programs to make children smarter, healthier, and more advantaged tend to hurry children. Like crash diets, they frequently create more stress and ill health than anything else. Similarly, "let the children do whatever they want" programs tend to have effects like "eat all you want and still lose weight" diets. They just don't accomplish the job.

National Policy and Children

No national policy regarding children exists in the United States. As a society, we no doubt want their needs for food and shelter met, and we want them educated and prepared for productive lives in society. A host of national policy decisions, however, affect children in ways that create crisis.

Children, perhaps by default rather than intention, are not a national priority. For example, comparisons with other industrialized nations show the United States to be the only country in which as many as one fourth of its children are being raised in poverty. The percentage of children being raised in households with incomes below the poverty line increased from 1970 to 1980.[10] One study has estimated that per child expenditures of the U.S. federal government for children are less than a tenth of the per person federal expenditures for senior adults.[11] The struggle that states and school boards have in raising adequate funds for education probably reflects society's inattention to the needs of its children.

The Yankelovich study of American values, *New Rules,* found two thirds of American parents now agree that "parents should be free to live their own lives even if it means spending less time with their children."[12] The increasing numbers of married adults who choose not to have children are not only exercising their right of choice, they may also be reflecting a subtle cultural value. These attitudes reflect a cultural stance toward children which transcends, and perhaps explains, the lack of aggressive governmental spending and programming on behalf of children.

Perhaps the greatest crisis children in American society face is that they have so few advocates. They are the citizens with little power to plead their case and are without votes to exert their will. Of course, they are without the needed maturity always to know what is best for them. They need a society that will take on their case with parental responsibility. They need churches who see them as valuable members of the community of faith. They need persons, in addition to their parents, who will see to their well-being.

Of the many developmental needs children have, one of the most theologically informed is the need to be welcomed. Welcome includes acceptance, provision, nurture, and care. If children are denied these, they are doomed to the most crippling of developmental problems.

A Concluding Word

Amid these particular concerns about the developmental process, it is important to remember that children are very resilient and durable human beings. American children managed to develop successfully in the midst of terrible nineteenth-century orphanages and sweatshops, through two terrible twentieth-century wars, and during one devastating depression. Each of these cultural events influenced development, placed unique stress on the process of growing up, and took its toll of many children. However, most children developed acceptably. Some even learned to excel because of these stresses in their childhood. Caregiving adults must do what they can to keep a society from unnecessarily and unduly stressing children. But they must also give their care with the realization that children have strength and resilience. Human development celebrates the gifts of each stage of life but realizes that the skills and sensitivities of one age must give way to new ones for the next stage. To be aware of development is to be sensitive to the drama of life and to experience the confirming and transforming character of human growth.

NOTES

1. An expanded resource for understanding the development of the school-age child can be found in David Elkind, *A Sympathetic Understanding of the Child: Birth to Sixteen,* 2nd ed. (Boston: Allyn & Bacon, 1978). Iris V. Cully provides an extended analysis of child development and religious issues in *Christian Child Development* (San Francisco: Harper & Row, 1979).

2. Erik H. Erikson first proposed these ideas in *Childhood and Society* (New York: W. W. Norton & Co., 1950) and most recently reflected on them in *The Life Cycle Completed* (New York: W. W. Norton & Co., 1982).

3. Virginia Satir, *Peoplemaking* (Palo Alto, Calif.: Science & Behavior Books, 1972).

4. Jean Piaget's work may be best summarized in Jean Piaget and Barbel Inhelder, *The Psychology of the Child* (New York: Basic Books, 1969).

5. Robert J. Havighurst, *Developmental Tasks and Education,* 3rd ed. (New York: David McKay Co., 1972).

6. Ibid., p. 2.

7. U.S. Bureau of the Census, "Projections of the Population of the United States, by Age, Sex, Race: 1983 to 2080." *Current Population Reports,* series P-25, no. 952 (Washington, D.C.: U.S. Government Printing Office).

8. U.S. Bureau of the Census, "General Population Characteristics: United States Summary." 1980 Census of the Population, PC 80-1-B1.

9. David Elkind, *The Hurried Child: Growing Up Too Fast Too Soon* (Reading, Mass.: Addison-Wesley Publishing Co., 1981).

10. *Source,* vol. 11, no. 3 (August 1986), published by Search Institute, Minneapolis.

11. S. Preston, "Children and the Elderly in the U.S.," *Scientific American,* vol. 251 (1984), pp. 44–49.

12. Daniel Yankelovich, *New Rules: Searching for Self-fulfillment in a World Turned Upside Down* (New York: Random House, 1981), p.104.

3

Faith Development and the School-age Child

Freda A. Gardner

Our own understanding of the genesis, nature, and meaning of faith will, of course, determine our perception of faith in children. If we believe that faith is a gift from God, given freely to persons whom God has created, then we will expect to see faith or traces and intimations of faith in children. If, on the other hand, we believe that faith is given by God in response to a person's belief or commitment, we will probably look for readiness for commitment or for evidences of belief in the children with whom we live and work.

Faith may be thought of as a noun or a verb, either something one has or a way to be. If it is something one has, we may listen for particular expressions that affirm ownership and then watch for evidence that such is the case. If faith is thought of as a way to be in the world, we might look first for perspectives, attitudes, and actions before listening for descriptive words and phrases.

In faith communities the prevailing convictions about the nature of humankind and of God's actions for the redemption of the world shape the forms and processes of ministry to children. Such convictions are integral to each community and provide significant determinants for the way those communities exist in and for the world.

Like any dominant perspective, beliefs about faith and lack of faith can shape our way of seeing and deciding about other people, including children. However, they may lead to tunnel vision, which rules out of bounds that which does not seem to fit. We often see and hear what we want to find in the children in our midst, that which fits our convictions.

If we think the dominant characteristic of a person is sinfulness, we may see in a look or hear in some hasty remark evidence of the evil marking that person's life. A child's outburst of "I hate you!" to a parent

Freda A. Gardner is Professor of Christian Education and Director of the School of Christian Education, Princeton Theological Seminary, Princeton, N.J.

or sibling in a moment of high frustration may be regarded as evidence of that child's sinful nature. On the other hand, to one who believes that goodness resides in the child until he or she is taught to be sinful, the same comment may be totally ignored or simply chalked up to a phase that the child is going through, with no meaning in the present and no implications for the future.

Awareness of what we might easily notice and what we might overlook is important when we encounter children in crisis. We must grow in our understanding of what may be true for children as they develop as persons of faith. We must be aware that our understandings are limited and do not exhaust the mystery in every child. However, growth in understanding and awareness allows us to live more faithfully with children, to be both more helpful and more humble about our own roles in their lives.

A Look Backward

We may think that children grow toward faith or we may think that their lives unfold in the context of faith already given. Either way, experiences of childhood seem to make a difference in the ways in which children come to know God and to hold the beliefs of their religious communities.

A baby may be thought of as helpless and acted upon by the world. Indeed, a baby is largely dependent upon others to fulfill both basic and secondary needs. But one need only have a baby in the family or visit a family with a baby to realize that, helpless and dependent as babies may be, they are certainly more than that. They make demands, elicit and shape the behaviors of others, affirm and reject, comfort and confound. They are transacting with their worlds and, in their own ways, are attempting to make sense of those worlds and of those transactions.

Long before children are school age they have established a way of being in the world. Very young children have been confirmed again and again in their sense of themselves, of life, and of the world in general. Beginning in the cribs of their infancies and in the arms or lack of arms of their earliest days and nights, they have developed a sense of who and what can be counted on. Before they can think, they may be said to know trust and hope and worth and goodness and their absence. Because their capacities to think are limited to present experience and not involved with the world of thought as we know it, what they know is very much centered on how they feel about what happens or doesn't happen to them.

If a baby is left wet, hungry, frightened by noise or confusion, abandoned to frantic and random motions, that child will have little basis for hope. Such a child may not easily be persuaded in times of later stress that patience will sustain until a better outcome can be achieved. Such a child will be hard pressed to hear a promise from a well-meaning adult that indeed the child's needs will be met even in a time of crisis. Encouragement to do or be all that one can be under stress will fall on deaf ears if the child's early attempts at initiating action or asserting his or her own rights have met with derision or punishment.

A few simple descriptions may remind us that what a child knows is a mixture of what that child has experienced and what that child has been taught. As we know well from experiences in pastoral care of adults, even adults may revert under pressure to primitive feelings and thoughts that in less stressful times they would try to hide. Children too may regress, but often their words and behavior in times of stress point to the fact that, for them, knowledge and belief are primarily what life has been for them rather than what the world of ideas has come to mean to them.

Children Speak and Act Out Their Faith

Let's examine quotations from five children that reveal something about their faith, yet must be studied if a more complete understanding is to be gained.

"Does God know to love my grandma? I do (love her), I really do."
"Will there be anyone I know in heaven?"
"When do I lie on the table and get cut?"
"God knows I'm moving a long ways away."
"You can't really believe in someone or something you can't see."

Children's talk, in both ordinary and stressful times, cannot be taken at face value or as the next logical thought in an apparently straightforward conversation. Parenting, teaching, and counseling children calls for caring, attentive listening and for invitations to say more if the child can say more. In tense situations, however, parents, teachers, pastors, and counselors are seldom without some stress themselves. A young child's bewilderment may remind us of our own vulnerability, and an older child's hard questions about the fundamentals of faith may expose our own uncertainties. In a crisis, therefore, we tend to deal with ambivalences, fears, and doubts swiftly and finally in order to end the tension of the immediate situation. We may deal with it later by labeling the child and his or her faith as immature, or even sinful, and may in subsequent interactions with the child be prone to introduce content and activity to correct, admonish, or create guilt about their expressed or acted-out faith.

What might those children have been saying?

The little girl talking about her grandma, God, and herself was speaking to her pastor, who was visiting after the grandmother's death. Careful conversation revealed that the child was concerned about two things. She had heard people say that God was taking care of Grandma when the grandmother had to go to the hospital. This five-year-old was trying to reconcile a caring God with what she had been told, which was that Grandma had died and would not be coming home ever.

It became clear that she also was bothered by her own feeling that sometimes Grandma's presence in the house robbed her of her mother's attention. This came out when the pastor said to her, "You really loved your grandma but sometimes you wished that your mom didn't have to spend so much time taking care of her?" and the little girl nodded her head. At five this child is not yet ready to separate thought from action, and so she fears that she was the cause of her grandma's death. At five she can't think about two things being true, and so a God who cares and the reality of death don't fit together in any way. She wonders about God, but she wonders in very concrete terms. She has learned that if you care for someone you do good things, and, although she doesn't understand death, she picks up from the emotion that death has triggered and the unusual activity and tension in the household that death is in no way good. A characteristic way of thinking at this age is evident in both of the child's statements. The child processes experience from the self outward. What she experiences is how it really is.

The six-year-old who asked about heaven had heard enough about it and about people who had died and gone to heaven that he had begun to picture it and to fantasize about being there himself. His mother responded to his question by saying that the child's grandfather, her father, was there. The child did not pursue the question further, but later in the day he came to his mother with a picture from her bedroom of his grandfather, whom the child had never known. He said, "May I have this so when I get to heaven I can know which one is my grandfather?" This child still has some of the younger child's way of thinking. He is concerned about himself, and the question he raises reveals that he has incorporated some ideas about heaven, but they are still very concrete as he deals with them. Heaven is a place and people go there. He isn't, at this point, concerned about the nature of heaven or the activities of any life after death. He isn't questioning the reality of life after death. He wonders if he will be OK there. The child has taken on faith what he has learned about life after death but is trying to make sense of it in concrete terms that will satisfy his unconscious needs for security and hold his fears at a manageable level.

A pastor was visiting in the home of a nine-year-old girl who was to be baptized. The pastor had made a special effort to be sensitive to the possible self-consciousness of a group of school-age children who had not been baptized as infants for one reason or another and whose parents had now requested baptism for them, so he visited them before the service. After reviewing what would happen, the pastor asked if this child had any other questions. She responded hesitantly, "When do I lie on the table and get cut?" Startled, the pastor asked her what she meant. She said that on TV she had seen a boy put on a bed in the church and they had a knife to cut him. Still in the dark, the pastor asked if she was sure it was a baptism. The child was uncertain but knew it was "something that happened to children." She thought it was in church because "a lot of men in dark suits talked about the Bible before they did it to the boy." Slowly the pastor and the parents discovered that the girl had witnessed a circumcision ceremony in some movie. The actual circumcision had not been portrayed but the intent had been clear. The solemnity of the movie scene matched the girl's own sense of solemnity about her baptism, probably her way of keeping her fears of mutilation under control.

In her fascination with the event, she missed the fact that circumcision was related to males. All the preceding explanations had not eradicated this central and compelling image associated in the child's mind with the event she was to experience. You can imagine the pastor's relief when the child's expectations and fears could be alleviated. Then she came to baptism with an appropriate sense of its importance, knowing the joy inherent in the church's celebration of the sacrament.

"God knows I'm moving a long ways away." A bit less frightening, but nonetheless real, is this seven-year-old child's affirmation of God's awareness of his impending move to another state several hundred miles away. The child is well aware that the move is away from the familiar. He knows that he is not coming back and he won't be known in the new place. Stating such a conviction may be the child's way of testing its truth with people who are bigger and older and supposed to know, or to show the world he isn't afraid. The child needs more than simple confirmation or applause for his faith. Without denying the truth of what he says, a listening adult can respond with an acknowledgment that knowing God knows what's happening in our lives and cares about it makes it easier to face a scary thing. Children want to believe what the important people in their lives believe, but they also need support when that belief doesn't quite take care of the feelings experienced under stress.

An older child may reveal some of the same ambivalence as the previous seven-year-old, but the ambivalence may come from the child's thinking instead of from feelings. The eleven-year-old who said, "You can't really believe in someone or something you can't see," is not having a crisis of faith but is trying to understand prayer. Her newly achieved ability to reason and to draw conclusions makes her question an earlier and simpler explanation of prayer. We must respect the child's mental struggle. If we want the child to grow to love God with the whole self, we must respond with affirmation to the difficulty in doing that contrary-to-reason thing of believing. The child is ready to explore what it means to believe without the evidence that is usually relied on. Beginning in the middle years of childhood, a child begins to press for evidence. Being able to think through cause-and-effect relationships, the child cannot easily put together an apparently unseen God and a form of contract with that God. The child is on the threshold of a long quest for his or her own faith and needs encouragement for the search. Even in times of stress, and especially when a child's compliance would ease our own distress, the child needs support for the new ways to be in relation to God.

Changes During Childhood

Before we look at some of the specific ways children seem to perceive God and God's actions in their worlds, it may be helpful to identify some of the changes in perception and thinking that occur as children grow.

Younger child	*Older child*
Moves into a larger world . . .	. . . and a still larger world
Accepts the authority of parents and teachers	Recognizes the limitations of those authoritative figures
	Recognizes that other people have ideas and feelings about God, church, right and wrong
"Knows" what he or she experiences	Is beginning to think about what is not encountered directly
Has feelings about self and an individual place in groups that motivate questions, concerns, affirmations	Begins to explore how others see and feel and react
Believes God is there, good, powerful (for many children), but may see God as vengeful and destructive	Believes God is different from people and evokes different responses, is complex and not easily described
"Jesus loves children and is different from God"	"Jesus was loved and hated and is something like God"
"Church is where I do things"	"Church is made up of many people and activities, and I can do many things there"

"Prayer is something you do and it has something to do with God"	Prayer moves from asking God for specific things to talking with God about many things
Feels bigger people are better and worth more and right	Begins to take into account motives, circumstances, goals, etc.
Apt to concentrate on one aspect of an event or story	Able to see more than one aspect; uncomfortable with paradox, however

The kindergarten and early primary child is moving from a time of knowing by intuition, imagination, and feelings which were evoked in the child's actual experiences. An early sense of disorder and chaos has, for most children, been displaced by an awareness of some order and trustworthiness in relationships and in the world. Even in situations of deprivation, some things have come to be counted on. As observed earlier, we look hopefully for signs of love and sacrifice and dependability, but a child may be counting on hunger, abuse, and illness.

With the sense of self and the meanings constructed in early childhood, the child moves into the larger social world represented by school. Earlier explanations that served the child's desire to understand and be in touch with significant others are now challenged by an increasing capacity to see that others are centers of experience and makers of meaning as well. The rich powers of imagination that provided the child with fantasy as real as reality, and the explanations that combined disparate experiences and images, are now met by generally accepted facts and contrary-to-imagined realities. Research suggests that even unchurched children are surrounded by symbols and language providing some image of God by the time they enter school. What the child has taken from the culture and the family and the church may be a rich mix. The truth of a particular faith community, the notions that help the child deal with fantasy and fear, the parts of rituals in which the child has participated—these may be what the child now "knows."

This younger school-age child, described by John Westerhoff in his book *Will Our Children Have Faith?* as being a person of faith in terms of experiences and affiliations with others of faith, may have internalized many rituals of faith. The child may have been a praying child long before he or she can explain anything about prayer. The child may have sensed, in the family's religious community, the presence of God in the liturgy or the place of worship. He or she may feel like a child of God because of what is experienced while participating in the activities of faithful people into which the child has been welcomed.

Lingering traces of the earlier way of thinking, from the self outward, make it appropriate to see that the child's faith is not so much in God but results from what the child has experienced as one of God's children. That God is there "because I pray" or "because we sing" or "because we give our money to God" may be seen as the basis for a younger child's faith.

Often the younger child will develop ways to avoid questions that push her or him beyond the capacity to respond. "I don't know" or "That's all I know," a shrug, or a deft change of subject may be a statement that our questions are simply beyond the child's capacities to think or articulate. Asking questions that depend on logical thinking may evoke such answers or behavior. Better to ask the child, "Do you have any more thoughts about that?" or "That's quite a lot to know about God." If there is more, this opens the way for the child to share it.

Recognizing that the child's statements or questions usually represent something he or she is trying to integrate will prevent us from hearing them as firmly held convictions or a basis for reasonable argument. Tragically, some children's earlier experiences have resulted in a picture of God as a punitive and frightening presence. Interactions with such children in times of stress may include speaking and acting in ways that contradict their negative beliefs. Embracing the child and speaking of both the child's fears and the God of love you know may be only a pale hope for the child, but it might become a step on the long road to a new understanding of God. Avoiding condemnation of parental or church teaching by simple words and acts of our own convictions will keep the child from having to deal with the additional stress of divided loyalties.

It cannot be stated too often that for children faith is a matter of feelings far longer than many adults would care to think. Feelings about God and prayer and religious communities, feelings about right and wrong and love and justice, shape behavior until a child is almost into adolescence. Approaching the teen years, children begin to go in thought where they could not go before, in spite of the feelings attached to the experience. To say that a child is more like adults in feeling and less like adults in thinking is to give us a clue as to what children are expressing or grappling with as we interact with them.

A younger child thinks in concrete terms; that is, in terms of life as he or she experiences it. The child of early school age is full of questions and curiosity and begins to develop ways of dealing with feelings. Some ways may be constructive and help the child with important growing relationships; others may serve to isolate the child and do harm to desired relationships. The child begins to see that big people are not always powerful, that parents have limitations. Disappointment or anger may accompany that realization, but the child is ready anyway to know about a trustworthy God. Though the connection between God and Jesus may be vague, in Jesus the child may come to see how God acts in trustworthy, loving ways to help all people. Iris Cully, in her book *Christian Child Development,* gives helpful illustrations of the ways children grow in their understanding of Jesus' relationship to the Creator and the Spirit.

Representations of God may reflect certain gender differences, as described in David Heller's interesting book *The Children's God.* It would appear that girls tend toward a more aesthetic deity while boys describe a more rational deity. Girls talk of and depict a more relational God who acts toward them in personal ways while boys describe a more active God who does things in the world. Without going into further and deeper research, a simple noting of these matters may lead us to greater understanding of the girls and boys with whom we live and work.

The child's experiences of God in words and stories, both in the home and in rituals of the faith community, will become part of the mix of messages to which the culture will add. Older children will draw from this mix the meanings that makes sense to both their limitations and their capacities. A strong force will be exerted, however, from those communities in which the child wants most to participate, to be accepted and valued. The family and church that welcome the child's efforts to know God and to be known as a child of God will make a strong case for the God who is significant to them. They will be a powerful model of what it is to live as that God's child.

Using Stories

Because children are, for the most part, still in touch with imagination, still drawing on images, still constructing from feelings more than thought as adults know thought, stories are a vehicle of communication not to be overlooked. Stories that give language to feelings and fears and fantasies provide the child with raw material for growth in faith. Reading a story in which a child is the central character in circumstances such as illness, death, divorce, separation, moving, or handicapping conditions may open the door to conversation that points to beliefs about who God is and how God deals with people. Even if no conversation ensues, the child may be enriched and equipped for continuing the search for understanding.

Bible stories that point to God's way with people may also be offered to the child as gifts for life's journey. The younger child will not generally grasp the underlying meaning of many passages or respond to the complexities and interactions of the human situation described. One striking facet of the story will probably capture the child's attention, usually that which is most closely related to the child's fears, fantasies, or actual happenings. Bigger, more powerful characters will be seen as being right and deserving of better treatment. Actions that are threatening to the child's own sense of well-being will be fascinating and may evoke requests for repeated retelling as the child tries to deal with the fears they provoke or with the affirmations the story or storyteller makes about them. Our questions about the story implying that a child should see the truth that the storyteller believes the story conveys will add to any sense of doubt or guilt the child may already have about his or her own worth. An invitation to retell the story or act it out or draw a picture of it may offer younger children a way of expressing what they have heard and offer the adult the opportunity to see what may have become new material with which a child can or must deal.

Older children will often want to describe in minute detail all that happens in a story or an experience. They are beginning to reflect on the probable meanings of the actions described. What happens in the story is the meaning, and stories become ways of knowing about themselves and others. A simple statement of what the story means to the storyteller, such as, "I like this story because it helps me to remember that God cares for all of us very much," may offer assurance to the child who is caught by one element of the story.

Summary

A child's faith, like an adult's, is not easily described and categorized. Faith has many expressions, but surely some of those expressions are shaped and perhaps largely determined by factors that can be identified and analyzed. General expectations of a child's capacities and of our abilities to communicate in terms of those capacities are in order. For the most part we can prepare for interactions with children in light of insights derived from knowledge about their age, their family situation, and the nature of the stress they are experiencing. We can, with the same knowledge, help children to prepare themselves for some crises, but three things will probably remain true.

One is that some crises will be beyond our belief and our capacity to take them in. Prepared by statistics that tell us the way the world is today, a ten-year-old pregnant girl, an eleven-year-old attempted suicide victim, a nine-year-old drug addict, or a raped six-year-old are simply shattering realities for which even the most experienced of us may need help before we can offer it.

Second, some of the children we meet, for no apparent reason that we can discover, will speak or act faithfully in ways that belie their years and circumstances. Robert Coles's beautiful book *The Moral Life of Children* gives eloquent testimony to this surprise that upsets our careful formulations of when and how a child should develop.

Finally, the child, like the adult, is never wholly ours, to have or to know. We are given only the ministry of participating with God's creation and re-creation of that other's life.

FURTHER READING

Coles, Robert. *The Moral Life of Children.* Ed. Peter Davison. Boston and New York: Atlantic Monthly Press, 1986.

Cully, Iris V. *Christian Child Development.* San Francisco: Harper & Row, 1979.

Fowler, James W. *Stages of Faith: The Psychology of Human Development and the Quest for Meaning.* San Francisco: Harper & Row, 1981.

Heller, David. *The Children's God.* Chicago: University of Chicago Press, 1986.

Rogers, Fred, and Barry Head. *Mister Rogers Talks with Parents.* New York: Berkley Books, 1983.

Westerhoff, John. *Will Our Children Have Faith?* New York: Seabury Press, 1976.

Guides to Children's Books

L'Engle, Madeleine, with Avery Brooke, anthologist. *Trailing Clouds of Glory: Spiritual Values in Children's Books.* Philadelphia: Westminster Press, 1985.

Thomas, Virginia, and Betty Davis Miller. *Children's Literature for All God's Children.* Atlanta: John Knox Press, 1986.

4

What Children Need
from Significant Adults
Kathryn N. Chapman

His eyes never left the teacher's face. He read every movement of
her eyes and pondered each turn of her head. She knew by his atten-
tiveness that her response was important and that the future of their
teacher/student relationship was dependent on the dynamics flowing
between them. She closed his homemade book about Old Testament
heroes, their eyes met, and she said, "John, what a good job! Pull up a
chair and tell me about your project." He pulled a chair close to hers.
With heads almost touching they pored over the completed project.
She listened as he told her the story of his successful work. An excellent
Bible project, yes. More important, John, age ten, had experienced
some of his crucial needs being met by a significant adult, in this case
a Sunday school teacher. He was accepted, affirmed, embraced, and
delighted in by a significant person.

Significant adults, persons who relate to children with love and concern, join God in the sacred task of creation. God is present both in
developmental processes and in the surges of growth that pervade a
child's life. God's automatic involvement is apparent as we bear witness
to the marvelous creation and maturation of each young life. Part of our
task as persons who nurture children is to be in step with God's timing,
a creative pacing divinely led. An awareness of God's plan and presence
in everydayness and in ordinary circumstances invites our participation
in a most sacred process. Such awareness will be a source of strength
for children in times of crisis. God's open invitation to join in shaping
a child's life offers every significant adult a responsibility and a challenge.

All children have needs. The basic needs of children must be met by
significant adults, especially ministers, rather than through the peer

Kathryn N. Chapman is Associate Professor of Childhood Education, The Southern Baptist Theological Seminary, Louisville, Ky.

group and its subculture. How we respond, or fail to respond, is related to our level of awareness about what children need. Through sensitivity to children and relationship with them, we can intentionally strive to meet their basic needs. Knowing both what those needs are and how to meet them is crucial for us as significant adults.

Emotional and Spiritual Needs

Children need love and acceptance. Love goes far past the daily hug and the occasional "I love you." A child needs a climate of psychological safety where love is not only spoken but lived out, an environment that sets limits but provides for love to never be withdrawn—no matter what. A home or a classroom is a safe haven when unconditional love and acceptance ensure that a child's worth is never questioned.

We love a child when we listen without interrupting, when we make up first-grade questions for a child who can't compete in the adult trivia game, when we hear and take seriously questions like, "What is it like to look out of blue eyes?" and "What if I can't do the hard work in second grade?" We love children when we focus our whole attention on their concern, call their names, look in their faces, and help them learn how to cope with their world. Loving says "Come over here, I'll help you do that" rather than "Can't you ever do anything right?"; "I'm sorry your friends hurt your feelings," not "Serves you right for being bossy!"; "I'm glad you are doing things in a different way" rather than "Why can't you be more like your brother?"

Love and acceptance communicate to each child a much-needed sense of belonging, a message that says "I not only know you're here, I delight in your presence and treasure you more every day. No one else can take your place. You belong to me and I belong to you. Lucky us!" Children who feel they can put both feet down in a safe place, and with people to whom they belong, experience the true measure of love and acceptance. Grace flows freely in their lives. In times of crisis like those discussed in this book, children need an extra measure of love and acceptance.

Children need affirmation and support. Professional teachers know the importance of teaching and guiding children through positive direction. That means leaving out many of the nos and don'ts. As long as things are moving smoothly, our pleasant, affirming words come easily; however, under stress we may revert to sharp, terse, negative words.

Children need to hear the encouraging word and the uplifting comment. They need to see the affirming smile and the confident nod. The key to meeting a child's need for affirmation and support is remembering how *we* feel when we are acknowledged and praised. Each of us can recount a time when a sincere affirming word literally made a difference in our day. We should re-create that good feeling we internalized and translate it into a meaningful event for a child.

Children need significant adults to be their advocates, to be supportive in an adult world that may not always view children from a friendly perspective. Support needs are met when an adult constructively intervenes at school or assists a young child in returning unpaid-for bubble gum to the store. Support means being present for meaningful life events (recitals, ball games, choir concerts) and also being emotionally available to children as well as physically available.

Verbal affirmation is very important to all of us, especially children. How many of us have longed for the verbal blessing of a significant other! Even though the rent is paid and food is on the table, children need emotional nourishment, too. Hearing positive words of affirmation about their daily presence and the delight you have in them lightens the heart. A secret smile of approval between adult and child is special; a sincere word of praise will reverberate through the head and the heart for several days to come. A sensitive minister who says to an early-comer at church, "Hey, I heard your steps in the hall and I hoped it would be you!" will notice the little shoulders lift and the walk become more confident. We have within our control the power to lift or crush a child's spirit.

Children need our model of stability. As with other personal attributes such as love, trust, and acceptance, the example of steadfastness we provide for children has deep theological implications. We say by way of our relationships with them that we can be trusted, we are predictable, we can be counted on in every situation. The stability we model in human relationships indicates to children that the God we love and serve is a God who is constant and faithful. Children learn a powerful lesson of security through the faithfulness they see in adults, the faithfulness they learn to live, and the faithfulness they attribute to God, the Most Significant Other. So being a model of stability is more than providing a psychologically safe environment and being an emotionally healthy adult. It is teaching children through our very lives a mature way of living in relationship with God and with humankind.

Children notice moods and emotional cycles, of course, and because school-age children are still quite egocentric, they often internalize our roller-coaster behavior and feel that *they* have done something wrong. Bad feelings and withdrawal may result and communication breaks down. Imagine the eight-year-old who literally dances with excitement over the anticipation of speaking to the minister after morning worship but finds him or her preoccupied and distant. It is easy to become preoccupied with adult parishioners, but think how much healthier our relationship with children is when they can count on our warm, genuine embrace and greeting *every* time we meet. Knowing what to expect and what is going to happen next is especially important for children in crisis.

Stability is modeled when ministers are predictable in presence and in mood and are genuinely happy to see each child. In a crisis, when stability is automatically challenged, it is particularly important for ministers to provide a stable environment. We are important examples of God's faithfulness and loving steadfastness. Being who we say we are and providing a consistent model for children meets a critical need children have for stability.

Children need to derive from us a sense of hope and promise. Current events made available for us daily through the news media convey a pervasive sense of sadness and doom. It is difficult to believe in the survival of a world that contains so much chaos and defeat. Children at a young age may begin to wonder where to look for a sense of hope and promise. This is particularly true when a child is in crisis. As significant adults, we can demonstrate for children a form of resiliency against the hard knocks of the world. Part of what we can teach are coping skills, healthy balanced ways of dealing with the world and its problems. Rather than conveying to children a perfectionist attitude we can offer a theology of grace lived out, a way of saying that second chances are available. We have erasers on pencils, second and third times at bat, apologies for mistakes. These opportunities signal to children that grace is present in life, a chance to begin again. They are and will always be accepted. This good news is critical for children in the midst of crisis because they frequently feel guilty and responsible for the crisis.

In the face of today's difficult world the attitudes of significant adults can teach—or fail to teach—hope and optimism to children. When toddlers stumble and fall they are verbally coached by loving caregivers to hop up and start again. In a similar way school-age children must learn to lean into their world with feelings of hope, hope that rests in God's eternal strength revealed in the optimism they see demonstrated in the attitudes of significant adults. When children question the origin of their hope in a world darkened by crisis, ministers can bear witness to a personal faith and hope centered in God through Christ. Belief in God's promises as revealed through scripture can be modeled for children as the foundation stone for having a sense of hope and promise. When promises made between adult and child are broken, children need to know that God's promises never fail.

Children need our example of religious faith. Being a congruent Christian where "the walk fits the talk" means providing for children a model that is lived out as well as talked out. Inconsistencies, which children are very astute at observing, shatter the example, which should convey that we are who we say we are.

In a world where Christian heroes are rare, and inappropriate figures from the media are overwhelming, it becomes increasingly important for ministers to be worthy of children's emulation. School-age children not only are internalizing feelings and attitudes about church, they are observing rituals, listening to Bible stories, and attempting to begin their own prayer life. Families may participate in Christian education opportunities together, and in those particular families the walk *may* fit the talk. Frequently, in today's society, children will not be part of an intact family unit and may, in reverential awe, relate to the minister as their model. As significant adults, we ministers can be an example of religious faith and worthy of imitation. Children in emotional distress may be doubly impacted by who we are.

Through involvement in corporate worship via litanies, children's sermons, and leadership in seasonal events, children can deepen their understanding of religious rituals and experience the joy of belonging to the family of God.

Hopeful Outcomes

All children have needs, and significant, caring adults have the key to meeting many of those needs. As children's needs are identified and met, several hopeful outcomes will result. One hopeful outcome is *high self-esteem.* Feelings of respect for self and faith in one's ability will enable a child to move into the ever-widening social world with confidence. Children's posture, language, and attitude will convey to their whole world how they feel about themselves. With a consistent diet of support, affirmation, love, and unconditional positive regard we help children develop the most valuable tool necessary for dealing with their world of relationships. High self-esteem can be a well-developed aspect of life on which children will rely for many years to come.

Often in conferences parents of "busting out all over" six-year-olds will ask tentatively, "What do you do about a six-year-old who has too *much* self-esteem? He's full of himself!" My response is, "Don't do anything. That's part of who sixes are developmentally. The peer group in first and second grade will handle it for you." One's peers have a way of shaving down an ego that has grown too large too rapidly. When other children painfully cut a child down to size, our task is to welcome the wounded child into a safe haven where worth is never up for grabs. Adults who determine to carve a child down to size are creating an unfair and perhaps cruel situation. It's not a fair match—child versus child, maybe, but never adult versus child. Children who emerge through childhood with a strong sense of high self-esteem are better equipped to take whatever the world hands out.

Another hopeful outcome, when children's needs are met by significant adults, is *feelings of competency*. Erik Erikson identifies industry versus inferiority as the psychosocial task in which school-age children are involved. When the child learns to work and to have a sense of accomplishment about that work the hopeful outcome is competence. If the effort to learn how to be industrious is met frequently by failure, the end result will be feelings of inferiority. Of course, no child's effort ever results in total competence or in complete failure. Each of us has feelings across the middle of that polarity. It is crucial for school-age children to practice, rehearse, and become reasonably competent in all areas of their development.

The everyday lives of children present hundreds of opportunities for us to observe their efforts in perfecting skills: reading library books, playing baseball, riding bicycles, and attending slumber parties where relationship skills are being honed. The stepping-stone concept involved in skill development encourages children who succeed to build upon each success. Every small success contributes to feelings of competence, thus enhancing a child's self-esteem.

Another hopeful outcome resulting from children's needs being met is *the healthy development of personhood*. Children in preschool years begin the task of becoming independent, autonomous human beings— learning that they are separate from the primary nurturer. They begin a lifelong journey of becoming a unique, separate self. The development of personhood continues in school-age children as their world expands and widens to include the peer group and other persons in the school, church, and community. Fortunate is the child whose home territory celebrates the unique specialness of personhood. A child whose sense of self is strong and secure would feel, "Just think, as long as I live I will never be anyone else but *me!*"

When children's needs are fulfilled, a foundation for faith development emerges where belief in a Supreme Being is fostered and the child is invited to see God in everydayness. In their daily interactions with children, significant adults demonstrate the attributes of God. In the familiar cycle of days, months, and seasons children see a fulfillment of promise. In the dependable orbit of sun, moon, stars, and planets, children are reminded that we have a God who is in control of an orderly world. We adults model for children love, grace, forgiveness, and redemption through the way we interact with them every day. As significant adults, we can be god for children in some ways until their god becomes God. Wise adults in touch with God in their own lives will best know when that transition can be made.

Specific Needs of Children

In order for us to review what specific children need from significant adults, school-age children will be divided into groups identified as younger children (ages five to eight) and older children (ages nine to twelve).

Younger Children

Younger children, specially, need our support in a widening world. From the first day of kindergarten well into the primary grades, children experience ever-widening concentric circles that broaden past the primary family unit to include other persons. Church may well be their first significant involvement with community; then come friends in the neighborhood and, finally, classmates at school. Every year children's lives branch out to include others in their personal circle of friendship. That desire to reach out to others must be supported by caring adults who guide and assist children as they develop appropriate social and emotional skills.

On a hot fall day two years ago my whole family waited anxiously for the outcome of a crucial experience. Time crept by very slowly all day. Grandma crocheted more than usual. Daddy glanced frequently at the clock in his office at the company. Aunt Jane fidgeted at her desk in her fifth-grade classroom. Time for lunch. Midafternoon, and the extended family gathered on Grandma's porch. Each car that turned the corner caused the family to pause and hold their breath. Suddenly, their interest froze as a familiar car came into view. The rocking chairs stilled, each family member leaned forward with anticipation, the car pulled into the driveway, the front door flew open, and Lendy, age six, flew into the open arms of her daddy. "I did it. I did it!" She had left home that morning a tiny little girl of six. She came home a woman of the world. Her head held high with newfound confidence, even her legs seemed longer. She had tasted success. *Lendy had successfully completed her very first day of school!*

Much preparation and support had gone into making that special day one in which Lendy would succeed: many long talks about what school would be like, a visit to the classroom, meeting the teacher, finding the right desk, and daily reassurances that she would be just fine. Support from loving adults is crucial for younger children. Support ensures a firm stepping-stone steadied by loved ones for the faltering foot of the child just venturing out.

Akin to support in a widening world is another need that younger children have, and that is help in ordering their world. With a widened world will come a rush of varied expectations and creative opportunities. Younger children may feel overwhelmed and become overly fatigued from so many demands, thus making it necessary for adults to set limits and to help the child make wise choices. Some young children may be finishing the preschool task of separating fantasy from reality. Fears will be in transition from the imagined world of ghosts, wild animals, and things that go bump in the night to a more realistic world that holds terror too, the world of school and teachers and peers. Helping children to order their world means learning to choose, putting things in their place physically and cognitively, determining priorities, and balancing a world of play among siblings and peers. Accompanying the establishment of order in their world, children need to experience an appropriate degree of independence. Innate in each child's nature is some measure of knowing how far and how fast to move emotionally.

Younger children need our help in learning how to compete. Currently, popular game books that encourage cooperation in order to win rather than winning by way of competition are available for purchase. For example, the longtime favorite Musical Chairs, popular among younger children, is reorganized so that a chair is left out of the circle rather than a child, making it necessary for many children to discover creatively how to sit on fewer and fewer chairs. Imagine the delight of eight children balancing precariously on one or two chairs! Cooperation is valued, rather than competition. However, back in the real world of one against another, children face competition in every facet of their lives. Win the spelling bee, hit the ball out of the park, run to be first in line, wear the latest style, be the best, the prettiest, the strongest . . . what pressure children experience when there is a strong message that to be worth anything they have to win! For children who are more often normal or average than outstanding in their attainment, society's word about achievement can be defeating. At least one teacher in public school conveyed the right attitude about competition to her class. Karen came home wearing a large blue ribbon and explained excitedly to her parents, "I won! I won!" The glow on her face was a look to be treasured. Actually, as the story unfolded at supper, Karen had come in last, but every child was given a ribbon and declared a winner. Significant adults need to respond to children in many competitive arenas with attitudes that reward each child. What more special way can we convey to children the manner in which each of us is viewed by God? Each of us is a winner!

Children's feelings, just like adult feelings, need to be respected and accepted. Handling the whole range of feelings is an ongoing process that needs the support and understanding of significant others. Some adults believe that children should be allowed to express only positive feelings while negative feelings are suppressed and pushed under the surface. Expressions of anger and subsequent conflict may be viewed as "bad" and in many cases seen as unchristian. Rather than acknowledging and channeling negative feelings into constructive avenues of behavior, children may be taught unwittingly to be less than whole persons in regard to their emotional expression.

Even young children can be encouraged to solve problems and make their own decisions. Teaching children how to cope with life's ambiguities and frustrations not only provides tools for coping but contributes to a heightened sense of self-worth. These skills will help children creatively cope with the acute crises that arise. Being successful in solving a problem, or realizing that our choice was a good one, makes us feel good about being able to handle our own life. On the other hand, realizing that inevitably some poor choices will be made and learning to live with the result of less than ideal circumstances is part of the choosing process too. The key to success in helping children mature in the choosing process is being in touch with who they are developmentally and how much appropriate freedom can be given.

Children need to be released to make appropriate choices. Caring adults will supply children with support, information, and skills for making decisions. Part of the process of preparation is honoring the decision made as well as helping the child to know in advance its full ramifications. Sometimes the natural consequences of a decision may afford a child a teachable moment not possible for adults to contrive. As long as no health or safety hazard is present, and no serious threat to the child's sense of self-esteem, seeing what happens as a result of choosing is one of life's important lessons.

Limits equal love. While the child is learning to make appropriate choices, rules need to be set firmly in place. The child who pushes against those rules needs the security of knowing that some persons care enough to hold the line. Eight-year-old Mark liked to flirt with danger on his bicycle by seeing how close he could come to moving cars without being hit while his parents watched passively from the porch. After a narrow escape Mark burst into tears and shouted to his parents on the porch, "Make me stop! Can't you see I'm going to hurt myself?"

Children often lead us in a nonverbal way to an understanding of how much independence they can tolerate. In a society where children are pressured to grow up and become adult at younger and younger ages, our challenge may not be to hurry children along but to slow children down so childhood can be savored and preserved. Children of today may not remember their childhood as idyllic, as slow days of reading on the porch swing and daydreaming about the future. Significant adults who can assist children in creatively pacing their lives can enter the child's widening world of independence as a partner in discovering "how much—how soon." Children's behavior may cry out for limits, for a little more luxury of dependency before the burden of the world becomes completely theirs.

Older Children

Older school-age children (ages nine to twelve) shift somewhat in their focus concerning needs that can be met by significant adults. Although many of the same needs younger children have will continue to be the needs of older children, the added dimension of the widening world, the extended impact of external forces, and a mounting invasion of internal forces pervade their lives. School becomes increasingly more sophisticated, peer influence and pressure intensify, media messages bombard the mind, and activities increase, making it necessary for the child to decide about the use of time. Simultaneously, the child is faced with new feelings and moods, body changes, increased hormonal development, spurts of growth, and conflictual feelings. Growth begins to accelerate in preparation for teen years, and with renewed growth comes renewed conflict. Older children need a great deal of support from significant adults in this time of rapid growth and change.

Fourth-, fifth- and sixth-graders need significant adults to give them support and encouragement in their academic endeavors. The breadth and depth of subject matter at school is increasing, and the child is experiencing demands to excel. We hope that the child who reads poorly and the socially or physically immature child has been helped in overcoming hurdles in the younger years and now can keep pace academically and relationally with his or her peers. Ministers can recognize the older child's desire for encouragement and support. They tell us in any number of ways what they need. For example, through recognition of giftedness among older children at church we can provide opportunities in areas where they are certain to succeed. The poor reader may delight in designing banners, the gifted child who memorizes easily will enjoy the speaking part in a musical, and the shy child may become involved in a peer group where the task rather than the relationship is central. Sensitive ministers will note that after-school programming may need to focus on alternative ways of learning rather than on the more traditional emphases of reading and writing skills. Relief must come from the academic pressure older children endure.

Accompanying the increased academic challenge, older children are experiencing an inordinate amount of pressure in peer relationships.

Close same-sex friendships (chumships) are in full bloom now. Children need our models of relationship as well as our help interpreting, clarifying, and defining what relationships can and do mean. What friends think and say becomes more important every day, and adult understanding and acceptance of these relationships is critical. Asking a child to choose between an adult's wish and a peer's demand may cause a struggle that is not worth the issue.

Older children need the assistance of significant adults in preparation for adolescence. Taking advantage of a calmer growth year for teaching (age ten, for example) in contrast to a year when turbulence is high (age eleven) will aid significant adults in helping children to know what lies ahead in teen years. Good preparation for change lies in talking and teaching when children *can* listen, rather than when they must listen. All of us can remember being too upset to be reasonable and responsive to suggestions for change.

James Dobson, in one of his helpful books, *Dare to Discipline,* tells of his own family and how in their preteen years he took each child aside and spoke of how the years ahead would hold much change and what those changes would mean. In the peaceful, loving relationship between father and child, each could hear the other. This would be the anchor conversation that would reassure and hold family relationships steady in the months and years ahead. Dobson said that inevitably the turbulence of early teen years arrived. In a stormy session one night between his daughter and himself, she said through her sobs, "Do you remember the time you told me that change was coming and that it wouldn't be easy, but that you would always love me? Well, I think that time has come." She couldn't hear and be reasonable *that day,* but she remembered a day of calmness and strength in which she could anchor her hope.

Both ministers and parents need to recognize the importance of helping older children to prepare for adolescence. Greatly beloved ministers who love, understand, and enjoy fifth- and sixth-graders can plan retreats where openness and good dialogue are fostered and where every question is respected and addressed. Materials which not only give accurate sex information but which support Christian choices and values can be dealt with among peers and with trusted Christian leadership. All-night talk sessions after the lights are out and a climate of psychological safety develops will invite women and girls to "really" talk and men and boys to confide. Within a Christian context they can determine what kind of woman or man they want to be. Sex, drugs, peer pressures, thoughts of suicide, and struggles with parents and peers could well surface. Older children have a right to expect from us, as significant adults, honest and forthright dialogue. Having answers is not nearly as important as being willing to deal with the questions. A weekend of this type with preteens may well be one of a minister's heavier moments—and a most rewarding one.

Older children have very ambivalent feelings about "growing up," as reflected in their vacillation between the silliness of earlier years and sophisticated behavior beyond their years. Departing from childhood may have strains of sadness as children glance first to the past and then into the future. The wise minister will offer opportunities for play as well as for mature, structured experience. I am reminded of a group of four preteens who announced to me one fall at church that they thought they would rather stay in the children's division than to move up with their group into the youth division. Fighting my momentary panic over what an unusual dilemma this would be, I chose to trust the pull of the peer group. Within a very few days they were waving to me from the balcony, where they were well ensconced with their peers. Such ambivalence is temporary. We, their significant adults, must hold steady.

David Elkind, in his book *The Hurried Child,* tells us that children are growing up too fast too soon. Activities favored several years ago as good and appropriate for senior highs have now become favorites for junior highs; elementary-school children are now involved in junior high activities. Children are "doing their thing" at younger and younger ages. We have a critical need for adults to intervene in this hurried cycle and help children learn how to pace their lives creatively. Needless to say, this proverbial chicken-and-egg cycle affects adults as much as it does children, both within church life and in secular life. The whirlpool of hurriedness contributes, and perhaps causes, what Neil Postman has identified as the disappearance of childhood. Ministers can help in several ways. We can encourage children to play, an antidote for hurrying, Elkind says. We can plan times for families to slow down, to be together, to anticipate more, and to rush less. An understanding and acceptance of what hurrying does to children may call us to do ministry differently. We may find ourselves slowing the program pace at church and inviting families to stay at home and enjoy each other's company. Who knows? Savoring life as it comes, rather than rushing to its end, may be the best gift we can give our children.

Conclusion

She is only eight, but she had looked forward to my annual visit to Grandma's with great anticipation. Her parents had spoken often of my coming, and to have an aunt whose one joy in life was to bring gifts and spend time with her was really very exciting. The vacation week finally came, and our joy in being together was very nearly complete. We played games and sang songs and told jokes and explored the country-side. Everywhere I went the eight-year-old shadow was not far behind.

One late afternoon in Grandma's den, as she cuddled close on the arm of a big chair, she said, "I was thinking today about how much I love you. I love you right next to God. I really do." The seriousness of her comment was reinforced by the solemn expression on her face. She had thought this through. Actually, I am an ordinary everyday aunt, but to her I was a very significant adult.

To be significant adults who give children what they need, expect, and deserve calls forth our very best. We can't find all the necessary knowledge from books, though they do enlighten us. We can't collect a bag of tricks, though know-how is important. What matters is the kind of person we are. We must, therefore, take responsibility for nurturing ourselves and all the relationships that feed our selfhood, including our relationship to God. We nourish children from overflow, not from emptiness. Children will recognize the minister whose primary source of strength is the love and grace of God. Because we are loved and accepted by the greatest love of all, we too are able to love and accept.

FURTHER READING

Dobson, James. *Dare to Discipline.* Glendale, Calif.: Regal Books, 1970.

———. *Hide or Seek.* Exp. and updated ed. Old Tappan, N.J.: Fleming H. Revell Co., 1974.

Dreikurs, Rudolf, and Vicki Soltz. *Children: The Challenge.* New York: Hawthorn Books, 1964.

Elkind, David. *The Hurried Child: Growing Up Too Fast Too Soon.* Reading, Mass.: Addison-Wesley Publishing Co., 1981.

———. *A Sympathetic Understanding of the Child: Birth to Sixteen.* 2nd ed. Boston: Allyn & Bacon, 1978.

Gleason, John J. *Growing Up to God.* Nashville: Abingdon Press, 1975.

Hendricks, William L. *A Theology for Children.* Nashville: Broadman Press, 1980.

Kersey, Katharine, ed. *Helping Your Child Handle Stress.* Washington, D.C.: Acropolis Books, 1986.

Oates, Wayne E. *On Becoming Children of God.* Philadelphia: Westminster Press, 1969.

Price, B. Max. *Understanding Today's Children.* Nashville: Convention Press, 1982.

Williams, Joyce Wolfgang, and Marjorie Smith. *Middle Childhood: Behavior and Development.* 2nd ed. New York: Macmillan Publishing Co., 1980.

5

Understanding and Caring for the Child in Crisis
Olle Jane Z. Sahler

I once knew a girl named Sandy. She was eleven years old and had just been diagnosed as having a seizure disorder. I got to know Sandy when she was assigned to me as a patient in our Behavioral Pediatrics clinic in Rochester, where I was a medical student. She had been referred to our clinic because she had a very poor self-image stemming from her feelings that she was defective. She tried to deny that she had seizures by refusing to take her medication. She was a behavior problem at home and was failing in school.

I met with Sandy weekly for more than a year. During our meetings, which she told me she was forced to attend by her mother, Sandy was sullen, uncommunicative, and angry. Despite my best efforts, we seemed to make only a little progress and her situation at home and school improved minimally. At the end of the year, I graduated and told Sandy of my plans to move to another state to continue my training. She withdrew from the treatment program, refusing to continue with another counselor.

I returned to the University of Rochester four years later and eventually joined the faculty. Last year, fifteen years after graduation, I received a call from Sandy. She told me that she was living in a city about fifty miles away. She had been married but was recently divorced. Her major concern was her two-and-a-half-year-old son, who was displaying a lot of acting out and negativistic behavior. She wanted me to provide counseling to her and her child.

"But, Sandy," I responded. "There must be someone nearer to your home whom you can see."

"There probably is, Dr. Sahler, but you helped me so much when I

Olle Jane Z. Sahler is Associate Professor, Departments of Pediatrics and Psychiatry, University of Rochester School of Medicine and Dentistry, Rochester, N.Y.

was younger that I feel I can trust you, and I really want *your* ideas about what I should do."

The Impact of Crisis on Children

One of the most universal feelings at times of crisis is the sensation of being alone. Frequently, people who have suffered loss or hurt ask for space—physical and emotional distance from others—to sort out feelings, grieve, and be angry. After a period of time (temporal space from the event) comes a rejoining and with it the opportunity to gain strength from others.

As was the case with Sandy, it is much easier to separate than it is to rejoin. This is particularly true for school-age children, for whom going through a significant crisis may represent a first encounter with some of the deep emotions arising from turmoil. For them the words "time heals" have no meaning, because they may never have weathered a similar experience and in any case their sense of time is poorly developed. To understand that in a few days, weeks, or months the hurt of a stressful event will be eased is beyond their cognitive ability. Such children may not know that, once they have separated or withdrawn from those caring persons around them, they can move back into a positive and supportive relationship when they are ready, and so they remain estranged, coping poorly and unaware of the roots of their unhappiness. The role of the minister is to reach out and move into their space, usually unbidden, to fill the void they have unwittingly created between themselves and the world.

To understand how and why children frequently find it difficult to cope with crisis, it is important to understand that youngsters are egocentric during the school-age years. They have a strong sense that they are somehow central to, and therefore responsible for, events in the world around them; that through some act of theirs, especially one perceived as bad or negligent, some disaster has occurred. School-age children, who are struggling with the mastery of skills and believe they must be competent in all tasks in order to feel good about themselves, are particularly vulnerable to feelings of being inferior or lacking and thus responsible for a bad event.

Actually, children this age enjoy tackling and completing projects and are becoming increasingly adept at working cooperatively. They are also, however, stringent critics, quick to be cruel in their estimation of the work of both themselves and others if they find it unfit or lacking. Because these children do not fully separate the person from the product, a less-than-completely-acceptable product translates into being the work of a less-than-completely-acceptable person. The major danger of this age is that a sense of inferiority may overcome those children who think that what they do or produce—and therefore what they are—is inadequate.

If we examine the school or social life of children this age, it is very easy to see that the opportunity for feeling inferior presents itself almost continually. Unlike older students, those in junior or senior high school who can pick and choose courses according to interest and talent, the elementary-school child must be good at everything: math, drawing, spelling, soccer, music, and a myriad of other diverse activities. Although it is hard to disagree with the basic educational tenet that children this age should be considered undifferentiated and thus exposed to all educational, social, and physical activities possible, it also must be remembered that stern critics (the children themselves) will be merciless in their evaluation of anyone not up to par. School and neighborhood are such potent forces in the life of children that even minor shortcomings are disproportionately significant in their negative effect on self-esteem.

The cognition of school-age children is distinguished by the gradual stepwise development of logical thinking, which, during this period, is restricted to learning about "concrete" (physically present) concepts. Manipulation of the environment, therefore, whether in a specifically designed experimental situation in the classroom or through informal experimentation in the backyard ("If I throw this rock this hard, it will go this far; if I throw this same rock harder, it will go that far") is a constant activity. Every day is filled with new discoveries children make all by themselves. They experience a sense of "eureka" almost daily as they discover a concept for the first time. This sense of single-handed discovery of the universe has, among other potential pitfalls, the associated sense that "no one has walked in my shoes before," "no one knows exactly how I feel," "no one can understand me completely." This sense of uniqueness is further strengthened by children's inability to take fully the point of view of another. And what they do not or cannot do, they cannot conceive of others doing.

Being inadequate is a shameful thing for which one is taunted by peers in the classroom or on the playground. It leads to withdrawal (Leave me alone), aggression (I'm really better than you are), hostility (You don't know anything, anyway), somatic symptoms such as headache or stomachache (I can't help what I do if I'm sick), disrupted sleeping (Why do I have so many bad dreams?), poor school performance (I can't remember what the teacher said), apparent unconcern (If I don't think about it, it will go away), daydreaming (I want to think about how it might be, not how it is), hyperactivity (If I keep moving, I don't have to think about it), and, occasionally, truly antisocial behavior such as stealing and truancy (Let's talk about how bad I am so we don't have to talk about that other thing).

At times of crisis, children will display a wide variety of behaviors. Any given child may display marked fluctuations in emotional state, vacillating among many intense, seemingly disparate behaviors in quick succession trying to find the emotion that fits. Although such maladaptive behaviors are common as initial reactions, they are worrisome when they become persistent. For example, transient withdrawal from peers for a few days or a week after a best friend has moved away is common and allows the child the emotional and physical opportunity to mourn the loss by remembering shared experiences, writing letters, and planning a visit during the next school holiday. Coupled with this, however, should be consistent, even if slow, movement toward establishing new relationships or strengthening other old ones. Helping the child does not mean suggesting that the friend who moved away should be forgotten, but that other close friends need to be made.

Ministry to Children in Crisis

What is a crisis to a child? The list of crises is different from that which would be drawn up for an adult and includes many seemingly minor events that are crises merely because they have not been experienced (and mastered) before: entry into or change in school (What will happen in a new place?), death of a pet (What will things be like without my dog?), move of a friend (Will anyone else play with me?), as well as the major calamities of life such as divorce or the death of a parent (Who will take care of me?). Note that many of the questions children this age are likely to ask involve concerns about separation from, and loss of, familiar beings and surroundings. Loss of relationship in particular— because of the child's persistent egocentrism—carries with it a sense of somehow being responsible for precipitating the crisis situation. However, children are loath to admit that they cannot cope and are unable to comprehend that others have faced similar situations and can understand their thoughts and feelings. This situation, which can ultimately lead to permanent withdrawal and isolation, can be easily understood as a potential hazard stemming from their normal, age-appropriate developmental stage. The challenge for the pastor is to recognize the potency of the psychological and cognitive forces at work and to strive to overcome the natural reticence of the child to seek help.

Crisis represents a period of disequilibrium of sufficient magnitude that usual coping mechanisms are ineffective or inadequate. Crisis results in emotional turmoil and psychological disorganization while the individual casts about, often in a trial-and-error fashion, to find some way of managing the situation. As we are reminded by the Chinese characters for crisis, both danger and opportunity exist as possible outcomes. The significance of the Chinese characters becomes very clear when we consider that, by definition, a crisis is a short-term and self-limited state; resolution or movement into another steady state, for better or for worse, will occur after a period of days or weeks. The time of opportunity for adaptive resolution is short-lived and accompanied always by the danger of maladaptive resolution.

That the individual in crisis is aware of the immediacy and urgency of the crisis state is well illustrated by the fact that, after a momentary time of seeking space, people in crisis are actually quite receptive to outside intervention, although once the period of disequilibrium has passed and the situation has stabilized, they become very reluctant to seek help. Thus, the ability to recognize that a crisis either is occurring or is an expected outcome of a given situation is an important skill for the intervenor. To wait until "things have settled down" will make intervention more difficult and sometimes impossible. Thus, prevention of maladaptive behavior, by providing more adaptive alternatives right away, is a primary goal in the treatment of any crisis.

Erikson has identified a sense of basic trust in the intrinsic goodwill and worthiness of others to be the cornerstone of all human relationship. Trust evolves in infancy through feelings of familiarity, inner goodness, and comfort and from contacts with the people who are associated with these feelings. Consistent, continuous, and predictable role models in the environment teach infants how to display these same traits themselves. Basic trust also includes for infants the sense that even though relationships might be tested by them, individuals in the environment will remain constant in their demonstrations of love, affection, and attention. Through this early nurturant phase, then, infants learn to become and remain confident that cries for help, or just for loving, will be heard and responded to by someone who cares for them. They, in turn, respond by cuddling and smiling and gazing intently at those who provide them with care.

Infants bond to those few people who, through close and sustained contact, provide nurturance. This bonding is actually a mutual process in which each individual—infant and caregiver—both gives and receives. From this early process comes a feeling of attachment—a bonding over space and time that is filled, predominantly, with love.

We know that human nurturance is a necessary ingredient for life. The studies of René Spitz, for example, which investigated an almost 75 percent death rate among infants and young children in a foundling home in South America fifty years ago, revealed that infants who are given adequate food and kept clean but not played with or caressed will eventually die of inanition. In other words, when receiving little or no human contact outside of feeding and diapering and being confined to spotlessly clean but otherwise bare cribs, completely normal infants lose their zest for life and actually starve to death from lack of interest in food or eating. Simply put, a person devoid of human relationship may have no will to live.

Let us apply the notion of relationship or nurturance—human caring modeled on God's love—to the pastor's role in crisis intervention with children. Five steps in this process follow.

1. Recognition that a given event truly represents a crisis. The pastor must recognize that even that which may seem trivial to an adult may be major to a child. Denigrating a child's concerns immediately places the pastor in jeopardy of being labeled as not understanding and therefore not caring. Pastors are in a truly unique position to know about real or potential crises because of their ongoing relationships with families in the congregation and the willingness of many families, who would not otherwise seek professional psychological help, to share such needs with clergy. Because it is an accepted and desirable practice for clergy to visit in homes, both as a routine part of ministry as well as at times of problems, what more natural way is there to reach out to children who may not know that help is available or where to turn for it?

2. Recognition that young school-age children rely heavily on the existence of relationships as markers of their own intrinsic self-worth. Unlike the infant who is accepted, loved, and nurtured regardless of behavior and demands, the school-age child is beginning to learn about rejection. Although most rejection comes from peers, because of poor skill in some area, for example, children also have learned that rejection can come from adults, such as parents and teachers, for the same reason. Because their self-concept is tenuous and therefore vulnerable, few children will wittingly lay themselves open to possible ridicule and further rejection by admitting they are unable to cope with a stressful situation. Coupled with this is the feeling that no one has ever faced this particular dilemma before. The pastor must reach out, not by saying "What's wrong?" or "What are you feeling?" but by saying, "I was once in a tough spot just like you are and I felt hurt (angry, alone). I thought there was nobody who could help me. More than that, I didn't think I needed any help. I wanted to figure it all out by myself. I wouldn't be surprised if you've been thinking about (how to make new friends, how you'll get along with the new teacher)." Putting oneself in the place of the child and stating probable feelings is a powerful tool. It also removes from the child the burden of having to put feelings into words because, for the child, the situation may be indescribable, either because it has never been experienced before or because it is too terrible to speak aloud.

3. Recognition that school-age children are basically good kids.
Undesirable behaviors arise because a child has not learned other, more adaptive ways of dealing with stress. To ask the question "Why?" ("Why aren't you doing your work in school?" "Why are you fighting on the bus?" "Why are you giving your parents such a hard time?") may be to ask the unanswerable. How can I tell you, at age ten, that my anxiety that my father's illness may be fatal is so great that I can't concentrate? How can I tell you that I have to beat up the kids who tell me that my parents are bad because they're getting a divorce? How can I tell you that I'm jealous of my baby sister when my mom and dad tell me I should love her? Again, the role of the pastor is to use imagination and creativity in trying to assume the child's role in whatever the crisis might be in order to understand why certain behaviors are occurring. To chastise the child for the behaviors is to perpetrate what has already been done. Many people, from bus drivers to parents, have already said the behavior is unacceptable, apparently without effect. The pastor, however, is neither the bus driver (whose job it is to keep order, with little time for discovering why certain behaviors are taking place) nor the parents (who may not wish to know why their child is acting out because of their own need to deny or because they lack the extra emotional energy necessary to deal with their child's crisis at the same time they are dealing with their own).

A better approach is to suggest an explanation of why the child is acting a certain way. The child will agree or be neutral, if the guess is right, and disagree if it is wrong. In the latter case, the child is more likely to give the real reason if the pastor has already made an honest attempt to understand. It is not a matter of one-upmanship; instead it is a matter of the child's setting the record straight for someone who truly wants to understand the behavior. This is an extension of a nurturing relationship; the pastor is not put off and does not reject the child because the behavior and the child are two separate entities. The pastor says, "I approve of the child; at this stage I neither approve nor disapprove of the behavior, I merely want to understand it better."

4. Problem-solving and helping the child adopt adaptive behaviors. Anyone in crisis is having trouble problem-solving; otherwise, the situation would not be a crisis. For the school-age child, providing the opportunity for self-mastery is a crucial ingredient to successful, healthy resolution. Figuring out (with help) what can be done about the situation helps to restore self-esteem. Breaking the enormous problem down into its component parts and dealing with each in small, manageable steps is essential to the restoration of adaptive equilibrium. Dispelling the feeling that they are alone in trying to work out solutions by sharing that others have felt similarly—and have been successful in overcoming their feelings—helps to alleviate the anxiety that there is no end point or that resolution is never possible.

The important question for the pastor to ask is "Does what you're doing get you what you want?" The way is easy if the child says no. Sometimes, however children will say yes if their initial aim was to hurt someone whom they perceive as hurting them; the "eye for an eye" ethic can be very strong among school-age children. The maneuver, then, is to move them toward some other goal than hurting others. Fortunately, school-age children are in the process of becoming capable of understanding negotiation as well as reciprocity. In many instances, helping them to do something good for someone, either in return for something good (a tangible reward) or even for something as abstract as approval, is possible. Having them determine the good actions and the rewards increases the chances of compliance and, again, enhances their sense of self-mastery ("I can come up with good ideas; therefore, I am a good person").

In addition to direct help from the pastor, some children profit from bibliotherapy, using reading material to help solve problems. If children who are experiencing a crisis can read about others who have also had a similar problem, they may see alternatives for themselves. By identifying with characters in a book, children come to realize they are not alone in their struggle with reality and gain insight into their own situation. Encouraging children to do some work on their own to sort out feelings, using tools such as books, encourages independence and self-mastery. The technique is most useful when child and pastor discuss the story together, after it has been read, to clarify the issues and apply the insights the child has gained to the problem at hand.

5. Solidification of the caring relationship between the pastor and the child. A single successful intervention, no matter how small, in which the pastor has acted as the child's advocate (for a goal desired by both), helps assure that the child will develop a sense of trust in the pastor and return either to complete work on the current crisis or to seek help in the event of some future crisis.

The ultimate goal, of course, is for children to work toward mastery in crisis situations out of a sense of intrinsic self-worth and a belief in the integrity of the attachments they have with others in their life. It is a natural feature of crises, however, that these ties, to ourselves and others, are stretched, sometimes beyond the breaking point. The resulting sense of separation and loss leads to withdrawal and isolation. As a temporary maneuver to gain strength and perspective, separation is an adaptive phenomenon. If it persists, however, it can be overcome only by our actively seeking these children out, identifying with them, and joining with them in the process of resolution. Children usually do not know that they can come to us for help. Those who are sent may be resentful and uncooperative. What they need to learn from us is that we are willing to meet them where they are, even if it means going all the way to them while they stand still waiting to see just how far we will go, to hold their hand and tell them they were worth the walk.

Epilogue

I once knew a boy named David. He was twelve years old and had cystic fibrosis, a progressive fatal disease affecting the lungs and digestive tract. I first met David one January when the nurses asked me to speak with him because he seemed depressed at having to come into the hospital again only five months after his last admission. He knew, they believed, that increasing frequency of hospitalization is a sign of deterioration.

When I met David, he was truly sick with pneumonia. As I sat by his bedside he had little strength and even less desire to talk. He agreed with me, by nodding his head, that he was disappointed to be in the hospital again so soon but said little else. When I saw him again two days later, he was much better and directed the conversation to what he planned to do during the spring when he went fishing with his father. As I saw him daily for the next week he never talked about being sick, seemed unhappy that I had come to see him, and never called me by name.

David was readmitted in May and I went to see him. Again, he would not talk about his disease and seemed to resent my presence. Once he was feeling better he told me, somewhat defiantly, all about his plans for the summer. In June, David was again hospitalized. This time his conversation focused on his teachers for the following year and the fact that his best friend was in his homeroom. Once again, however, he seemed to resent my visiting.

In July, on a Thursday, the day before I was scheduled to leave for a two-week vacation, I was told that David was in the hospital again and that perhaps I should see him. I went into his room where he was sitting with an oxygen mask on, hunched over his bedside table, hardly able to breathe. The moment I said "Hi" he looked at me and said, "Dr. Sahler, I don't want to die." I sat down to collect my thoughts. "You've been thinking a lot about dying, David?" "A lot," he replied. "Have you talked to your mom and dad about it?" "Oh, no, no one." After a moment, he asked, "Do you think they'll find a cure for cystic fibrosis this weekend?" "I know they're working on it very hard, David," I replied. "I'm sure they're trying to find a cure just as fast as they can. I'm not sure if they'll find it this weekend, but I sure hope they do."

And then I asked him, "Has Dr. Jones from the CF center been straight with you, David?"

"No."

"Do you want him to be straight with you?"

"You tell Dr. Jones to be just the same as he always is. No different now from what he was before."

I promised that I would, and since I was going to be gone for a long time, I gave David a big handshake which he returned with more feeling than he ever had before, looking directly into my eyes. Each of us said the single word "good-bye."

David and his family were members of a strong Fundamentalist church. He asked that the minister and his many friends in the congregation come to see him and pray with him. After a long weekend of visitors, he died quietly on Sunday night.

It is a privilege to be allowed to share the frightening and unutterable, to help put terror into words and so help it to be mastered. Coming from David, who had always seemed so rejecting of my presence, it was a rare gift indeed, attesting to the strength of the trust that existed in our unspoken relationship. That he derived his strength from God was clear; that he allowed me to minister to him in the broadest sense was then, and continues to be, my joy.

FURTHER READING

Dreyer, Sharon S. *The Bookfinder: A Guide to Children's Literature About the Needs and Problems of Youth Aged 2 to 15.* 3 vols. Circle Pines, Minn.: American Guidance Service, 1981.

Erikson, Erik H. *Childhood and Society.* 2nd ed. New York: W. W. Norton & Co., 1963.

Ginsburg, Herbert, and Sylvia Opper. *Piaget's Theory of Intellectual Development.* 2nd ed. Englewood Cliffs, N.J.: Prentice-Hall, 1977.

Gnagy, R., B. B. Satterwhite, and I. B. Pless. "Ministry to Families of Chronically Ill Children," *Journal of Religion and Health,* 16:15–21, 1977.

Sahler, Olle Jane Z., and Elizabeth R. McAnarney. *The Child from Three to Eighteen.* St. Louis: C. V. Mosby Co., 1981.

PART II

Ministry with Children in Particular Crises

6

Children Whose Parents
Are Divorcing

Benjamin T. Griffin

Divorce has become almost commonplace in American society. Except for a few small Christian groups and the major exception of the Roman Catholic Church, most American religious communities no longer consider divorce the moral scandal it was a few decades ago. While one may applaud this trend away from considering divorced people social outcasts, one fact remains unchanged. The children of divorce continue to be the innocent victims of the breakup of their parents' marriages. One study of 131 children of divorce noted, "The most pervasive fact to emerge from our research was the enormity of the grief all the children felt over their parents' divorce, whether it was obvious or not. They were sad beyond measure. The pain was there—hard and hurting—in every one of the 131 youngsters."[1] That has also been my observation over more than twenty years of pastoral counseling with children of divorce.

Clergy and other marriage counselors who are not experienced in working with children have often failed to communicate to parents the sad toll of divorce upon their offspring. Too often parents are told, "Children are very resilient. In time, with love and understanding, they will get over it." Research and clinical experience reveal another picture. In the survey of the 131 children under age thirteen, not one of them wanted the divorce to happen—"not even those who had witnessed acts of terrible violence. They longed for the absent parent with an intensity that says something about a youngster's capacity for love and loyalty."[2] I am not trying to deny that many times circumstances warrant a divorce. The fundamental point I wish to make is that in the rush to meet adult needs one should not so easily pass over the feelings and needs of the children. This chapter is an attempt to offer pastors

Benjamin T. Griffin is President, United Theological Seminary of the Twin Cities, New Brighton, Minn.

and other concerned persons ways to help these children and their parents who are in the crisis of separation or divorce.

The Nature of the Crisis

The separation or divorce of parents precipitates what may be the most critical crisis a family can face. The intact nuclear family is blown apart. Parents and children will view and experience this crisis from different perspectives.

Separation from the Child's Perspective

Adults, including the affected spouses, will primarily view the crisis as *husband* and *wife* no longer living together. The child will see what is happening as "Mommy and Daddy no longer live with *me.*" The difference is not one of semantics. Think of your own parents. Do you primarily think of them as husband and wife or as your mother and father? A child experiences parents primarily as mother and father, both individually and as a unit, and only vaguely, if at all, as a marital pair. Failure of parents and counselors to grasp this essential point may be a major contributor to the inability of both parents and counselors to grasp that divorce is a major life trauma in the lives of children.

A child experiences a major crisis, yet is almost totally powerless to affect its course. The child, furthermore, is in no sense responsible for this event, which will forever change his or her life and that of the family. In a profound sense the child is the innocent victim and "orphan" of divorce. When ministering to children of divorce we need to keep in mind that the separation of parents breaks up the basic world the child has always known. The child is born into and grows within a family that the child expects to remain intact. This world, centered in mother and father, provides the child's basic security. With the separation of parents the child feels abandoned not simply by the departing parent (usually the father), but in a profound sense by both mother and father, who have abandoned their conjoint role as parents, *together*. While there has been clinical research on the feelings of abandonment when the "absent" parent leaves home, more research needs to focus on the sense of abandonment the child feels toward both parents as they abdicate their joint responsibility.

When a person's family falls apart, basic trust in the world is called into question. In his classical study of human development, Erikson pointed out that the first developmental stage through which humans pass is that of basic trust versus basic mistrust.[3] This is also the stage that is ultimately religious, since trust leads into faith. The baby learns either to trust the primary parent (usually the mother) for food, care, and love, or not to trust. To a lesser but still significant extent the child learns to trust or not to trust the father. The separation of the parents seriously threatens the child's basic trust in both mother and father. As a result the child's sense of security is under attack. The child asks the fundamental question, "Who will take care of me now?" The feeling of abandonment by the parental couple is one of the reasons children of separated parents have been called "the orphans of divorce."

Separation from the Parents' Perspective

While the focus of this chapter is ministry to children whose parents are divorcing, one of the major ways we can help these children is by helping their parents in their relationships with the children during and after the divorce. This is an essential part of that ministry, whenever possible. I assume most couples with children do not come easily or quickly to the decision to separate. We are frequently asked, "What effect do you think a divorce will have on my children?" This question gives us entrée into assisting the parents in their relationships to each other and to the children during this stressful time in the life of the family.

Regrettably but understandably, couples in the process of deciding to divorce focus primarily upon their unhappiness as wife and husband. If the marital relationship appears unredeemable to one or both spouses, the agenda of the couple may be to dissolve the marriage. A great deal of rationalization will then be expressed about how much "better off" everyone will be, including the children.

Nevertheless, rare is the parent who does not feel guilty over the breakup of the family. Scapegoating and self-blame are not unusual. A role of the counselor is to assist the parents in examining and dealing with this guilt. I agree with Richard Gardner that the counselor has a responsibility to correct the myth that divorce is relatively benign and to confront the parents who believe that "the children will be better off not living in an unhappy home, etc."[4] I believe that a marriage counselor must not slide too easily or quickly over the effects of divorce upon children. Parents who would otherwise "do anything for their children" often will refuse to work at resolving their marital difficulties. I have a standard comment to such couples: "No, you should not stay married simply because of your children, but surely your children are powerful reasons to work hard in therapy to put your marriage back together."

One of the great difficulties in working with parents who are in the process of separating is that hostility, even hatred, for each other is often present. Indeed, no description of the nature of this crisis is complete without the inclusion of hostility. It is the major factor that prevents rational and compassionate discussion of the current and future welfare of their children. If a counselor can assist one or both parents in defusing hostility, or at least keeping it suspended where the children are concerned, I believe the counselor has helped the couple achieve a major breakthrough. Hostility is also a primary reason that custody and visitation issues become so nasty and why children are put in the middle of an ongoing marital struggle, a struggle that often extends beyond the legal divorce.

Parents may have to be reminded of the obvious: you may cease to be husband and wife to each other, but you will always be father and mother to your children. This leading question might be asked, "I wonder how you think the two of you will carry out parenting tasks together after you are no longer husband and wife?" Couples, because of their hostility, are often resistant to any suggestions that they need to share anything, including any form of joint parenting. By asking this question the counselor brings another perspective and may open the parents to suggestions or coaching about better ways to relate to each other and to their children. The counselor should always take advantage of such opportunities.

In counseling with divorcing parents I bring a bias that I freely admit in sessions: I am an advocate for the children, who are not represented in either the counseling or in the divorce and custody litigation. Children are the weakest and least powerful members of any family system. In being an advocate for the children, the counselor must avoid becoming triangulated with their family system. As the counselor seeks to help parents and children of divorce, attention needs to be given to understanding the impact of divorce on children.

Children's Responses to the Divorce of Parents

Considerable clinical research has been done on the emotional responses of children whose parents are divorcing. The fundamental response is separation anxiety.[5] Separation anxiety is defined as "a threat to instinctual need which is symbolically linked to earlier threats that resulted in vulnerability and conflict."[6] Separation anxiety in a child is the threat of the loss of a person significant to the child, usually a parent. The temporary or permanent loss of a parent causes the child's basic sense of trust, security, and self-identity to be seriously threatened. How this anxiety manifests itself depends on the stage of the development of the child, the child's environment, and the actions of significant persons (parents). How a child will react also depends upon age, custody arrangements, coping mechanisms, and the relationship between father and mother. While each child will experience the crisis in a unique way, certain general responses may be expected.

Denial and silence. A child who has been informed about the parents' coming separation may lie about it when confronted by another child who says, "Your parents are going to get a divorce." Parents are sometimes bewildered when, after informing the child about their decision, they are met with, "OK. Can I go out and play now?" That does not mean the child is indifferent, but that the thought of a major family disruption is too great for the child to accept. The child may fantasize that somehow the parents will get back together. The child should be helped out of the fantasy, the unrealistic hope for reconciliation, and into an acceptance of reality. As will be seen later in this chapter, the fantasy of reconciliation of parents does not easily die.

Regression. Children may regress to an earlier level of development, such as thumb-sucking or bed-wetting by children who have already passed beyond those habits. Such a child may not be able to master the new anxiety. When regression occurs, the child is probably saying, "Don't leave me. See, I'm only a little child. Please love me and stay with me."

Hostility or anger. A child may see the breakup of the home—the place of basic security—as abandonment. Not only is one parent physically leaving the child, both parents are giving up their joint parenting roles. A normal human response to events over which one feels helpless is anger. The hostility may be directed at the parent with whom the child lives. "You sent Daddy away," said one ten-year-old girl to her mother.

Bodily stress. Anxiety may express itself in trembling, restlessness, loss of appetite, increase in pulse rate and respiration, diarrhea, urinary frequency, fitful sleep, frightening dreams—all symptoms of acute anxiety. The child fears that the most basic things needed will be lost: food, shelter, and love.

Panic and confusion. A child quickly perceives that a divorce will result in the disruption of normal relationships with at least one parent and that homelife will be different. A child has two basic questions: "Who will take care of me now?" and "How and where will I now live?" Children may "experience confusion about the absent parent, difficulty in school and . . . health difficulties."[7] Some children feel humiliated— especially older children of middle-class families—at being abandoned by a parent.

Blame and guilt. In seeking to gain some self-understanding to the breakup of their parents' marriages, children will often blame themselves. "I must have done something really bad to make Mom and Dad split up," a ten-year-old said. Children have been known to run away from home in hopes that with the child's absence the parents will come back together, or at least be united in the search for the departed child.

One of the sad side effects of divorce is that a child is often placed by parents into a conflict over loyalty. Usually the child needs, loves, and is loyal to both parents. No child should ever have to choose between parents. As parents continue their marital warfare after the divorce, however, the child often becomes a pawn who is pressed to "side" with one parent. The child feels the conflict of divided loyalty and the resulting guilt about the deception such loyalty demands.

Mourning and depression. Divorce has often been called an "emotional death." One should not, therefore, be surprised that those most closely affected by divorce, particularly the child, would experience the process of grief. In a profound sense the "way things always have been" has died for the child. The child has lost the day-by-day presence of one parent and the joint parental presence of mother and father. One common aspect of mourning is depression. Unfortunately, children are given little public, or even private, opportunities to express grief. The custodial parent may view such expressions as disloyalty. While our society has social and religious rituals and support systems when a person dies, few exist for the emotional death of divorce, and none for children. Therefore, the child's grief and accompanying depression are borne in solitary and internalized ways. One opportunity open to the pastor is to be an accepting person who allows the child to express grief.

Reconciliation fantasies. Children have strong and persistent preoccupations that parents will effect reconciliation and the family will be together again. So strong is this desire that even after one or both parents have remarried some children retain this wish. Some children will become directly active in efforts to bring the parents together. These actions have ranged from discouraging the mother's dating to stealing a parent's money so that "they cannot afford the divorce."

Changing relationships. Following separation of parents, children will become aware that the nature of their primary relationships changes. Siblings may be drawn together through their shared pain and anxiety over parental separation. The custodial parent may be overfocused and overinvolved with the children for several reasons: to compensate for the departed parent, to respond to their guilt, and to meet the adult's own emotional needs. The noncustodial parent may for a time give the children more attention than when the family was still intact. The norm, however, is that with the passing of time there will be less contact and involvement.

These are the general and normal reactions of children to divorce. The pastor should be sensitive to distorted reactions in these children. If the symptoms become severe and protracted, the pastor should not hesitate to recommend referral to a child psychiatrist or some other qualified counselor/therapist who works primarily with children.

Children whose parents are divorcing have many specialized needs as they endure the dissolution of their families. Perhaps the most basic need is assurance that they will continue to be loved and cared for. In a time of great insecurity, the manner in which parents and other significant adults interact with children is of central importance. A child has no greater need at such a time than for parents to be helped to deal rationally and compassionately with each other and their children. No easy ways exist to help children through the trauma of divorce, but some approaches may limit the damage to the children. Parents need to learn that they play the critical roles. Therefore, the counselor will attempt to assist the parents whenever possible.

Gardner maintains that children can be most effectively helped if the therapist can work with one or both parents by "coaching" them about their words and actions in relationship with the children.[8] He sees the role of the therapist to be one of clarifying the issues involved and alleviating pathological behavior in the parents. Among the issues with which parents should be coached are: when and how to tell the children, what should be included in the telling, postdivorce parental relationships with each other and the children, custody and visitation arrangements. A pastor who wishes specific suggestions on parental coaching may consult the suggested readings at the end of this chapter.

Children need honesty and love from both parents. They also need both parents, despite their separation, to continue to interact with them as the most significant persons in their lives. Children need to feel secure and supported, especially after their world has been torn asunder by the separation of mother and father. The faith community and its symbolic representatives, usually the clergy, have roles to play in the lives of such children.

Faith Issues

We who work within the context of a faith community are concerned not only with psychological and sociological issues of persons encountering life crises but also with spiritual or religious issues. We need to be reminded that there are stages of religious development just as there are stages of a person's psychosocial development. Unfortunately, many who are counselors with a religious orientation know more about psychosocial development than they do about stages in religious growth. In many of its major themes Christianity is an "adult" religion. From a psychological point of view, a person probably needs to pass through the crisis of adolescence before he or she can begin to grasp such themes as guilt, forgiveness, alienation, and reconciliation. The religion of many preadolescents is, for example, quasi-magical. The pastor, on the other hand, is normally thought to be the most theologically informed person within a congregation. The pastor must be aware of both the child's psychosocial developmental stage and his or her level of religious maturity. The question is not whether the child is religious, or whether the child participates within the faith community, but the nature of that religious participation.

Basic trust, in the Eriksonian sense, centers in confidence by the infant that the parenting persons will provide food and love to the baby. From this basic trust in the primary parent comes trust or faith in the world and, in religious terms, in God. A child's sense of self-worth and sense of security derive from this basic trust. As a small child develops, this basic trust is invested in both parents as the caring and supportive world in which the child lives.

It might be argued that if a child's trust in the parents is challenged by their separation, then the child's faith in what he or she considers to be divine is also challenged. Put simply but truthfully from a child's perspective, the question becomes, "If I cannot trust my parents, how can I trust God?"

A nine-year-old boy was in conversation with his pastor not long after the boy learned of his parents' decision to divorce:

PASTOR: I know how hard it is when you feel someone let you down.
BOY: I'm tired of people letting me down. Mom and Dad say everything
        will be fine. Sure, maybe for them. They're grown-ups. I'm not.
PASTOR: Well, God doesn't let us down. That's not how God is.
BOY: What do you mean?

How is the pastor to respond? It will not do to launch into a theological explanation, even on a "child's level." If the child has trust in a grandparent or a trusted youth leader, however, the pastor might point out that the child still trusts some people and can also, perhaps, trust God. However, in my opinion it is better not to press this issue too soon with children.

Another religious issue encountered by children of divorce is related to "magical prayer." This is closely tied to the child's fantasy of the reconciliation of parents. More than one child has prayed that God will somehow "make Mommy and Daddy love each other again." When this prayer goes unanswered, and it is a deeply expressed prayer, the child's faith in God is severely tested.

CHILD: I don't like God.
PASTOR: Is there some reason you don't like God?
CHILD: Yeah. He never, never gives me what I ask. I asked for a new bike for Christmas and for my birthday. Didn't get it yet. And now every single night I pray we will all be together, but Daddy moved to an apartment.
PASTOR: Sometimes we don't get what we want or need, even if it is something we want very, very much. It's hard to take, I know. I don't understand that myself, but a person can still love us and want to help us even if that person will not give us what we want. I think God is like that.
CHILD: Huh?
PASTOR: Your mom loves you even if you didn't get the bike.
CHILD: I guess so.

Often a pastor will meet with a child who feels a sense of overwhelming loss, low self-worth, and a reduced sense of belonging. A ten-year-old girl, born of Korean parents, was adopted at age three by an American family. Now the parents are separating.

GIRL: Nobody loves me. Nobody ever loved me.
PASTOR: Your parents love you. I have heard them tell you that.
GIRL: Which parents? The ones in Korea? They gave me up. The ones here? If they loved me, they wouldn't get divorced.
PASTOR: You seem to feel you've lost a lot.
GIRL: I'm tired of losing things. I lost my parents in Korea. I'm going to lose Daddy. I'm going to have to move with Mom from our house and have to go to a new school.

The alert pastor will know that this little girl, who has already suffered anxieties of abandonment by natural parents, will need ongoing pastoral care and probably professional counseling.

With families who have regularly attended the same church, the divorce of parents will usually result in one parent's dropping out of that church. Churches, even the more "liberal" ones, have been unable to convey to both divorced parents that they are accepted and welcome. To be sure, discomfort and embarrassment on the part of one or both parents play a part. For the child, however, the message communicated is that church is no longer a place Father (or Mother) feels welcome and at ease. What does that say about a child's view of the church as the family of God? A pastor stopped to talk to an eight-year-old in the hall before Sunday school.

PASTOR: It's good to see you today. I saw your mother and sister a while ago.
CHILD: Thank you.

PASTOR: How are you doing these days?
CHILD: OK, I guess. I wish Daddy would come with us to church like he used to.
PASTOR: It's tough. I wish he'd come too. You know, it is just as much his church as it is yours or mine. Maybe some Sunday soon he can bring you and your sister and sit with the two of you. Would you like for me to talk to him about it?
CHILD: If you want to.
PASTOR: I do.

In this conversation the pastor seeks to communicate to the child his understanding of the church, but he is also willing to take pastoral initiative with the father. If the father fails to respond positively, not only has the effort been made but the child has been told by words and action that the pastor believes the church is for everyone.

A pastor may also help children deal with both anger and grief. Children often believe they cannot directly express anger to a parent over what has happened. An eleven-year-old girl was brought in by her mother "to see the minister." The girl and the pastor sat around a table in her Sunday school room.

GIRL: Sometimes I hate my folks. I love them too.
PASTOR: Do you think you can love and hate something at the same time?
GIRL: I don't know. Can you?
PASTOR: I don't know about you. I can. Sometimes when I had to go to school I loved recess (lunch, gym), but I hated English and history.
GIRL (*laughing*): Me too!
PASTOR: So shouldn't we be able to do that with people too?
GIRL: I don't know. I do love them, but I don't like what they do.
PASTOR: Well, I think that's OK. But you know, I really did love school more than I hated it—most of the time.
GIRL: I still don't like my folks, but I guess I love them—sometimes.

A mother called the pastor reporting that her seven-year-old son "has me worried. He doesn't seem to respond to the divorce. He's just quiet. He will not talk about it." When the boy came to the pastor, the minister offered to read the boy a story. It was a story about a boy whose father went to live in a hotel. As the story was read the boy began to cry and then sobbed heavily. The pastor picked the boy up and held him. When the tears stopped the pastor took the boy back to his mother. Later the mother reported that the boy no longer seemed as withdrawn. Grief had been expressed and accepted.

These opportunities for pastoral care were possible because the pastors had previous and ongoing relationships with those children. Where that is not the case, the pastor may need to spend some time developing a solid relationship with the child. As has often been mentioned, we pastors can take initiative denied in our society to most other helping professionals. We do not have to wait for people in need to come to us; we can go to them. In the case of children of divorce, I believe a pastor has an obligation to take such an initiative. Rarely will a child ask to speak to the pastor. Often a parent may ask the pastor, "Will you please talk with Jimmy? He's having a hard time and I don't know what to do." Certainly the pastor may wish to respond to such a parental request, but how much better if the pastor initiates the contact. It says, among other things, You matter to me just because you are you.

Ideally, the pastor will seek to stay in a relationship of pastoral concern with all parties—father, mother, and children. In predivorce counseling the parent-child relationship should be addressed. Parents have a natural anxiety about what divorce will do to their children, and most parents are eager for the pastor's insights and counseling. The pastor should no more hesitate to speak directly with a child than with an adult member of the church who is in a personal crisis. The pastor may be one of the few "neutral" and emotionally uninvolved figures to whom children can express their feelings, knowing that they will still be accepted.

Here is a model of a conversation I have had with many children whose parents are divorcing. I seek to have such conversations not in my office or counseling room but in an informal setting such as the floor of a Sunday school room. Usually I assure the children that Mother or Father will be waiting for them in the next room. Indeed, I show them the parent in that room.

The conversation begins with a question:

PASTOR: Do you know why you are here with me today?

CHILD: Well, no. Mommy just said I was coming to talk to you.

PASTOR: I'm glad you're here. I know that your mom and dad have not been getting along and that they are unhappy. Both of them have told me that they love you very much. (This can be said to the child *only* if it is true.) I also know that they told you they are getting a divorce. Do you know what a divorce is?

CHILD: I think I do. I saw it on television. People aren't married anymore. Oh, yeah, I have a friend whose parents are divorced. She really hates it.

PASTOR: Most kids hate it. It's a hard time for everyone.

CHILD: I don't know why they have to do it. Why can't they just stop fighting? They tell us to stop when we fight. And they're grown-ups!

PASTOR: I know. But sometimes people who are married just stop loving each other and don't seem to be able to get along.

CHILD: It's not fair. I may have to go to that other dumb school where I don't know anybody. I hate it.

PASTOR: I'm sure things will be different, and that isn't always easy.

CHILD: Why do they have to do this divorce thing?

PASTOR: Let me tell you something you may have not thought about before.

You always think of your folks as Mom and Dad, not as husband and wife. We think Mom and Dad will always live with us; after all, they are our mom and dad. We don't ever think that Mom and Dad are not going to live with us, but Mom and Dad are also husband and wife. What has happened is that husband and wife cannot live together anymore. But one thing will never change.

CHILD: What's that?

PASTOR: They will always be your mom and dad. Always. They may stop being husband and wife, but they will never stop being your mom and dad. Never.

CHILD: Oh, but Dad is moving out forever.

PASTOR: I know. And that is tough and it doesn't seem fair. And things will be different.

The conversation will continue usually on the themes of how things might be different, but also on how some things will be the same. Seldom is the conversation more than thirty minutes. I usually end by saying, "I'd like to talk with you again, and I hope you will too. Let's talk with your mother and see what would be a good time for you." I treat these conversations with the same confidentiality I do all counseling.

The pastor of children of divorce may find himself or herself used as a parent figure. In small congregations a pastor may be willing to accept this temporary role, but the better wisdom is to encourage other adults to assume it. A pastor should try to remain in the primary role of pastor to the child. This role, of course, can include being a "significant other adult," a friend to the child.

As in all crisis ministry the pastor understands that follow-up is necessary. Once the immediate crisis is passed, the minister should assume that supportive counseling is still necessary. This is especially true of children, who may appear outwardly to be making an adequate adjustment, but who inwardly have unresolved feelings. More frequently than with adults, a pastor will have to take initiative with children and be able to discern symptoms that point to inward turmoil.

Summary

Marital counseling is one of the major forms of pastoral counseling performed by the parish minister. A pastor can be one of the resources available to provide sound information on the effects of divorce on children. A minister can also engage in "coaching" of parents in their actions and words with their children. Furthermore, a pastor can be an advocate for the child, who is usually absent when these discussions take place. One of the most troubling aspects in the whole tragic business of a family breakup is that few persons, if any, speak for the child.

A pastor should not hesitate, if the symptoms are in evidence, to recommend that the child receive professional psychotherapy. Even when counseling is indicated, the pastor or other professional counselors should never forget that the primary focus should be on the parents. If the two parents can act in healthy ways, the child's own dis-ease will be helped. As the pastor counsels with the parents, the minister should always remember that he or she is also the child's pastor. This means that the pastor will be as available to a child as to an adult.

NOTES

1. George R. Plagenz, "The Orphans of Divorce." News service article in the *York (Pa.) Dispatch,* July 9, 1986.

2. Ibid.

3. Erik H. Erikson, *Childhood and Society,* 2nd ed. (New York: W. W. Norton & Co., 1963), pp. 247–274.

4. Richard A. Gardner, *Psychotherapy with Children of Divorce,* p. 4.

5. Benjamin Griffin, "Pastoral Care of Children in Crisis" (unpublished D. Min. dissertation, Lancaster Theological Seminary, 1975), pp. v–vii.

6. Ibid., p. vii.

7. Earl A. Grollman, ed., *Explaining Divorce to Children,* p. 28.

8. Gardner, *Psychotherapy with Children of Divorce,* p. 15.

FURTHER READING

Friedman, Edwin H. *Generation to Generation: Family Process in Church and Synagogue.* New York: Guilford Press, 1985. A helpful book on understanding "family theory" not only within the family but also within the congregation and the clergyperson's own family.

Gardner, Richard A. *Psychotherapy with Children of Divorce.* New York: Jason Aronson, 1976. The psychiatric authority on the subject. Useful for those wishing to explore the subject in depth.

Grollman, Earl A., ed. *Explaining Divorce to Children.* Boston: Beacon Press, 1969. Despite its age, still one of the best general introductions to the subject by a rabbi widely known for his care of children.

Hart, Archibald D. *Children and Divorce: What to Expect, How to Help.* Waco, Tex.: Word Books, 1982. A general introduction by a professor of pastoral psychology at Fuller Theological Seminary.

7

The Bereaved Child
Andrew C. Puckett, Jr.

For everything there is a season,
and a time for every matter under heaven:
a time to be born, and a time to die;
a time to plant, and a time to pluck up what is planted;
a time to kill, and a time to heal;
a time to break down, and a time to build up;
a time to weep, and a time to laugh;
a time to mourn, and a time to dance.
(Ecclesiastes 3:1–4)

I want to share with you at the very beginning of this chapter the most important and powerful advice I know in working with children in grief or any other crisis: Let the child take you by the hand and show you the way. If you let this image be your guide, you can be a helpful companion on almost any path a child has to walk. Providing ministry with children in their grief calls for entering into their world and appreciating their perspective. Within their perspective you will find that what they do and say makes sense.

The Nature of Grief in Children

As with adults, grief in children can come from many sources. Often our inclination as ministers is to assume that "grief" refers to death. Some kind of death or loss, of course, is related to any grief experience. But grief doesn't always imply the loss of life. Grief includes the wide range of losses the school-age child can experience. There are the obvi-

Andrew C. Puckett, Jr., is Chaplain for Pediatric Hematology/Oncology and for the Cancer Rehabilitation and Continuing Care Program at the Medical College of Virginia, Richmond, Va.

ous losses such as the death of a parent or sibling or the separation stemming from a divorce. As ministers we are usually aware of these. The less obvious losses might be the death of a close relative, the loss of a pet, a friend who moves away, a teacher who changes jobs, a Scout leader who gives up the troop, or a sibling who changes schools in moving to a higher grade. You could add other losses to this list.

Grief is a part of life. You and I read the verses from Ecclesiastes and recognize that just as there are times to be born, to laugh, and to dance, there are also times to die, to weep, and to mourn. We accept this as part and parcel of the human experience—or at least we are in the process of recognizing this as we experience more and more of life. School-age children are just beginning this pilgrimage. Primarily they experience the world in concrete terms: what they can see, touch, feel. They are moving toward being able to experience and describe the world in both concrete and abstract terms. They are not as skillful with their words, but they more than make up for it with a refreshing honesty.

Understanding grief in children involves some understanding of how they view death. Current literature still relies heavily on two classic pieces of research by Sylvia Anthony and Maria Nagy.[1] These findings can be summarized as follows:

0–3 years No obvious perception of death. Separation of any kind is threatening and is viewed as death.

3–5 years An awareness of death, but not death in a permanent sense. Attributes life and consciousness to the dead. Considers death as gradual or temporary. A departure of sleep. Physical death is recognized, but child cannot separate it from life. Death is reversible. The dead can come back again.

5–9 years Death is personified (e.g., the grim reaper, the angel of death, or perhaps the boogeyman), is invisible, and works in secret at night. Death may also be identified with a person who had died. Children have an increasing sense of reality and acceptance of death which at the same time is held in tension with a denial of death. At this stage, death also is associated with magical thinking, aggressive feelings, and punishment. Death can be perceived as the result of evil or a bad thing. If you are good you live, but if you are bad you die.

9 years on Children begin to recognize that death means the end of physical life as we know it. They begin to believe that death is irreversible and biologically caused. The child begins to see death as a part of the life process within each person and within the universe.

Children experience stages of grief similar to those of adults, but the stages are less clearly defined and usually intermixed with each other. Emotions generally are more fluid in children than in adults. A child can be dreadfully upset at one moment and outside playing at another. Often adults are uneasy with the child's emotional extremes and respond by trying to stifle the child. As a minister, you can anticipate this kind of easy flow of emotions in children and not be thrown by it.

The Impact of Grief on Children

I want to use four stories to illustrate some of the possible impacts of grief on children. As you read these, imagine the child in this situation. Ask yourself what was happening to the child. What impact did the loss have on the child? As minister, how might you have helped this child deal differently with his or her loss and grief?

John, a first-year medical intern, stopped me in the hallway. He heard me talk to the new interns during orientation and wanted to talk with me. We went for a cup of coffee and he began telling me how anxious he was about the pressures of his internship. Always before he had felt on top of things, but now he was beginning to feel overwhelmed. In the following weeks we had several counseling sessions. John's level of anxiety about his work as a young physician became so intense that he was granted a brief leave of absence from his assignments. As he related the events of his life, he told me about his older brother who had died when John was nine years old. I asked him how he had dealt with his grief. He thought that he had, although it was not something discussed openly in his family. A picture gradually began to emerge. John had taken it upon himself to make up for the loss of his brother. He tried, in a sense, to live two lives at the same time. Because he was bright and highly motivated, he had been able to manage this, but the rigors of medical internship proved too much. His superhuman efforts to make up for his brother's absence, both with himself and with his parents, finally became overwhelming. John began to grieve more openly, let go of his brother's memory, and discover who he, John, was as one individual.

Shirley sat before me expressing her concerns about her eleven-year-old daughter who "once was just a normal little girl but has been a handful for years. I don't know what happened to her. It seems to have started when she started school. She's been too much to deal with ever since." In the course of the conversation, I asked if she had any other children. She said that she had had another child who died when he was six years old. Her daughter was four at the time. Two years later, when her daughter started school, she started this overactive behavior. Then Shirley said, "It's almost like having a houseful of children." We began to explore the possibility that her daughter was trying to take care of both her mother's and her own grief by filling up the space with noise and activity, by making enough noise for two children.

Christina's eight-year-old twin brother, Chris, was in the final days of dying with a terminal cancer. Chris was being cared for at home by a home health care hospice team. As I sat by his bedside talking with him and his mother, Christina bounced into the room with a girl-friend of hers. Both were chatting and seemed only a little uneasy with the rather difficult circumstances facing all of us. They wanted to tell Chris good-bye before they left for a school activity. Later I asked her mother how Christina was dealing with Chris's dying. She told me that Christina had said the day before that she had cried every night for the past week and that she just couldn't be sad any-more for a while. She had to be happy for a little while.

Now a personal illustration. Cora, a small, wiry woman, provided child care for me most of the first ten years of my life. Then we moved away. In many ways she had been my surrogate mother. I was about eleven years old when she died. It's hard to remember clearly just how old I was. At her funeral I showed very little emotion. In fact, I remember very little about the service other than our filing by the casket for one last viewing and our singing the hymn, "Precious Lord, Take My Hand." Afterward, our family rarely talked about her or her death. Sometimes at night I would think about her and wonder if she was really gone. It was hard to be sure. Sometimes I would imagine that she was coming back again. After about a year or so, I finally decided that she was really gone.

These feelings rarely surfaced afterward. But looking back through old journals, I found a three-page entry about Cora and her husband, William. Twenty-six years after her death I wrote these words that illustrate how long a child's unresolved grief can continue:

How much can a man of thirty-seven look back through the eyes of a small boy? The difficulty in doing so, I think, lies more in the pain of recall than in the lack of ability. . . . Can a thirty-seven-year-old man still feel pangs of guilt for once calling Cora "you old dodo" in a rush of little boy's anger or for the many ways I took her love and generosity for granted? Sounds silly, and yet the guilt is still there. Even more, can I still feel the weight of guilt for not stopping by to see her on my last visit to town before she died? . . . For one thing, to go see her was always to be faced with the loss of her, my surrogate mother. Also, it was to be faced with the pain, sympathy, and concern I felt for this very dear lady who loved me and who was suffering with her health. I didn't know she was dying. I intended to go back sometime later.

These four examples tell something about what we as ministers look for as signs of the impact of grief on children. With children the impact is both immediate and potentially long-term. They may show very little immediate response to a grief situation, but the impact may be delayed and show up later in other ways. Children sometimes become quieter and more withdrawn. Sometimes they express anger over their loss by getting in fights at school or by disobeying their parents. They may start making noticeably lower grades in school. They may start showing signs of physical distress.

Consider the kinds of feelings people have in their grief, such as anger, denial, a sense of losing touch with reality, confusion, depression, or impulsiveness. How would children who were just learning how to sense and express their feelings express these? The language of children may be limited mostly to actions and behavior. Help them to translate these feelings into words.

The Particular Needs of Children Facing Grief

Remember, first of all, that school-age children are in the process of learning how to be in touch with and express their feelings. They are also learning how to conceptualize what is happening both inside them and around them as they experience life. They look for clues in their world and try to piece them together. They are looking for solutions. The significant people in their lives, such as parents and siblings, have a great deal of influence on them and how they react. It is not unusual in a grief situation to find children focusing most of their energy on taking care of the adults around them.

Children are highly intuitive and can usually sense what is going on. Well-meaning parents may want to keep painful information from their children. Experience in chronic care hospital situations, however, has shown that children not only know most of what is going on with their own illnesses, but they also know what is going on with the other children on their unit. The problem for children who are having to intuit what is happening in their world is that conclusions are often drawn from inadequate information. That which is hidden from them by silent adults can easily become exaggerated. Children see the facial expressions and nonverbal communications of grief and pain in the people around them, but unless someone sits and talks with them and hears them out, they are left to their own conclusions. They may decide, like John, the medical intern, that they have to live double lives to take care of their parents and make up for a sibling's death.

One of the primary needs of children facing grief, then, is honesty. Be open and honest with them. Remember, that which is hidden gets exaggerated. Things are better dealt with in the open. Children need help in distinguishing between fantasy and reality. Try to provide simple and straightforward answers to their questions. This is a crucial, though not easy, task both for concerned adults and for you as the minister.

Children facing grief need stability. Their sense of security is threatened when they experience significant losses. Their daily routine of life is disrupted. As adults we experience some of the same threats. However, our world is larger than the child's world. Also, we are better able to see beyond the immediate concrete situation.

In the face of grief, children need to be included rather than excluded. Often children are shuffled aside in an effort to insulate them from the grief situation. Feelings of being excluded or possibly abandoned, however, are much harder on children than feelings of grief and sadness. Families often want to know if it is all right to bring children to the hospital when someone close to them is very ill or dying. Families may ask you if they should bring children to the funeral service. This is easier to handle, of course, if family members have talked openly among themselves and with the children from the beginning. Even if they haven't, however, children can be included in hospital visits or in the funeral service. Children need to be prepared in advance. Tell them about the hospital and the ill person. Tell them about the funeral home, the service, the casket, the hearse, the gravesite. Let them ask their questions.

Children are naturally curious. This is the way they learn. They will want to know about death, dying, funerals, burials, heaven, and grieving—aspects of grief that we may take for granted. Children may ask questions that cause adults to feel uncomfortable. Realize that this is the way children learn, understand, and come to accept death and grief. Children may want to know what the inside of the hearse looks like. They may want to know what happens to the deceased person's body once it is in the ground and covered up. Children may ask why people are so upset at the funeral. After the initial grief response, children may ask why they still cry or think about the person sometimes.

Children need to express their feelings when they face grief. The admonition "Big boys don't cry" is destructive. All children need permission to cry, to be angry, to talk about feelings of guilt, to hurt, and to express any other feelings they may have. Sometimes they don't know what they feel or how to express it except through their behavior. They may need help in describing and expressing these feelings.

Faith Issues Focused by Grief

I walked into Bubba's room early that morning. It was obvious that a drastic change had taken place. Several times in the past couple of weeks different ones of us had tried to facilitate an open conversation between Bubba and his family about his terminal condition. They just weren't ready. Two weeks before, however, Bubba talked with Will, one of his favorite nurses. He told Will about his pet rabbit and showed him a picture. Then a little cautiously he asked, "Will, do you think you'd like to give a rabbit like that a home?" Bubba knew! This morning all of us knew, but the conspiracy of silence was like a brick wall. Finally I asked if I could talk about what was going on. Each of the adults standing around his bed gradually nodded "yes." I told Bubba that he had fought it with all his strength, but his illness was finally winning out. He looked at me and asked, "You mean I'm dying?" He cried softly a few moments. There was a profound and liberating sense of release throughout the room. Then he turned to his grandmother and asked, "Grandma, will you still talk with me at night?" Then he asked me, "Do you think I'll be able to drink sweet milk in heaven?" As the day passed, he was able to talk with each of the members of his family and they with him. Bubba was able to express much of his grief and say his good-byes. That night he died.

Fortunately, most of the children in your congregation will not be facing that kind of crisis. But when they do experience grief, they are likely to face similar barriers and will have similar open, refreshingly honest questions. A problem for the minister is that our society tries to insulate children from the harder realities of life. We even try to insulate ourselves as adults from these realities! Often it takes a crisis to break through the protective barriers. Not until then do we ask the questions "Why?" "Why me?" "Why now?" "What does it mean?" or "Where is God in all this?" Observations of faith development in children indicate that they are the same way.[2]

Writings on crisis intervention frequently refer to a Chinese symbol for crisis which includes both danger and opportunity. A grief crisis presents an opportunity for growth in a child's faith pilgrimage. At this time, a child is apt to ask theological questions if there is an adult who gives permission and is willing to really listen. "Grandma, will you still talk with me at night?" "Do you think I'll be able to drink sweet milk in heaven?" Such innocent questions translate into theological inquiry. What will it be like for me when I die? What can I expect from God? What is it like to be with God? Will I be remembered when I'm gone? How am I part of the creation? Despite the depth of the questions, only straightforward and simple answers are required. "Bubba, you can be sure that I'll talk with you each night in my prayers." "I don't know about sweet milk in heaven, Bubba, but I'm sure God will provide you with something just as good if not better!"

In the face of grief, you have the opportunity to walk a special pathway with children. You are challenged to share your own faith in clear and simple terms. You have the opportunity to say you don't know all the answers to their questions, and that's all right too. Sometimes a Bible story may come to mind. For example, consider the story of the Prodigal Son. How did the father feel when his son left home? How did the older brother feel? How did they feel when he came back? What would have happened and how would they have felt if he had never returned home again? Then ask the children if they have ever had someone or something leave and then come home again or never come back. The parallels are there. Children love stories and are willing to enter into them with you. Often it is helpful to relate your answers and responses to something that the children already know, something that is familiar to them in their world. Who you are as a person with a child speaks louder than your words. Allow yourself to relax and speak from your heart. You'll find it an enriching experience.

The place to start with children in your congregation is now. Begin laying the foundation for talking about their faith concerns and spiritual development right away. Where and who is God for them? How is God a part of their everyday lives? How can God be a part of their lives when a crisis hits them? Look for opportunities, such as children's sermons, when you can talk with both the children and their families at the same time. Speak honestly to grief and losses that occur in your community, in the public media, in Bible stories, in the change of seasons, and in everyday events. In your own way, whether or not you think you do it with ease, you provide a model for these children and their families. In reality I expect that none of us do it with ease, for we are talking about deep questions of faith and the spiritual life. We are speaking from the child within us to the children sitting around us. When you do this, however, you open the way for better communication with them about their grief.

Ask yourself what children's faith means to them in facing grief. Let me suggest some possibilities to consider. Facing grief with their faith can help children face the realities before them. It can help them express their feelings in healthy ways. Their faith can help them grow closer to God and feel a closer tie to the whole of creation. It can help them gradually to reinvest themselves in life and other relationships.

Look for opportunities to talk with the children in church school classes or in other less formal circumstances. You don't have to spend a whole hour with them. Ten to fifteen minutes may be more than enough. Your time with them as their minister will be significant. As much as you can, relax with them, sit at their level, and talk openly. They will remember it, and it will be a warm memory for them. As their questions surface out of their own natural curiosity or out of a crisis, they will feel freer to talk with you about them.

Ministry with the Child Facing Grief

Telling a Child About Death

Here are some specific suggestions for telling a child about death. (1) Talk with the child as soon as possible, for he or she will sense that something has happened. (2) Be straightforward and to the point. This is the way children express themselves. (3) Remember that children take things literally and concretely. Avoid clichés like the person has "gone to sleep" or "on a long journey," has "passed away," has been "taken away by God." Place yourself in the child's place and take each of these literally and in concrete terms. Where does it lead you? What conclusions do you draw? The child will do the same. (4) Do not just say that someone was sick. Reassure the child that many people become sick but only those who are very, very ill may die. (5) Listen to the child's questions and concerns. Be sure you understand what the child is telling you and what it means. (6) Let your answers be simple and to the point. Stop when you have answered the child's question.

Helping Children Cope with Death

Avis Brenner[3] has summarized generally agreed-upon suggestions for helping children cope with death. All the authors she summarizes caution that any activity should be brief and should be continued only when the child seems ready for more. Brenner's material is paraphrased in the chart below. The left-hand column describes typical ways children try to deal with their grief and the right-hand column provides a current synthesis of recommended therapeutic responses. Many of the helping strategies mentioned are discussed in more detail by Claudia Jewett.[4]

Suggestions for Helping Children Cope with Death

Child's Behavior	Helpful Adult Response
Protest Stage	
Appears to not hear or not understand the news of the death; acts dazed.	Talk with the child later in the day or the next morning. Questions should be answered clearly, openly, and honestly. Give the child time to become aware of what has happened.

Fears being alone; has a sense of panic; has nightmares.

Look for ways to maintain the child's usual routine. Children need to know who will be taking care of them in the days and weeks to come. At night provide some way for the child to hear sounds of life, e.g., a radio or an open door. The child needs someone near to provide comfort after a nightmare.

Wants to be the one who tells about the death; wants to be on center stage.

Provide the child some freedom to do this. It is a need that won't last long.

Denies that the death has occurred; avoids thinking about it by being overly active and boisterous.

Children need acceptance for this defensive behavior. Consult a therapist if this lasts more than three to six months.

Grief Stage

Shows sadness and tears, a sense of yearning, and feelings of acute loneliness.

Share your own feelings, tears, yearnings, and sadness with the child. Touch, hold, and cuddle. Review both pleasant and unpleasant memories. Make a memory book with children and collect photographs, home movies, videotapes, and other items to help review memories. Let these be springboards for communication.

Regresses to behaviors more characteristic of an earlier age.

Accept these behaviors as the child's attempt to handle grief. Allow these behaviors, yet support the child's attempts to regain skills more appropriate to his or her age.

Tries to look for and find the dead person.

Provide acceptance for this effort at resolving grief. Be willing to talk with the child about disappointments. Let these open the way for talking about grief.

Has difficulty with schoolwork, ranging from inability to concentrate to development of learning disability.

School problems may last as long as two years. Teachers can work with the class around death issues. The school counselor can work with the child on personal problems so he or she can concentrate during class. Help the child stick with studies, but do not neglect the importance of playtime.

Exhibits guilt or anger that may be misplaced and directed toward parent(s), siblings, and other adults in the child's world.

Accept anger. Understand that it is misplaced. Empathize with and respect feelings. Reassure the child that hurting is part of grief and eventually it will subside. Help the child find emotional and physical outlets for anger. Emphasize the importance of talking about guilty or angry feelings by setting aside adult activities when possible for such conversations. Encourage drawing, writing, and playing out feelings. Where possible, meet with siblings to talk about feelings of guilt and anger and reach solutions to their shared problems in their new living situation.

Feels helplessness and despair

Help the child to see such feelings as legitimate and painful. Reassure the child that these are temporary. Books and stories can help show how others have coped with death. Fairy tales where a child conquers adversity can be a way of helping to restore meaning and hope.[5]

Acceptance Stage

Accepts loss, seeks closer bonds with parent(s), and strengthens relationships with siblings.

Remember anniversaries, recall feelings and memories. Help the memory of the deceased person be an appropriate part of the child's life. Encourage efforts to go on with life.

Many of these suggestions seem obvious. Don't assume, however, that members of the child's family will deal openly with their grief. Parents tend to plunge into their work or other activities. Parents may not have the physical or emotional energy to be of much help to their children. Your ministry will come through your presence as a supportive friend, a provider of pastoral care, and a spiritual guide. Let the children take you by the hand, and learn from them as you seek to help them face their grief. Your willingness to walk this road with them will help develop their own spiritual formation as an ongoing part of their life pilgrimage.

NOTES

1. Sylvia Anthony, *The Child's Discovery of Death* (London: Kegan Paul, Trench, Trubner & Co., 1940); Maria Nagy, "The Child's View of Death," in Herman Feifel, ed., *The Meaning of Death* (New York: McGraw-Hill Book Co., 1959).
2. Robert Coles, "The Faith of Children," *Sojourners,* May 1982, pp. 12–16.
3. Avis Brenner, *Helping Children Cope with Stress* (Lexington, Mass.: D. C. Heath & Co., Lexington Books, 1984).
4. Claudia L. Jewett, *Helping Children Cope with Separation and Loss* (Boston: Harvard Common Press, 1982).
5. Bruno Bettelheim, "Reflections: The Uses of Enchantment," *New Yorker,* Dec. 8, 1975.

FURTHER READING

Adams, David W., and Eleanor J. Deveau. *Coping with Childhood Cancer.* Reston, Va.: Reston Publishing Co., 1982.
Grollman, Earl A. *Talking About Death: A Dialogue Between Parent and Child.* 2nd ed. Boston: Beacon Press, 1976.
Johnson, Joy, and Mary Johnson. *Tell Me Papa.* Council Bluffs: Centering Corp., 1978.
LeShan, Eda. *Learning to Say Good-by: When a Parent Dies.* New York: Macmillan Publishing Co., 1976.
Levine, Stephen. *Who Dies: An Investigation of Conscious Living and Dying.* Garden City, N.Y.: Doubleday & Co., Anchor Books, 1982.
Levy, Erin Linn. *Children Are Not Paper Dolls.* Caryl, Ill.: Publishers Mark, 1985.
Rosen, Helen. *Unspoken Grief: Coping with Childhood Sibling Loss.* Lexington, Mass.: D.C. Heath & Co., Lexington Books, 1986.
Sharapan, Hedda Bluestone. *Talking with Young Children About Death.* Part of a series produced by Family Communications, 4802 Fifth Avenue, Pittsburgh, PA 15213.
Smith, Doris B. *A Taste of Blackberries.* New York: Thomas Y. Crowell Co., 1973.

Video

National Center for Death Education. *The Death of a Friend: Helping Children Cope with Grief and Loss.* 12-minute video. 1985. 656 Beacon St., Boston, MA 02115.

8

The Hospitalized Child
R. Wayne Willis

Several developments in recent years have substantially reduced the emotional trauma of hospitalization for children. One improvement has been the proliferation of pediatric hospitals and of pediatric units within general hospitals. Here, environments have been created "just for kids," including architecture, artwork, furniture, and playrooms. Placed with fellow strugglers their own age, pediatric patients can be spared the dubious distinction of being a nonadult on a unit designed for adults only. Integration into the health care team of child life workers, expressive therapists, child psychologists, and other pediatric specialists has enhanced the staff's responsiveness to the special needs of children.

Visits by the child's family, including siblings, have finally been accepted by hospitals as a right instead of a privilege. Several years ago it was thought that the presence of parents in the hospital was essentially negative—they introduced germs, disrupted the therapeutic regimen, and upset the child—so parents were invited to visit the child once a week, once a month, or not at all. Now it is accepted that the presence of family and friends is so important to the child's healing process, and the danger of infection so small, that unrestricted access is the rule. The Ronald McDonald House movement, which provides housing for families from out of town, symbolizes this positive change.

Even with facilities and staff optimally attuned to the needs of children, however, hospitalization is an emotionally hazardous situation. How a child responds to this crisis will be influenced by several variables. In assessing a child's needs, the sensitive pastor will seek to understand the following factors.

R. Wayne Willis is Chaplain, Kosair Children's Hospital, Louisville, Ky.

Prior hospitalization. A child's first hospitalization, featuring scores of strangers entering the room, painful diagnostic procedures, sleep interruption, physical examination of genitalia, monitoring of eliminations, and restricted diet, is obviously anxiety-producing. The veteran, on the other hand, will have already developed idiosyncratic coping patterns.

Socioeconomic fit. Disadvantaged children are more likely to be admitted to hospitals, have unexplained admissions, have multiple admissions, and stay longer than middle-class children. Having a definition of acceptable behavior that is at variance with the middle-class staff will create extra stress (for staff as well as patient!).

Type of admission. A child battling cancer (or some other life-threatening illness) or whose body image has been radically altered (due to a burn or some other disabling trauma or disfigurement) is obviously dealing with a heavier set of dynamics than the child whose diabetes is out of control or who is having a hernia repair.

Quality of parental care. While separation from parents has been proven to be detrimental to the preschool child, the eight- or nine-year-old may be wanting to be less close to parents and may not need a parent to spend the night. The quality of the relationship of child to parents, when they are present, is most significant. The child will pick up parental attitudes, and overprotective or high-strung parents will have a negative influence.

Acquaintance with adversity. For families that are relative strangers to adversity, a hospitalization can precipitate a major crisis of the spirit: "Why me? Why my child?" Other families, already acquainted with loss, may perceive the current crisis as part of life. These "Why *not* me?" people often take a hospitalization more in stride.

Inborn temperament. Parents who have more than one child know that children are by nature difficult or easy, bold or cautious, docile or rebellious, aggressive or gentle. That basic nature of the child is going to manifest itself despite the best or worst of hospital life.

Time and timing. A lengthy hospitalization tests the character of child, parents, and staff. The serious student will worry about falling behind in school. "Serving time" over a holiday (such as Christmas or Hanukkah), cancellation of a family vacation, or interference with a kinetic program (such as Little League or ballet lessons) compounds the crisis of hospitalization.

Paying attention to these facets of a particular child's hospitalization can make the difference between performing a perfunctory pastoral visit and being effectively responsive to a child's real needs.

Crisis and Opportunity

I have deliberately chosen the word "crisis" to describe a child's hospitalization rather than the word "trauma." Much recent research indicates that stressors early in a child's life, such as a hospitalization, are not predictive of long-term problems. Thomas and Chess[1] followed

133 subjects from infancy through early adulthood in an attempt to assess the impact of childhood crises on later developmental stages. They concluded that neither divorce of parents nor parental death portended adult adjustment problems.

The British psychiatrist Michael Rutter[2] found that a surprisingly large number of children come through disadvantaged or even brutalized childhoods relatively unscathed and go on to become normal, successful adults. Norman Garmezy[3] found in working with stressed children that individual differences *in response to* stress are far more important in determining long-term effects than the *occurrence* of stress. Santayana once wrote that he wouldn't mind repeating his youth were it not for all those trapdoors. A hospitalization is one of those trapdoors, but one that can be successfully negotiated with a little help from parents, peers, pastor, and hospital personnel.

Growth Issues

Jean Piaget[4] observed the "general push to grow, to learn" in the school-age child. Erik Erikson[5] described this child as being dominated by the drive to be industrious, to gain approval by successfully producing things, to be a good little worker. The task of meeting the developmental needs of the hospitalized child is to find ways to help that child leave the hospital feeling like a success and not a failure.

One way to cater to the child's need for mastery is to invite the child to become your teacher, to teach you what it is like to be sick. I recommend to pastoral visitors that they assume the posture of student when they visit and in some way convey to the child, "You are the expert here. I have no idea what it is like to be where you are. Please teach me." Children love the opportunity to reverse roles and, for one brief shining moment, become teachers—authorities—with you as their admiring student.

In order to be a "successful" patient, a child may need to take periodic flights into fantasy. Children like to identify with the hero or heroine in classics such as *Little Orphan Annie, Huckleberry Finn,* or *The Wizard of Oz.* Telling children the story or giving them the book can inspire them to use their own creativity to overcome trouble and come out winners, as did Annie and Huck and Dorothy. Luke Skywalker and Princess Leia offer modern examples of "good" taking on "evil" and winning. Rocky Balboa and the Karate Kid model underdog-takes-on-bully-and-wins. It is easy to identify with Rocky upsetting Apollo Creed, or Luke Skywalker besting Darth Vader, as the child wrestles with the intimidating environment of the hospital, determined to hang tough and emerge the victor.

The One Within Is Greater than the One Without

No developmental stage of life is more crucial to the formation of a mature faith than that of the school-age child. The fact that in most Christian traditions baptism or confirmation takes place by age twelve stems from the awareness that this is a time of enormous personality reconstruction. If the church is to have a significant role in those changes, it must be assertive at this point in life. Otherwise, progression to an adult faith will be stymied or stillborn. Gordon Allport[6] describes this age as one of moving "from second-hand fittings to first-hand fittings."

In this connection, pastors should know that most school-age children conceptualize their illness as externally imposed punishment for wrongdoing. Brodie[7] reviewed all the studies between 1950 and 1960 on children's concepts of illness and found that illness or accident is assumed to be a consequence of "being bad." Bibace and Walsh,[8] in a study of the development of children's concepts of illness, saw movement from "contamination" to "internalization." By contamination (sometimes referred to as the "germ theory") they mean children's belief that a "bad" or "harmful" external agent has caused their health problems. This perception may be connected to an immature faith that thinks of God as the agent of sickness. By internalization they mean that children begin to understand their own body's complicity or malfunction as the major dynamic involved. With this insight come the first stirrings of accepting personal responsibility for their health. This period when the child is moving from an external to an internal focus of authority is prime time for the pastor to speak of God not as the Author of misery but as One who strengthens and fortifies and enables the sufferer to overcome.

> Todd, a twelve-year-old boy who was hospitalized for a broken leg sustained in a school bus accident, continued to be tormented by nightmares. In the accident, the drunk driver of the car that hit the bus had been killed, and Todd had seen his bloody, mutilated body hanging out the window of the car. In Todd's nightmares, the man, dripping with blood and brandishing a knife, would approach his hospital room with the words, "You took my life. Now I'm here for yours," at which time Todd would awake in a sweat, trembling, unable to return to sleep. In our first visit, which lasted over an hour, I learned that Todd felt some guilt over masturbation, some guilt over being the most severely injured of the children on the bus ("Why me?"), and some guilt at living while the driver of the car died. Those feelings, mixed with having viewed too many *Friday the Thirteenth* and *Halloween* movies, culminated in his room's nightly invasion of Evil.

Ascertaining the presence of some Christian faith, however elementary, I proceeded to teach Todd to exercise what faith he had. He and I read Romans 8:37–39. I instructed him, upon the next visit of the haunting spirit, to sit bolt upright in bed, point his finger at the spirit, and command, "In the name of Jesus Christ, you get out of here!" (a pediatric rendition of the exorcism ritual). Next morning Todd greeted me with a smile and the exclamation, "Thanks! I slept like a genius last night!" (I think he meant like a baby, or like a log.) The nightmares did not recur. The faith lesson for Todd was that faith is stronger than fear, God is greater than Satan, good triumphs over evil, or, to paraphrase scripture, "The one who is within you is greater than the one who is without."

Moving Alongside to Help

Two powerful related processes can either enhance or sabotage pastoral ministry to children. They are *empathic identification* and *transference.* Pastors who are parents or grandparents may find themselves identifying closely with the parents of the hospitalized child. If the child has a life-threatening illness or has been permanently handicapped by an accident, and the parents are appropriately distraught, the visiting pastor may find it easy to imagine being in their place: "There but for the grace of God go I." Such identification can unleash profound empathy for the parents and allow the pastor to relate caringly and effectively. However, such identification can overwhelm, immobilize, and paralyze the pastor with fear and sorrow.

Transference is a similar dynamic. Pastors who are parents may be able, using a little imagination when they look at the hospitalized child, to picture their own child in that bed, especially when that child physically resembles their own. Such a transference of affection may be either emotionally overpowering for the pastor, or a resource for in-depth pastoral caring, or both. What is crucial for the pastor is to recognize as soon as possible what is going on. After eleven years as a chaplain to children, I still have to say to myself, when visiting a boy who is critically ill or injured and who reminds me of one of my sons, "Chances are this will never happen to my boys." Having reminded myself of why I am experiencing such intense emotions, I'm not caught unaware if my eyes gloss over.

The goal of the pastor visiting the hospitalized child is to be an enabling presence. Barnabas, "son of encouragement" (Acts 4:36), is the model. The Greek word translated "encouragement" literally means "called alongside to help." The pastor called alongside sick children can offer a relationship in which children can seek truth, accept and manage personal responsibility, and be inspired to "rekindle the gift of

God" within them. When I enter a child's room, I hope to accomplish five tasks before I leave, all part of the enabling ministry. These five acts acrostically spell out "N-ABLE"—Nominate, Absolve, Bless, Lay on hands, Emote—and can be rehearsed on the five fingers of one hand before entering the room.

Nominate. Yes, nominate the child. The hospital, like a juggernaut, can run over children. Even the best hospital is impersonal and frenetic, a world where many people are looking at a child's eyes and ears but not necessarily at the child. Biaca Gordon[9] quotes a seven-year-old child as saying, "They looked into my mouth and into my ears; they looked into my eyes, and they touched my tummy; but they never looked at me."

The parents of one eleven-year-old who was unconscious following brain surgery taped a number of messages on construction paper over the head of his bed: "I like to be called Tag." "When you talk to me rub my hands and arms." "Wash your hands first. I don't need any extra germs." "Say only positive things to me, like 'You look good, Tag'; 'Keep Jesus on your mind, Tag'; 'Jesus loves you, Tag'; 'You are very strong, Tag.' " "My hobbies are rock music, playing clarinet, basketball, talking on the phone, reading comics, fishing, and swimming." We teach families and visitors (including pastors) to speak to and touch the unconscious patient, since the last senses one loses are hearing and feeling.

How important it is in the antiseptic, impersonal environment of the hospital to protect the humanity of the patients! Calling them by name, seeing them as subjects instead of objects, serves that end. One physician, who is a member of a group of six highly skilled pediatricians at the hospital where I work, is by far the most popular with parents. I once asked a member of the house staff the reason. She told me, "For one thing, he doesn't just talk to the parents; he talks to the child. He always calls the child by name. Even if it's a baby, he doesn't refer to 'the baby' or 'your daughter'; it's always 'Lauren' or 'Natalie.' Parents just get the feeling that their child is very precious to him."

Find out the child's preferred name. Is he Charles, Charlie, Chuck, or Chuckie? Does she like to be called Elizabeth, Liz, or her parents' favorite, Elizabeth Jane? Before entering the room, tell yourself, "I'm not going to visit Bill and Sue Thompson's son. I'm going to visit Danny Thompson." Call the child by name several times during the visit. In an environment where children tend to be thought of and referred to as "the heart" or "the broken clavicle in room 13," the pastor can help humanize and personalize things simply by addressing the child by name.

Absolve. Concrete-thinking ten-year-olds probably will not be struggling with the metaphysical "Why do bad things happen to good people?" kinds of issues that their parents may be experiencing. They may, however, want to connect concrete behaviors with concrete consequences. Equating food with love, they may wonder if their restricted diet is punishment for having been bad. They may have fantasies that their parents' absence is rejection, or that removal from home to hospital happened because they were mean to a sibling.

Maria Nagy[10] and Perrin[11] found in children under twelve no understanding of host defenses and no understanding of the presence of germs in healthy people. The children they studied thought of germs as omnipotent bearers of disease, their very presence bringing immediate sickness. Left to these understandings of illness, the hospitalized child is going to feel personally impotent and guilty.

The pastor will want to ask the child in private (away from family whose presence might influence the child's response), "Why do you think this happened to you?" If the child is hospitalized for an accident, the cause-effect relationship will likely be given: "I was striking matches" or "A drunk driver hit me." The child hospitalized for an illness may simply say, "I don't know." The pastor's work is to help the child sort out rational guilt from irrational guilt. Ask, "Do you think you deserved this? Do you think God is trying to get you?" All irrational guilt must be confronted: "No, you didn't get meningitis because you wished your sister dead." "No, God didn't cause your spine to grow crooked because you were hateful to your mother." "No, getting stabbed while on your paper route was not in any way a punishment from God." The pastor can seize the opportunity to impress on the child that God is a good God who doesn't do mean things and then follow up with a natural explanation for human suffering. The child will probably remember the theological interpretation that you, the spokesperson for God, offered in the *kairos*.

Some hospitalizations, of course, result from events that appropriately lead to some rational guilt. By rational guilt I mean appropriately owned responsibility for the conduct that brought on the suffering, such as the boy who shoots himself in the stomach while disobeying Father's rule never to play with the gun in the drawer, or the girl who takes a dare to swallow a handful of prescription medicine and goes into seizures. The pastor will hope to hear the child volunteer "honest confessions." Then the pastor will offer absolution, not a facile but a solemn absolution: "As God's minister, I want you to know and fully believe this—God has forgiven you whatever wrong you have done. Because God has completely forgiven you, you can now find it within you to forgive yourself. God doesn't want you to go on punishing yourself."

Bless. One day I met a new patient in our hospital's burn unit. He was wrapped in gauze from his waist up. He was five years old, Paul by name, and the day before he had been severely burned in a house fire. I noticed a beautiful medallion on his bedstand and asked what it was. He told me how a uniformed policeman had entered the unit earlier that day to visit someone else. Paul waved to him. The policeman was so touched by the suffering of this little child that he turned and left the unit, went home, got the Medal of Valor he had been awarded just two weeks earlier, and returned to the burn unit. He went into Paul's room, draped it around Paul's neck, and said to him, "You deserve this more than I do. You're a hero. This is for you." Then he turned and walked away.

That day Paul received "the blessing." By blessing I mean the affirmation that comes from an adult via word or deed or sparkle in the eye that says to a child, You are very special and I believe in you. Such an affirmation coming at a tender, impressionable age may be indelibly imprinted in the child's spirit. The school-age child, as noted earlier, is motivated by the desire to win approval, to master situations. When I work with a child who is meeting the threat of hospitalization successfully, I may say, "Justin, because of your bravery in the face of great danger, I now dub you Luke Skywalker [or Samson, or David the giant killer, or some other biblical hero]. From this day forward you shall be known throughout the land not as Justin Phillips but as Luke Skywalker, victor over Darth Vader and the dark empire"—a metaphor, of course, for the rigors of hospital life.

Koons[12] wrote, "Religious habits established in this formative period are so inwrought with the structures of the brain that they will likely abide for life." We would hope that one early habit established by children will be to think of themselves as blessed children, highly favored by God. Jacob said to the angel with whom he wrested, "I will not let you go until you bless me." The hospitalized child's need is the same, and the pastor will not want to leave the room without leaving behind a blessing.

Lay On Hands. Touch can be effectively used or abused in the care of children. I have never met a child who liked to be patted on the head. It musses up the hair and doesn't feel pleasurable. A pat on the shoulder or a handshake upon entering the room is probably pressing in too hastily, unless the pastor is very familiar with the child. The uninvited invasion of psychic space (the atmosphere surrounding the body) is an invasion of privacy. I once knew a minister from another country who was taking a sabbatical in America and was not being well received by his American parishioners. The reason eventually came out: he stood uncomfortably close, an acceptable distance in his country, but an invasion of body space over here. Children are people too, and we enter their private space by invitation only.

Having stressed the potential dangers of touch, the pastor will not want to miss well-timed opportunities to lay on hands. Power—spiritual energy—can flow through touch, as faith healers from the time of Jesus to the present have known. One eleven-year-old, who was left quadriplegic after being struck by a car, has feeling only one place on his body—his face. Every time I see him, in pretense of brushing the hair away, I make a point to touch his forehead. That is the only contact his sense of touch has with the rest of humanity. His friends have told me he likes it. Some children will enjoy thumb wrestling. Some will let you hold their hand or accept your offer to steady themselves by taking your arm while on a walk. Some will "give you five" at the end of your visit, older kids a "high five." Scientific studies conducted in intensive care nurseries have shown that babies who are regularly stroked take more nourishment and grow faster than those who are not. We do not yet understand how skin-to-skin contact is therapeutic, only that it is, for young and old alike. The pastor will await the chance to lay on hands—to anoint the child with oil, as it were—before terminating the visit.

Emote. Some have compared the role of chaplain in the hospital to that of the clown in the circus. Surrounded by highly skilled professionals such as trapeze artists, lion tamers, and tightrope walkers, the clown is busy tuning in on the laughter and tears of the audience. Similarly, the hospital minister who works alongside specialists and technicians concentrates on the humanity of those serving and served by the institution. The hospital minister's "territory" is morale, the spirit of the patient.

One of the chief needs of hospitalized children is to talk about their emotional response to the crisis. The effective pastor will want to ask "feeling" questions, questions that probe the emotions of the child: "Were you scared?" "Do you feel a little guilty about that?" "Do you get a little embarrassed when they do that?" The pastor's own humanity needs to be apparent to the child (the divinity is probably assumed). You may choose to tell stories about your own childhood, stories that let the child see you as a warm-blooded creature who just might be able to understand mortal experiences of being scared, angry, or uneasy about giving a urine sample. When speaking about yourself use "feelings" words—ashamed, mad, nervous, thrilled, upset, happy. Modeling realness is the best way for the minister to encourage children to be honest and open with their feelings.

Clergy may find this the most discomforting requirement of ministry to children. Clergy prize control and have historically taught by word and example that feelings—the negative ones especially—are not to be expressed. Working around honest children has a way of reminding us that there is a little child in each of us that has been stifled through years of acculturation, and we may need to spend some time getting back in shape for pediatrics. That means exercising the right hemisphere of our brains, our childlike, creative, playful, imaginative, intuitive self. Attending live theater, dancing, and listening to classical music can help. Being around children, playing with them, observing them, listening to them, enjoying them is better exercise yet.

Summary

Perhaps the trauma of hospitalization for children is overestimated, and hospitalization as a catalyst for personal growth has been understated. One must remember that the hospital, and the medical problems that require the hospitalization, constitute only one system in a child's life. Parents, friends, the church, you as a representative of God, and the child's own inner resources are other systems that can be mobilized to neutralize and overcome the negative fallout of hospitalization. A hospitalization is a lion's den for children for sure, but a lion's den from which they can emerge conquering heroes.

NOTES

1. A. Thomas and S. Chess, "Genesis and Evolution of Behavioral Disorders," *American Journal of Psychiatry*, vol. 141 (1984), pp. 1–9.

2. Michael Rutter, "Stress, Coping and Development: Some Issues, Some Questions," *Journal of Child Psychology and Psychiatry*, vol. 22 (1981), pp. 323–356.

3. Norman Garmezy, *Stressors of Childhood: Stress, Coping, and Development in Children* (New York: McGraw-Hill Book Co., 1983), pp. 43–84.

4. Jean Piaget, *Play, Dreams and Imitation in Childhood* (New York: W. W. Norton & Co., 1962), p. 273.

5. Erik H. Erikson, *Childhood and Society* (New York: W. W. Norton & Co., 1950), p. 258.

6. Gordon W. Allport, *The Individual and His Religion* (New York: Macmillan Co., 1950), p. 36.

7. B. Brodie, "Views of Healthy Children Toward Illness," *American Journal of Public Health*, vol. 64, no. 12 (1974), pp. 1156–1159.

8. R. Bibace and M. Walsh, "Developmental Concepts of Illness," *Pediatrics*, vol. 66, no. 6 (1980), pp. 912–917.

9. Biaca Gordon, "The Familiar Stranger," *The Family in Child Health Care*, ed. Pat Azarnoff and Carol Hardgrove (New York: John Wiley & Sons, 1981), p. 17.

10. Maria Nagy, "Children's Ideas on the Origin of Illness," *Health Education Journal*, vol. 9 (1951), pp. 6–12.

11. E. Perrin and P. Garrity, "There's a Demon in Your Belly: Children's Understanding of Illness," *Pediatrics*, vol. 67 (1981), pp. 841–849.

12. W. Koons, *The Child's Religious Life* (New York: Easton and Mains, 1903), p. 44.

FURTHER READING

Anderson, Peggy. *Children's Hospital.* Toronto: Bantam Books, 1986.
Faber, Heije. *Pastoral Care in the Modern Hospital.* Philadelphia: Westminster Press, 1972.
Herrmann, Nina. *Go Out in Joy!* Atlanta: John Knox Press, 1977.

9

The Terminally Ill Child
Barbara J. Prescott-Ezickson

Perhaps no experience in all of life carries more tragic weight than a child dying. It is one of those events we are aware of but pray that we never have to face. However, those who care for children in any capacity realize that children deal with terminal illness more often than we want to recognize. In our own hurry to deny the pain and tragedy, we may fail to develop the tools and skills to minister to children facing just such a reality. As a result, many children are dying without the opportunity for grieving that we regularly offer adults in our ministry.

Michael was ten years old and diagnosed with an inoperable brain tumor that would claim his life in a matter of months. His parents had not told him at first, fearing the knowledge would spoil his enjoyment of the time he had remaining. Then, after strong encouragement, they told their son the entire situation. I visited the following day and asked Michael to share with me what had been said. With many pauses and many tears he reported in great detail all he had been told. Then we cried together. A long silence followed before he said, "Now, what about that game of PacMan and those cookies you promised?"

Mary was eight years old and in the final stage of leukemia. We had numerous conversations throughout the course of her illness. On this particular day we were walking outside when she saw a butterfly and said, "Dying is like a butterfly." I asked what she meant and she explained. "You know, like the caterpillar gets in a cocoon and goes into a deep sleep and wakes up beautiful and able to fly. That's what will happen when I die. . . . I'll wake up and be able to fly in heaven and I won't hurt no more."

Barbara J. Prescott-Ezickson is Staff Chaplain, Hospice of Louisville, Inc., Ky.

Lynn was six years old and had a rare terminal disease that attacked the lungs. When I visited with her parents, they reported that the child knew nothing about her illness. They also noted with concern that Lynn was terrified of nighttime and of her bedroom door being closed. They said both of these were recent fears. After several conversations the issues were clear. Lynn reported a long list of "wrongs" she had done. She believed God was punishing her and that's why she was sick. Most of all she was scared of being "shut up in that basket and buried alive in the ground." The basket, of course, was a casket.

Cookies, butterflies, and caskets are clear examples that children face, understand, and interpret their death experience.

We are called to minister to all members of our congregation in their time of need. They call on us to help them understand, to find God, and to make sense out of life's circumstances. Our children have the same needs. Children, however, are at various developmental stages, and so we must expand our horizons to understand children and find meaningful and creative ways to meet their needs. In this chapter, we will explore the scenery, costumes, and props for ministering to the dying child. The unfolding script will depend on your commitment, creativity, and energy. My prayer is that you will find the love and courage to be a part of your children's drama, for your presence makes God an active member of the cast.

Getting to Know the Characters of the Drama

By the time children reach school age they have had various brushes with death experiences. They have seen death on television, perhaps a pet has died, and often a family member has died. Although death is an abstract concept, it now has some concrete connections in their life experience. They now struggle to understand and manage the experience.

What Children Think About Death

During the school-age years children are beginning to see and understand death as part of the life process. If we view childhood as a continuum, then the concept of death seeds at age six, grows during ages seven through nine, and is firmly rooted by age eleven. Death may be tragic and death may be unfair, but for children it is a real part of life that must be explored and examined. Two important concepts will help us understand what children think about death.

First, children view the world in very concrete terms. While we adults struggle with the philosophical questions about life, our children want to know specifics such as what death is, where you go when you die, what God looks like, how big the cancer is, and so on. Death represents an unknown assailant that is going to completely change their world. Children need to know, in words they can understand, exactly what death is, how it will happen, and how their world will change because of it. Because they are concrete thinkers, we must explain the situation in simple, basic, concrete terms.

Second, school-age children have a thirst to learn, to gather information, and to organize it in categories they can understand. Information and knowledge become their way to understand and control their world. When they are facing their own death, information becomes especially vital. Dying children experience increased anxiety and the need to find some sense of control in their lives. Children will attempt to lessen their anxiety and gain a sense of control by interpreting the situation with the information they have available. If they do not have accurate information, they interpret the situation from their distorted or inadequate knowledge, as in the case of young Lynn and her "basket" burial. When accurate information is provided by caring, informed adults, however, dying children are given the opportunity to manage their situation in an open and healthy way. This gives children permission to ask questions, clarify concerns, and express all their thoughts and feelings about what it means to be dying. Children feel less anxiety and a sense of control in an open, supportive environment that encourages such conversation.

A final point to keep in mind is that children's present coping with death is influenced by experiences in the past. Children have no basis of comparison except what they have already learned. It is important to talk with children and assess the healthy and unhealthy thoughts they have connected with death. This enables us to clarify their stage of mental development, to know what learnings to use and build upon, and to discern what learnings to help them discard.

What Children Feel About Death

One of the marks of childhood is energy and free expression of all emotions. As children move into the school-age years they begin to pay close attention to the adults and other children in their world. Conformity becomes an important part of a positive self-image. They want to look, talk, and dress like the rest of the children. They want to please the significant adults in their lives. Both desires have important implications when children are facing their own death.

Children who are dying are acutely aware that they are different. Three areas crucial for developing a positive self-image are affected: they usually have physical limitations, their school life is upset by hospitalizations, and often their appearance is drastically altered. Children feel isolated, afraid, sad, angry, and anxious. An added issue is not having developed adequate skills to identify and process these feelings.

A primary way that children learn about expressing emotions is by watching the significant adults around them. Children are natural imitators. They discover what is a "right or wrong," "acceptable or unacceptable" response by copying adults. When children are facing their death they need to be encouraged to explore and express their feelings. All too often, however, we adults set poor examples. We try to "remain strong" and act as if everything is fine. As a result children learn that it is unacceptable to discuss feelings or to cry. The end result is that their anxiety continues to escalate. Children are now isolated from peers and from caring adults who are mistakenly attempting to create an atmosphere of normalcy when children are feeling anything but normal. Mark's story illustrates my point.

Mark was a nine-year-old who had received a much-needed organ transplant. The operation was initially a success. However, Mark became weaker and it was clear the body was rejecting the organ. There was not time to get a second organ, and the family was told Mark would die. The family continued to tell Mark that all was well and he would be home soon.

Family members and friends were told the truth and began "dropping in just to say hello." One day Mark's uncle from Europe stopped in, making it seem like no special occasion. He stumbled over this explanation and Mark said, "It's OK, Uncle Jack, you don't have to pretend. I know I'm gonna die and you wanted to see me. Don't tell Mom and Dad I know 'cause it will worry them." At this point he and his uncle cried together. The family was extremely upset by this and asked for my assistance.

Mark told me he had known he was not getting well because he felt so bad. He said everyone looked at him weird but would not say anything about it so he guessed he wasn't supposed to ask. As we talked he was full of questions, fears, and much self-blame. He said 't was good to "get all this inside stuff out."

I had several conversations with Mark, helping him know how to talk to his friends and meaningful adults in his life. I had an equal number of conversations with his friends and family, helping them know how to talk to Mark. This provided opportunities for special times of sharing and good-byes before Mark died two weeks later. They were two weeks of tears, courage, and, yes, joy that I will always cherish.

Without appropriate pastoral availability and intervention this story would have ended very differently. Mark would have died alone though surrounded by caregivers. He would not have talked through that "inside stuff." Mark, his family, and his friends would not have enjoyed the chance to express their love, pain, and good-byes. Nothing was wrong with Mark or his family. Both were doing what they thought best. However, with information, support, and encouragement they found a different and more meaningful way to face death together.

The Spiritual Needs of Children Facing Death

Children in Christian homes are taught from the earliest years that God is love and that Jesus is their friend. By school age they can tell Bible stories, sing hymns, and quote prayers and scripture. They know that God made the world and are taught that God is in control of what happens in the world. They know that Jesus was a child once and grew up to do good works. They know Jesus died but is now alive in heaven. They know that Jesus loves the little children—all the children of the world. They also know that in God's good, created world, where Jesus is their friend, they are dying.

When we care for dying children it is one thing to provide information and encourage the healthy expression of feelings; it is quite another to explore theological concerns with them. After all, we adults have no answers about the senseless death of children. How are we supposed to help children with their questions and struggles to make sense out of a world turned upside down? The spiritual dimension does exist, however, and children look to us as ministers and spiritual caregivers to provide the information they need to understand. We have taught them the foundations of faith, and now we must help them let this faith speak to their death experience.

When death becomes a real factor in the spiritual development of school-age children, confusion is the order of the day. Remember, children are concrete thinkers and view the world in cause-and-effect terms. The only images of God they recognize are parent, shepherd, and friend. Without warning they now must face a tragic mystery of life and attempt to understand how the God they know fits into this new circumstance. In a true sense the facing of death calls these children to begin a faith task that is usually reserved for the adult years. This task is to walk through the valley of the shadow of death and see if God can be found there.

School-age children are somewhat ill equipped for such a journey, so the presence and intimate involvement of caring adults is vital. School-age children have learned that God is not their parents or their teacher. Children's concrete perception of the world still determines much about their understanding of God's character. They are observing the character of their pastor and other providers of spiritual care for clues about God's character. When children are facing death they become especially observant because they are unsure how God fits into their world at the moment. Our involvement communicates God's care and presence. Our absence may reinforce feelings of punishment and abandonment.

Children facing death have similar struggles and questions as do we adults. These children have a need to understand how God is involved in their situation. They have a need to grasp what happens after death. They have a need to celebrate the life they have had and grieve over what death will cause them to lose. They have a need to experience this process under the blessing of those who minister to them and therefore, in their understanding, under the blessing of God.

Directing the Drama: Developing a Pastoral Plan of Care

Initially one of the most important interventions you make is with parents and family. You will hear statements such as, "Children are too young to understand" or "We want to spare our child pain." Your ability to educate the family regarding the mental, emotional, and spiritual needs of children can be essential at this point.

Families rely on their pastor and other spiritual caregivers to give counsel in times of crisis. When children are dying it is extremely difficult for these family members to think clearly. If you take time to familiarize yourself with the basics of child development, your intervention can be an essential key to a healthy grief experience for family and children. Family members feel helpless to change the situation and long to have some control. In helping choose how to use the time they have with their child, you offer them a measure of control and the precious gift of time to share love and say good-bye.

Talk Directly with the Children Themselves

When children are diagnosed as terminally ill it is tempting to focus only on family members and ways to support them. Children are often forgotten for a variety of reasons. It is essential, however, to talk directly with children. They crave this one-to-one contact and interaction with their pastor and other spiritual caregivers.

The question is, of course, how do you talk with these terminally ill children about death and their experience? We live in a world that has made us question our own ability to conduct this type of conversation. A voice in our mind says we might do more harm than good, so why not leave such pursuits to the experts. If this line of thinking persists, then our children will have difficulty understanding why we preach to them and teach them but avoid talking to them about their death.

Pastoral care with children begins with conversation. We must overcome our personal inhibitions and allow ourselves to join our children in their drama. The only requirement is love for these children and a willingness to communicate that love in an open atmosphere that encourages trust and the expression of all thoughts and feelings. With this foundation let us talk about some practical ways to accomplish this task.

Create Situations That Allow a Child to Explore and Express Thoughts, Feelings, and Spiritual Concerns

Step 1 is to arrange to see the child individually. Make your appointment with the child and not through the parents or family members. Choose a meeting place that is on the child's turf. This could be the family room at home, the school playground, the park, or any number of places where the child feels comfortable. Visiting the child in familiar surroundings will provide an atmosphere of comfort and companionship for both of you.

Step 2 is to let the child know why you have arranged the visit. Children are very perceptive and, like young Mark, will see through any pretense. It is fine to let the child know you have heard the news and are concerned. Once you have expressed this reality then the child will set the direction by responding to your statement. This response —be it an abrupt changing of the subject, a flurry of questions, a joke, or an emotional outburst—will be a good indication of how the child is coping at that particular time. Allow it to direct you in how to proceed.

Step 3 is to begin conversation based on the child's response. If the subject has been changed, follow it; if there are tears, allow them; and so on. Keep your language simple and concrete. Use images and examples familiar to the child. When the conversation turns to spiritual matters be careful in using the "language of Zion," which is full of abstract ideas not readily comprehended by children. Pay careful attention to the child's facial reactions to check for understanding. Take time to check out whether a child understands by asking him or her to tell it back to you.

Step 4 is to be creative in relating to the concerns of the child. You do not have to be a play therapist to use toys, puppets, and stories to facilitate conversation or to make a point. Often a child is more comfortable using play to communicate because this is a primary medium of expression for children. For example, start a story and let the child finish it or vice versa. Or ask the child to put on a play with puppets, dolls, Masters of the Universe, or whatever is available at the time. If you pay close attention, the child will communicate clearly some of his or her concerns of the moment.

Step 5 is not to be afraid of having direct conversations with the child. Ask information questions to discover what the child is thinking. Provide information when the child asks. Use open-ended questions or make open-ended statements that require more than a yes or no response. Be willing to share with the child your questions, thoughts, and concerns. The same applies to the healthy expression of emotions. Be willing to show emotion with the child and provide an atmosphere where the child has permission to do the same.

Step 6 is to have regular and frequent contacts with the child. Grief is a process that must be encouraged and nurtured. Keep notes on the concerns of which you become aware during your visit. Take time in advance to strategize creative ways to follow up on these concerns. Have in mind a general framework of the child's grief process and what issues need to be addressed in your conversations. Have goals in mind for these conversations but be sensitive to the child's unique experiencing of the death process.

Encourage the Child to Find Spiritual "Answers"

"Does God kill people?"

"I was a bad girl and so God is making me die."

"Are there other kids to play with in heaven?"

"What's heaven like anyway? Will I be able to fly?"

Death and what it means are unknown elements in children's lives. Questions such as these reflect their need to understand and maybe regain some control. The child turns to the pastor or spiritual caregiver for assistance in clarifying and interpreting this experience. We can do this in three definite ways.

In the first place we can help children distinguish between correct and incorrect information. We can affirm that God still loves them and stays involved in their lives. We can help them begin to understand that life-threatening illness simply happens and is not brought on by anything they have said or done. We can use scriptures and stories to answer some of their questions, when appropriate. In short, we help remove the obstacles that prevent the child from relating to God in a constructive way.

The Bible has a wealth of helpful material for ministering to dying children: for example, (1) stories about Jesus and children, which reinforce God's love of children; (2) passages about Jesus weeping over Lazarus, Jerusalem, and his own death, which reinforce healthy expression of emotion; (3) stories about Bible characters who prayed to God about a variety of concerns, which reinforce God's care about all thoughts and feelings we have; (4) passages that describe God's goodness and love, which reinforce that terminal illness is not a punishment from God; (5) the Easter story and images of resurrection, which reinforce that God cares for us even in death; and (6) passages that describe what happens after death and what heaven is like, which give dying children a sense of reassurance. When these theological images are used appropriately and gently, in comfortable story form, they can be extremely meaningful for dying children.

Second, we need to be willing to admit that for some questions there are no answers. At the very least the tragic, untimely death of a child is an unexplainable mystery. It happens, but the reason behind its happening is elusive at best. Just as we find ourselves struggling without answers, so we must allow the child to do the same. What is important is to create a supportive atmosphere where the questions can be examined even if they cannot be completely answered.

Finally, we must be sensitive to the deeper need that these questions represent. The child is needing the reassurance of trusted adults that God still cares and that the child has done nothing to bring about this catastrophic event. Our continued involvement and willingness to share in the child's questioning communicates God's involvement and presence in the process.

If we are honest with children and encourage their questioning and exploration of ideas, they will arrive at conclusions that work for them. The test is whether these conclusions are constructive, promote healthy faith development, and support a positive relationship with God. If the opposite is the case, then it is a signal for further conversation.

Conclusion

Pastorally caring for children requires energy, commitment, intentionality, and an openness to spontaneous happenings. It is an art that is learned through involvement, practice, and continued reflection on your interaction with children. The script written is a joint project between the child and the significant adults involved. Our willingness to be involved contributes to the development of the characters, the direction of the plot, and, of particular importance, the play's outcome. Most of all, our involvement makes God a key figure in the drama. May we find the love and the courage to journey alongside our children as they face death.

FURTHER READING

Bernstein, Joanne E. *Books to Help Children Cope with Separation and Loss.* 2nd ed. New York: R. R. Bowker Co., 1983.
Grollman, Earl A. *Talking About Death: A Dialogue Between Parent and Child.* 2nd ed. Boston: Beacon Press, 1976.

Jewett, Claudia L. *Helping Children Cope with Separation and Loss.* Boston: Harvard Common Press, 1982.

Lester, Andrew D. *Pastoral Care with Children in Crisis.* Philadelphia: Westminster Press, 1985.

Shelly, Judith A. *The Spiritual Needs of Children.* Downers Grove, Ill.: InterVarsity Press, 1982.

Vogel, Linda Jane. *Helping a Child Understand Death.* Philadelphia: Fortress Press, 1975.

10

The Chronically Ill Child
Gary Brock

When parents take their child to a doctor they expect to leave with the assurance that "she'll be over it in a few days." They hope that modern medicine will again work one of its magical cures. Very few parents expect to be told that their child has significant physical or mental problems. Some problems (i.e., spinal bifida) will be diagnosed at birth or shortly thereafter. Most wait to suddenly announce themselves as the child matures. Found here will be the progressions, complications, and exacerbations of illnesses such as asthma, juvenile diabetes, juvenile rheumatoid arthritis, renal disease, hemophilia, congenital heart disease, and a variety of neuromuscular disorders.[1]

Parents will soon notice, with frequent and lasting shock, that the physician is using words like "care" instead of "cure." Unfortunately, the mental image many parents have for understanding the impact of a chronic illness is based on telethons or institutions. For many, therefore, the words "chronic" and "hopeless" will be synonymous. Almost all studies show that parental attitude is a major factor in how children cope with their illness. To this the minister must be seriously and sensitively attentive.

In providing pastoral care to sick children it is important to keep in mind a working distinction between acute and chronic illness. An acute illness is typically of short duration and has little or no lasting effects (excluding any serious complications). Once it has run its course, children go on about the business of growing up. A chronic illness, on the other hand, is of long duration and frequently insidious in its impact.

One helpful way of thinking about a chronic illness is by describing its "behavior" and "effects." First, although the intensity of the disease may be reduced by treatment and therapy, or because of the age of the

Gary Brock is Director, Department of Pastoral Services, Vanderbilt University Medical Center, Nashville.

child, it never really goes away. Second, because of the frequent disruptions in the life of the child, impairment in emotional and cognitive development is a probability. Third, children with these diseases are at high risk for psychological problems involving identity and the ability to relate to others. Fourth, all studies agree that chronic illness is a major "hazard" to the stability of the family. Neither parents nor siblings escape its impact. Because of these four dynamics, chronic illness has biological, behavioral, social, and theological dimensions.

Impact of the Crisis

Childhood is supposed to be a time of happiness, fun, and freedom, not a time of pain, suffering, and increasing limitations.

Beverly is twelve years old. She is just at the right age to begin that delicate transition from childhood to adolescence. Most of her friends are having a "really fun summer." She is not. Beverly's kidney disease has put her back in the hospital for the fourth time this year. The preteen sits on the foot of her bed and reflects:
"I guess I'll have to repeat my grade again. I just got so far behind. . . . I had a homebound teacher." She giggles. "Sounds like *she's* the one stuck at home, don't it? Well, anyway, we didn't get along too good. . . . Mom said that I should've been nicer, but, you know, sometimes when you don't feel too good, homework is the pits." Pausing, she glances in the mirror. "Uncle Jay came over last night. He said I looked like 'death warmed over.' . . . I'll be glad when Mom lets me start wearing makeup . . . most of my friends do already."

This brief vignette points to the impact that a chronic illness can have on a child. Her education has been delayed, and valuable time lost. Peer relationships, suffering from frequent disruptions, have a long-distance quality about them. Problems with adult authority are evidenced in the difficulties with the teacher. Beverly's self-image is seen through the disparaging comments of her uncle and, perhaps, even in the "refusal" by her mom to let her grow up. The desire to use makeup may be viewed as both a "masking" of who she is and a statement about approaching adolescence. Learning, peer relationships, child–adult interactions, identity—these are just a normal part of the day-to-day life of the child. The complicating factor with this particular twelve-year-old is the overlay of her chronic illness. Her adaptive[2] capacity will be put to the test. Chronically ill children must learn to cope with the normal developmental crises appropriate to their age group *plus* the stressors of their particular illnesses. Ironically, and sometimes tragically, the child will be a young adult before success or failure can be determined.

In order to minister effectively to these children, an underlying influence shaping what they experience must be appreciated. In their view, nothing happens by chance. This "infantile omnipotence" is able to "move mountains." That is, children believe themselves to be in possession of a unique power and/or responsibility. Everything is caused by something that in some way, directly or indirectly, involves them in the process. This means that all events will have a reason or meaning that is "consistent" with the facts at hand.

One recent study[3] looked at fifty chronically ill children, ages five to twelve, who were hospitalized. The purpose of this research was to gain insight into how children conceptualize their illnesses. Researchers found a three-stage sequence in conceptualization that was directly dependent upon the child's chronological age. At Stage I (ages seven years or less) the children saw their illness as something for which they were directly responsible. One child with juvenile arthritis stated that his problems were caused by playing in the snow and not taking care of himself. By Stage II (ages seven to ten) the children began to differentiate between internal and external causes. The most common cause was germs. A seven-year-old girl with multiple congenital anomalies suggested that these germs come from people "coughing in your face." In Stage III (not seen in those less than nine years of age) multiple causes were described. A twelve-year-old with congenital scoliosis suggested that people get sick by not taking care of themselves, by catching something, or by being born with the problem.

The primary significance of the research (also corroborated in other studies) is in its demonstration that *what* children think about the events in their lives is directly determined by *how* the child is able to think. The child-as-patient must be considered in relationship to the child-as-developing-person. To ignore either dimension will keep the minister from understanding the child. Although the study cited did not deal with moral judgments, it is easy to see how the Stage I child might feel guilty for what was occurring, or how the Stage II child might be angry and want to place blame on someone else for making her sick. This matter of "placing blame" becomes particularly evident in the older child who has a genetically linked problem.

To know about children in general is not to know about a particular child. Until the particular child is understood, very little ministry can occur. What are Benjamin's feelings about his condition? How does Julie's fear color what she thinks is happening to her? What does David state as the cause of the problem? Answers to these questions will give significant clues to, and information about, the degree to which the child has been able to integrate into daily life what it means to be called "well" or "unwell." If in doubt, ask! Children will tell you only what they want you to know.

In a hospital visit with six-year-old Jenni, it was apparent that Raggedy Ann was "speaking" for both of them. Helping to retie the ribbon on Raggedy Ann's pigtail, the minister asked the doll, "What have you and Jenni done today?" Raggedy Ann "talked" of the playroom, of her mother having to go home "and rest 'cause she was here all night," of coloring pictures, and of the woman who "hurt" Ann. Paying close attention to the Band-Aid on the doll's back, the minister heard that during a very painful test Ann had "been bad and tried to kick the doctor. And Mommy was real upset about that." When asked, very gently, "Why do you think Ann acted that way?" Jenni said that Ann was afraid of all the "strangers" in the hospital. "Everybody hurts her and makes her cry." If there had not been pastoral care for Ann, there would not have been pastoral care for Jenni.

Seven-year-old Henry said he had a "pretty rough morning . . . Mom and Dad were real worried about me." He was not sick, but his brother had leukemia and Henry was feeling ignored by his parents (a feeling that was quite accurate). A pastoral visit with him took the form of sitting on the floor and playing with Matchbox cars. A toy ambulance, "driven" by the minister, kept having to "rescue" this young boy from one "disaster" after another. Henry's play revealed the crisis atmosphere that was surrounding him.

The child's fantasy world is a rich resource for the doing of pastoral care. A common problem that interferes in caring for children is treating them as if they were little adults, with emotions comparable to the adult, only in smaller amounts. Eleven-year-old Michele was tired of being "polite" to all the adults who constantly invaded her world, always without permission and frequently without introduction. Her anger spilled over as the minister from her grandmother's church happily said as he left the room, "Can you tell me 'bye?" Her response, though considered rude by her parents, revealed the need to set limits. "I could," she said—but she did not. Listen to their world!

Faith Issues

Like other aspects of the child's development, faith is also in process. The fact that one's relationship to God is based on one's spiritual experiences is no less true for the child than it is for the adult. Therefore, faith issues must be approached in terms of the age and development of the child. Only by adolescence will enough spiritual, psychological, and physical maturity be gained to allow uniquely individualized faith affirmations about events in life and their effects upon the person.

The pastoral care of a chronically sick child is one of the more difficult parts of the church's ministry. Sickness has a way of creating emotionally and spiritually fragile individuals. Explanations and statements about God that are satisfactory to adults, who have a history of experiences with which to relate, may be totally meaningless to the child. Crises alter reactions.

Debbie is seven years old. Her tonsils were removed yesterday and her mom is feeding her ice cream when the pastor comes to visit. He reminds her that God took good care of her during surgery and will help her get well and go home. As is his custom, they all join hands and have prayer, thanking God for doctors and nurses who can take care of children like Debbie. He also thanks God for healing "this little one."

Catherine is seven years old and is back in the hospital because her diabetes is out of control. She was admitted through the emergency room last night almost in a coma. When the pastor comes to visit, Catherine is having blood drawn from a vein in her arm. He is there to remind her that God will take care of her and will help her get well and go home. She begins to cry.

Children will hear only what they are able to hear. The same message about God's care and concern was heard in radically different ways by these two seven-year-olds. Their immediate experiences were the primary difference. The emotional gap between having a sore throat and being a "brittle diabetic" is immense and hard to bridge. Debbie always felt warm and secure. Ice cream from her mother and a visit from the minister reassured her that all would soon return to normal as she recovered from an acute illness (tonsillitis). Catherine, with her chronic illness and frequent trips to the hospital, has an inkling that God may not be as warm and caring as the pastor indicated. The minister's assurance, on the basis of what his experience had taught him, ignores what her experiences have taught her. Before speaking on behalf of God, the caregiver should understand what children are asking, how they are asking it, what they have been told, and by whom.

Listen as other children share their experiences through the eyes of faith. A certain helplessness is experienced by each of these children that goes beyond their physical problems.

TOBY: Mom said that God loves me a whole lot . . . that's why I'm like I am. I'm God's special gift to my mom and dad.

How long can one be "God's special gift" without expecting this identity to bring with it special treatment? It may help the parents cope, but it will be of little value to this ten-year-old heart patient. As Toby moves beyond the security of the family, he will soon discover that not everyone will grant him the same privileges and status. The loss of these will only further complicate the developmental process of the child who is "sickly," trying to live with those who are not.

> GAVIN: I have a lot of trouble breathing when I think bad thoughts . . . you know, like when I get really mad at my brother. I heard the preacher at church say it's a really bad sin to be angry with your brother.

Has there ever been a brother who did not get angry at his brother over something? Perhaps it would be more helpful to assist Gavin in his theological interpretations. It matters little, at this point, what the preacher actually meant; what was heard is the source of difficulty. Angry feelings are normal. This nine-year-old asthmatic should not have the additional burden of labeling himself "sinner."

> LINDA: Before I was born, when I was in heaven, I could run and play just like the other kids at school; when I was born I had this thing wrong with my spine. Auntie said that it was God's will and that I should bear it like a good Christian.

This comment raises some rather major questions about how God works. Even if there was some kind of physical existence prior to conception and birth, what possible reason would "cause" God to take a healthy child and send her to earth paraplegic? This is a question that ten-year-old Linda will never be able to ask. Her "Auntie" has spoken on behalf of God and settled the issue of spinal bifida. To ask, therefore, will be to jeopardize her status as a "good Christian." How simple (and effectively uncaring) it is to provide the answers without even considering what the questions might be! The pastor must be constantly aware that sermons and classes are not the only religious information the child receives.

Four basic factors should be considered in understanding the faith of children. First, faith is a growth process. Second, a child's faith is concrete and objective; ambiguities will not be appreciated. Third, as we have observed, what is said about God reflects what they have been "told." Fourth, children are *now* oriented. Even if told that "Jesus loved you yesterday and will continue to love you tomorrow," the child will need some reassurance (usually nonverbal) that this is true. It is better to hold Toby's hand than it is to worry about holding his attention while a "message" is being proclaimed. It is better to read Linda's favorite story as a reminder that some things never change than to force your agenda. For one eleven-year-old boy, just to have the minister watch TV with him was a reminder that at least one adult cared. The love and the presence of God must be "incarnated" in the minister's behavior.

Children's faith should not become a hindrance to their struggles, a magic to make them well, or an oblique method of keeping adult anxieties under control. Faith should be able to "handle" the multiple emotions that have been observed in chronically ill children: denial, anxiety, guilt, fear, anger, doubt, depression, resentment, feelings of rejection or abandonment, and suicidal thoughts. In order to do this, their faith, which will be mediated primarily through human relationships, both verbal and nonverbal, must allow for and encourage love, acceptance, security, protection, dependence, independence, guidance, assurances of value, and trust. At issue is a pristine faith that if nurtured properly will grow with the child. It is holy ground and should be approached accordingly.

Ministry

The care of the chronically ill child requires a variety of professional resources. The nature and type of resource will vary with the illness. Regular attention will be received from doctors, nurses, and lab technicians. Since many of these children will need specialized care, they will also relate to special education teachers, physical therapists, social workers, dietitians, and (in some cases) hospital chaplains. Some treatments may take place in other cities or states. No matter who is taking care of the child, however, the goals will be the same: to minimize the effects of the illness and its potential complications and to maximize the child's ability to grow and develop. Therapeutically, this is referred to as "containing the disability."

Here is the setting for long-term pastoral care. On the one hand, the scientific and medical community will be working to enable both child and family to deal with the illness. On the other, the religious community provides the structure for care that will enable child and family to survive the various crises. With the issue being "care" and not "cure," the church is in a unique position to be the primary foundation for healthy integration of the spiritual, the psychological, and the physical. In fact, the church and its pastor may be the only predictable entity in this family's life. The pastor's presence, therefore, will remind them that in spite of all evidence to the contrary, God is still in control. The pastor affirms that the grace of God can be found in some rather ungodly situations.

Effective ministry will take both *time* and *commitment*—time for a relationship to grow through pastoral visitation, especially when the crisis eases, and a commitment to the "little person," who is indeed a child of God. Like any long-term relationship this one will have to be carefully and intentionally nurtured. The primary responsibility for this belongs to the minister. Every contact with the child will need to be considered a continuation of the initial one. Visits to the home, sitting with the child in hospital room or clinic, church picnics, church school classes visited or taught, children's sermons preached, grown-up sermons "heard"—all these are integral links in the pastoral conversation with the child. Treasure them as such!

The minister needs four areas of knowledge if effective pastoral care is to occur: know the sick child, know the family, know the immediate needs of both, and know yourself.

Know the sick child. The child cannot be known in isolation from the overall impact of the illness. Be aware of its immediate physical and emotional effects. Although this information can be obtained from the parents, talk to the child. Effectiveness in doing this will depend on five factors: (1) Be sure the child knows who you are. It is a long way from the pulpit to home or hospital. (2) Be sure the child knows why you are there. Was the last visit made when Grandmother died? Remember, children tend to make direct connections. (3) Be sure your attention is focused on the child's perspective. Children who have to deal with the problems of chronic illness become surprisingly knowledgeable and sophisticated. Honor their understanding of what is happening to them. (4) Be sure you bring a part of you to the conversation. A child will know if you are "for real." (5) Be sure you leave the blessings of the church. If you pray, pray *with* the child and *not about* him or her.

Know the family. Again, routine pastoral visitation is the key. Being present to listen to the parents' concerns, their direct or subtle pleas for help, asking both the difficult and the sensitive questions—these are the kinds of things upon which a pastoral relationship is built. Families in crisis become very narrowly—sometimes dangerously—focused. The minister brings the fresh, healing air of a new perspective. A child moves from a wheelchair to a walker, and the long and arduous hours of physical therapy that have left the parents exhausted become an occasion for a psalm of celebration. The after-school program at the church provides Mom a chance to return to work, and the presence of hope is once again made real. The minister arranges for the siblings to be involved in activities just for them, and long-festering anger finds resolution. The question of "Why did God do this" slowly evolves into an understanding of how "God can be with us" in painful situations. Effective ministry finds out what is essential. "A man's spirit may sustain him in sickness, but if the spirit is wounded, who can mend it?" (Prov. 18:14, NEB).

Know the immediate needs of both. The minister may need to take on the role of advocate. Is what the child needs readily available? Is the family having to take care of problems that others are more skilled in handling? What about the emotional and physical needs of the entire family? In many places the church may be the only resource in the community that can be helpful. With the role of advocate also comes the role of teacher. Given the tendency of medicine to focus on particular areas of the body or on specific limitations, the minister must consistently remind all involved that a whole child is at risk. In order to be helpful, the minister needs to have a working knowledge of what is happening to this child. The minister must be informed. Talk with other parents who have had to deal with a chronic illness. Can they be of help to your church members? Perhaps a network of parents can be established. Talk with local organizations that are dedicated to research on chronic diseases. Read the material that the parents have been given. Your objectivity will help them fill in the blanks with facts, not folklore. Add books to the church library that will be helpful to child and family.[4] Educate yourself and your congregation.

Know yourself. Why are you there: As pastor? As friend? As stranger? What can you bring them that no one else can—personally or professionally? How do they interpret your role as a representative of God in what is happening to them? What are your theological biases about how God does or does not work? In those crises that will inevitably come, will you be able to represent effectively the "ever-present help"? Sometimes children and parents get angry or disappointed with God. Can you handle this being directed at you? What are your own reactions, to illness in general and to sick children in particular? Some ministers simply are not able to enter into this kind of care. If this is true, be honest about it and let someone in the congregation minister in your behalf. Parents appreciate honesty much more than being ignored.

Termination of Ministry

A final observation needs to be made about terminating a ministry to children. The demands of a chronic illness bring many adults into the child's world. Some will be abrupt and disruptive, others will be long-term and supportive. Few will have the opportunity to be as present as the minister. Because of this, leave-taking must receive careful attention. The age of the child and length of the relationship will determine what needs to be said.

First, take time to explain why you are leaving. This is not the time to talk about the nature of God's call. Be practical. Most children are aware that people move and take other jobs. This may have happened in their own family. Keep the explanation within the child's realm of experiences. Second, on a map show where your new job will be. A picture of the church may help the child visualize that you will no longer be at "his" or "her" church. Third, tell the child that you will write after you move. Children enjoy receiving mail. They may not feel like talking on the phone. Fourth, if a lengthy period of time develops between ministers, try to maintain a minimal contact with the family. Be alert to impending illness-related crises. Fifth, anticipate your own pain over the leave-taking. Be careful not to overreact by changing your patterns of behavior. More frequent visits may only be confusing; less frequent ones may make the child wonder what he or she has done to keep you away. Sixth, since the child will eventually be given over to another's pastoral care, offer to make the necessary introductions.

Conclusion

Sick children are fragile. Their parents are especially fragile. Assumptions underlying one's pastoral care must be carefully considered. A cautious sensitivity must inform each visit. As a representative of God be mindful of the "kind" of God you represent.

NOTES

1. Intentionally omitted are the childhood cancers. Although their lasting effects are certainly chronic, they also have a life-threatening dimension that is absent from the others.

2. For an excellent study of adaptive and maladaptive behaviors the reader is referred to Rudolf H. Moos, ed., *Coping with Physical Illness* (Plenum Medical Book Co., vol. 1, 1977, vol. 2, 1984).

3. Arlene B. Brewster, "Chronically Ill Hospitalized Children's Concepts of Their Illness," *Pediatrics,* vol. 69, no. 3 (March 1982), pp. 355–362.

4. The Association for the Care of Children's Health (3615 Wisconsin Avenue NW, Washington DC 20016) publishes a pamphlet *Educational Resources for Pediatric Health Care.*

FURTHER READING

Belgum, David R. *What Can I Do About the Part of Me I Don't Like?* Minneapolis: Augsburg Publishing House, 1974.

Burnett, Frances Hodgson. *The Secret Garden.* New York: Dell Publishing Co., 1981 (reprint).

Fassler, Joan. *Helping Children Cope: Mastering Stress Through Books and Stories.* New York: Free Press, 1978.

Goldman, Ronald. *Religious Thinking from Childhood to Adolescence.* New York: Seabury Press, 1985.

Lester, Andrew D. *Pastoral Care with Children in Crisis.* Philadelphia: Westminster Press, 1985.

11

Abused Children
Virginia D. Ratliff and J. Bill Ratliff

Principle: The child shall be protected against all forms of neglect, cruelty, and exploitation. (UN Declaration of the Rights of the Child, 20 November 1959)

Recognition of child abuse as a social problem is a relatively recent occurrence. Throughout history children have been seen as the property of their parents, and parents could discipline them as they saw fit. Indeed, there were cultural and religious sanctions for physical punishment, since children were often seen as little animals who had to be tamed and socialized. One writer, after studying the history of child-rearing practices, stated that the methods used to discipline a large percentage of the children before the eighteenth century would today be called abusive.[1] Child abuse will continue in our society because it reflects the violence condoned in our recreation (in boxing and football, as witnessed by the injuries), discipline (in corporal punishment), personal relationships (in the personal assault statistics in this country), and international relationships (as shown by the forty-three countries fighting wars in 1986).[2]

In recent years we have seen tremendous increases in reports of families where there is maltreatment of one family member by another. Several major disciplines address abuse as it occurs in various family relationships—abuse of the elderly, spouse abuse, abuse or neglect of children. In the 1980s we are hearing more about sexual abuse of children. Our purpose is to focus on situations where children are targets for abuse within the family, whether it is at the hand of parent, guardian,

Virginia D. Ratliff, a therapist, was formerly Coordinator of Victim Assistance Network, Washington, D.C.
J. Bill Ratliff is Assistant Professor, Pastoral Care and Counseling, Earlham School of Religion, Richmond, Ind.

caregiver, or sibling. It is our opinion that in a family where active abuse of any member is taking place, the children are being abused in a subtle and covert manner. This abuse may be expressed in a number of ways:

Physical abuse involves nonaccidental injury to the child, ranging from slapping, pushing, and shoving to breaking bones and injuring with an object or weapon.

Psychological or emotional abuse includes withholding of love and affection, rejecting, teasing, degrading, and threatening the dependent child.

Child neglect results when the child is not provided the basic needs of survival (food, clothing, and shelter) or parental love, care, and guidance, or when the child is required to assume a caretaking role inappropriate to the child's age.

Sexual abuse by a family member of the opposite sex is called incest (for example, when a father has sexual contact with his daughter, or mother with son) and by a nonfamily member is called sexual assault.

Destruction of property and pets that have meaning to the owner are especially common by older siblings, who make it look like an accident, and by parents who use this abuse as a form of discipline.

While hard statistics are impossible to obtain, the National Center on Child Abuse and Neglect estimates that one million children are abused each year, resulting in two thousand deaths. No identifiable group escapes abuse. It happens in both wealthy and poor families, among all races and religions, in all geographic areas, at all socioeconomic levels, in all cultural groups, and among all educational levels. No matter what the circumstances, children are unable to escape the problem or often even to get any help.[3]

Child Abuse in the Family

Physical and emotional abuse, neglect, and incest have enough similarities, especially in terms of ministry, that they can be considered together. We have learned that abusive families usually have the following six characteristics:

1. Abusive parents usually have experienced abusive or neglecting behavior from their own parents. As children they may have been either victim or observer, but in either role they learned abuse as a style of relating that they bring to their own parenting.

2. Abusive parents generally do not understand the needs of a child and lack parenting skills. Consequently, they feel inferior, ineffective, and often guilty for their failures and frustrations. These feelings may then be taken out on the child.

3. Part of raising children requires a parent to be aware of the child's capabilities and limitations at different ages and stages. Because abusive parents lack this information, they may think the child is intentionally

being "bad" to hurt the parent; the parent then punishes the child for the imagined injustice.

4. The abusing family is often isolated from neighbors and extended family. Family members have few, if any, friends. They have no one, therefore, to whom to turn in times of stress. The abuse, of course, makes family members feel different and secretive, which heightens the sense of isolation.

5. The abusing family tends to be a family where independence is sacrificed for the sake of togetherness. Family members long for closeness but are afraid they might lose their sense of identity and feel swallowed up in a family that has no room for individuals. Enormous hunger for love and care is present, brought by each parent from a depriving background. This results in constant competition between the marriage partners to see who gets taken care of. The loser, then, in a desperate attempt to have needs met, turns to the child. When the child is unable to meet these inappropriate demands, a whole lifetime of the parent's frustration over unmet needs is acted out on the child in the form of overt aggression.[4]

6. Immature or insecure parents usually struggle with everyday problems. One distinctive feature of abusive families is that they are continually trying to adjust to changes.[5] We know something of the stress and pressure the average family is confronted with each day: money problems, work-related stresses, family relational problems, and the pressure of just getting it all done. At times of change—be it a job change, new family member, or sickness or death of a family member—life-altering stresses are added to the everyday pressures. Each family develops its own way of handling stress and conflict. Some people cry, others withdraw, some work hard, others get depressed, some turn to alcohol to escape, while others problem-solve. Some, of course, release the tension and frustration by assaulting a family member.

Child-battering, then, is an ineffective and destructive attempt to handle conflict and stress. The batterer has not learned to cope with feelings in a productive way but has learned to strike out at a family member. This behavior diverts the anger to an inappropriate target and releases it; in that sense it works. However, damage is done and the long-term cost is high.

Abusive episodes typically go through a three-phase cycle: the tension-building phase, the incidence of violence, and the calm, loving phase. The tensions come from a variety of stresses, although the abusive parent believes the child is the cause of all the tension. The child, in fact, may be causing some trouble or demanding attention at that time, but in no way is the child responsible for all the family tensions. Once the violence has erupted the parent feels more calm and often becomes loving and caring. The parent may explain to the child why the abuse occurred, interpreting events in a way that leaves the child feeling guilty and responsible.

In abusive families, often one child is picked as the primary target of abuse, the one identified as the problem, or the difficult one to handle. This may represent some truth. The child may have been born in adverse circumstances, may not behave according to parental expectations, or may have a special need that demands more from a parent. The parent's frustration is released by abusing the child. Once the scapegoating cycle has begun, both parent and child see the child as the problem, and this faulty view becomes ingrained in the parent's expectations and the child's self-image.

In other cases the abuse flows freely to all children in the home. The role of the abuser does not always remain with one parent. Sometimes the father is the abuser and the mother, as the nonoffending parent, may attempt to be protective. At other times she may be the abuser, taking out her frustration on the children. It is generally felt that in an intact family mothers and fathers abuse about the same amount. However, the total number of children abused by mothers is higher, a reflection of the number of female single-parent homes.

Impact of Abuse on the Child

Children who are abused by parent or caretaker learn a powerful lesson: the world is an unsafe place to be. The first-person accounts we have available, written by adults who were abused as children, give a compelling picture of the fear a child feels—fear of another beating, fear caused by not knowing what causes the beating or what to do to avoid one, fear of separation from the family, and finally fear of death of self or parent.[6]

All children love their parents. They are, after all, their parents, and parents are right in the eyes of their children. The children join the family belief system that denies the abuse ("It's discipline"; "It didn't happen"; "It's normal") or minimizes the importance ("They know I love them"; "It didn't hurt"; "It didn't happen"). Consequently, the child learns early that love and pain are indistinguishable. "My parents love me; they hurt me; therefore, love means pain."

As do children in all crises, abused children react by feeling guilty for events over which they have no control. This is in part a function of children's attempt to feel they have some power or mastery over part of their life. Children also tend to think, If my parents treat me badly, then it must be because I am bad. This natural tendency, coupled with parental explanations that it really is the children's fault, leaves the children in the bind of feeling responsible for their own hurt and pain, and having no way to protect themselves. When the children are old enough to understand, getting help is an option. They are also aware that asking for help could mean separation from family and the breakup of the family unit. They carry the burden of keeping the family intact by continuing to tolerate the abuse.[7]

The child learns to survive in the family, but there is more than one style of surviving. One child may withdraw, become shy and extremely quiet. Another child may be very active and on the move, as though saying, I can't be hurt if they can't catch me. A third child may actively attempt to please the parent, rigidly attempting to do everything right and, in the extreme, becoming parent to the immature parent. A fourth child may become angry, aggressive, and strike out at others. The common feature is the desperate attempt to learn to survive in and adapt to the child's lot in life.

How then do abused children come to our attention? It is very rare that children will ask for help. They are too loyal and faithful, and they need their family too desperately to take that risk. Sometimes a parent may find strength to ask for help for the family. More often the abuse is observed directly, by a neighbor or relative witnessing an event, or indirectly, by a teacher, minister, or doctor observing marks or bruises. Then questions are asked in a way that allows the child to disclose the truth without being threatened and feeling the necessity to lie to protect the family. The questioning is critical, since if it is not handled carefully it can cause the child to increase efforts at covering up the dreaded secret. Leave it to the professionals. Most states have child protective service units to look into such matters. In most states, any helping professional, including a minister, who observes behavior or marks that are suspicious, is required by law to report this. Childhelp operates a nationwide toll-free number, 1-800-422-4453 (1-800-4-A-CHILD), for help in reporting child abuse. The National Center on Child Abuse and Neglect may be reached at 1-202-245-2856.

Faith Issues

There is a spiritual dimension to the crisis of violence in families, in addition to the physical and emotional dimensions that have been discussed. Many times the family considers itself religious and is active in a church or synagogue. In one study of abusing families, 80 percent claimed religious affiliation, compared to 62 percent of nonabusing families.[8] The abuser may use scripture to justify the abuse: "Honor your father and your mother," or "Spare the rod and spoil the child." The nonabusing spouse, many times the wife, may feel that her faith will not allow her to leave her husband.

In the midst of this overt religiosity, abused children experience episodic chaos in the home that is painful and frightening. When the

abusive parent connects the abusive behavior with religious interpreta-
tions, a child's loss of trust in other people gets extended to God as well.
If God supports the parent's behavior, it is inconceivable to a child that
God is loving and protective. God must be a vengeful, wrathful, capri-
cious God. In return, these children may feel fearful and angry at this
God who punishes them through the hands of the parent.

James Fowler describes the stage of faith of elementary-age children
as the Mythic-Literal Stage.[9] At this age, the children are able to use
their minds to arrange a more orderly, linear world. They are clearly
able to perceive cause-and-effect relationships. The problem then occurs when their world at home is so chaotic. They may spend much time
at school, in what looks like a daydream state, attempting to make sense
out of the internal chaos they bring from home. They have little energy
to spend on school subjects, unless they have the ability to shut out the
family when they leave home.

Children also use stories to help organize meanings in their lives.
They love to read stories of the lives of great persons and great adven-
tures, and they often love to tell stories.[10] Religious education at this age
includes stories about the heroes and heroines of the faith. The problem
with abused children is that they cannot share the most important story
in their life because they feel bound by fear and secrecy.

Reciprocal fairness is the basic ethic of school-age children. They
abide by the rules and know the clear consequences when they do not.
Children perceive a natural kind of lawfulness in the world. Reciprocity
is also central in their relationship to God, whom they see in an an-
thropomorphic way, often as an old man with a white beard standing
on a mountain or sitting on a throne.[11] For abused children, the reciprocity makes them feel that God is a mean old man and that they must
deserve what they are getting.

Ministry to the Parents

The minister may hear from a neighbor, friend, or perhaps a religious
education teacher that abuse appears to be occurring in a particular
family. Of all professional people, the minister has the best opportunity
to initiate contact. The minister can call on the family and inquire in
a discreet, tactful way about the stress that may be present. If you are
uncomfortable in making a home visit, you can always call local child
protective services and ask them to investigate These persons are
trained to make careful, thorough investigations and then follow
through on their findings. In the case of violence occurring at the
moment, and you get a call from a neighbor, call the police. If you know
the family well and are comfortable going yourself, go, knowing that
you are at some physical risk.

Before such a crisis occurs, you need to know the community helping agencies. Many communities now have shelters where women and their children can go for a few days. Crisis child care and nurseries are available in larger communities, where mothers can leave their children for a few hours during a time of high tension. Many different kinds of therapy are now offered in almost all communities. The place to start with abuse, however, is with the local child protective services.

The church has a very important place of service to the abusing family, even after community agencies are involved. Being supportive through the entire process can be a real service, if the church expects nothing in return. Because the abusive family is isolated as part of the way it functions, few friends or extended family are available to help. Remember, each member needs attention and support. Many times the attention goes to the abuser, and the rest of the family, including the abused child, gets ignored. After the physical safety of all family members has been ensured, the listening is very important. As we have said, this kind of family is enormously hungry for emotional attention and in competition with one another for whose needs get met. Listening to each one gives each person important nurture.

Decisions will need to be made about jobs, school, child care, and other details of living. You can be with the family members during this time and offer alternatives and information about possibilities of which they may not be aware. Your own knowledge of the community will be useful. If they are involved in the legal system, they may need a companion to accompany them to court and through the complex legal process. Having an advocate is helpful in reducing the threat from the unknown and making the legal process productive.

You can understand the offender's feelings, but make it clear that behavior must change. Forgiveness must be tied to repentance so that no cheap grace is offered. It is not uncommon for the offender to confess, promise it will never happen again, and then expect that to be the end of it. The person is sorry it occurred and sincerely believes the behavior will not recur. You need to make clear that violence is like an addiction; without treatment it will happen again! You can help the person overcome the shame of admitting the need for assistance. You can also present self-control as a challenge and a way to avoid being controlled by the court and other authorities. The primary defenses of the offender are minimization and denial. The church has tended to use the same defenses in dealing with family violence. It is easy to fall into the same trap with the offender.

The nonabusing spouse may need to talk about guilt, either of not knowing about the abuse or of knowing and not being able to stop it. If the person, typically a woman in our culture, feels she cannot leave because she married him "until death do us part," you can point out that the marriage died when the abuse occurred and may only be resurrected with treatment and long-term change. Just as adultery breaks the marriage covenant, so does physical violence. The actual decision, most likely, will be whether to leave him until he changes, not about divorce. Your authority as a minister of her church might be helpful in giving her permission to consider separation for her safety and that of the children.

Additional help can be found in groups for women who have been battered and other kinds of support groups available in most communities. A referral might be very helpful and supportive in her struggle to become a whole person and more assertive in her rights. Parents Anonymous is a self-help group for abusing parents. With 1,500 chapters and 10,000 members around the country, its goals include redirecting anger away from children, learning to reach out to other people for help, and changing destructive ways of viewing oneself and one's children.[12]

Ministry to the Child

Dealing with abused children is a long process that requires care and commitment. The following needs are guiding lights for your ministry with them:

Protection. An abused child needs some help in disclosing this vulnerable secret. A report to child protective services is appropriate, useful, and often mandated. Obviously, steps need to be taken to ensure that the abuse stops.

Support. Once the abuse has been disclosed, the family will be in crisis. Every family member needs care, and the children are easily overlooked. Pay attention; inquire about their feelings and fears; acknowledge them as valuable and important persons.

Ventilation. As the child feels safe, and if it is appropriate, you may become the person to whom the child feels free to talk. Listen! Use your best active listening skills to keep the child talking. Abused children are ambivalent about their parents and may quickly move from hating to defending them. That's all right; it's part of what needs to happen. Accept it as their reality and the path of their healing.

Reassurance. The child needs to hear repeatedly one all-important message: "It's not your fault. You did nothing wrong. I'm glad you have survived [or weren't hurt worse]."

Consistency. Be available to the abused child in a consistently caring way. Abused children need someone who can tolerate their low self-esteem and the attempts to clarify the love-pain confusion. If you become an important person in the child's life, those mixed messages will be tested on you. Consistency is the key.

Because the world of abused children is so chaotic, you need to be a person of your word, responsible, steady, and faithful in your promises.

You can follow the child's guidance on how to be of help. The child may need to do things with you or talk with you about what happened. The child may want to hang around with you and your family and see what a normal family is like. Once children get to know and trust you, you may begin to hear about their anger at God and the church. When a child expresses these deeper feelings, you are on holy ground. As one older child in an institution for delinquents told Bill, "I don't want to hear about the love of God for me. I want to know if *you* love me, and then I will decide for myself if I think God loves me." As children grow older and approach the teen years, the question of suffering and the nature of God naturally arises.

Here are some specific guidelines for ministry to abused children.

1. Do not be afraid. The abused child is basically similar to other children and may be more resilient because of the experience.

2. Treat the child as a human being, with kindness and consideration. The child has no position or power in the church and contributes little to the budget, but "as you did it to one of the least of these . . . , you did it to me" (Matt. 25:40).

3. When speaking to the child, either sit or kneel at his or her level. This shows respect, keeps you from overpowering the little person, and increases the chances for communication.

4. Observe the child's demeanor and behavior in the church building. If you sense that something is troubling the child, invite the child to your office for privacy. Walk side by side as you go to your office; an abused child will tend to follow behind you. Again, you are showing respect and offering a corrective to the way the child has been treated. Be sure to have a chair in your office on which the child can sit comfortably.

5. Comment on what you observe about the child's mood. If the child agrees with your observation, you can ask if he or she would like to talk. Do not probe or push. Take your time.

6. If the child's story unfolds, listen! Do not try to talk the child out of his or her feelings, or give the other side of the coin, or provide reasons for the way things are.

7. Thank the child for sharing personally with you. If the child asks you not to tell the parents because that will get the child into trouble, reassure the child but do not make promises you cannot keep. You may be required to tell the authorities if abuse is suspected. If they are already involved, you will want to let them know if abuse is continuing to occur.

8. Let the child feel free to come talk to you again whenever the child would like.

An accepting class in the religious education program can be a stable point in the abused child's environment. Due to the isolation of the family and the secrecy involved, the child may have few friends and may not know how to relate to a group of peers. Because of these issues, the child may not be easy to have in class. However, if the teacher understands the nature of what is going on, loving patience and gentle teaching can be of real assistance in a child's adjustment to the painful realities and the process of recovery.

Nonfamilial Child Sexual Assault

A child is sexually molested every two minutes in the United States. Most of these children are between eight and thirteen years old, boys as well as girls. Half are molested within the family and half are molested by nonfamilial assailants. We have been discussing child abuse within the family, but it is equally important to consider the molested child whose parents are not involved in the abuse. It is important for the minister to be prepared to assist these parents, since we can help in caring for their child through this crisis.

Sexual abuse or molestation is defined as any sexual touch by force, trickery, or bribery between two people between whom is an imbalance of age, size, power, or knowledge. The power imbalance and intimidation results in the child living with a dreaded secret, while the molester continues to abuse many more children before being stopped. The hardest and most important step for the child is disclosing the secret. Only infrequently will a child volunteer the information; more often the child responds to direct questioning by someone who has noticed changes in the child's behavior. These symptoms may include a wide range of behaviors: withdrawing and becoming uncommunicative; problems with sleeping, eating, or bowel functions; excessive masturbation; making sexual advances toward other children in an attempt to regain some of the lost power and control; reluctance to go a certain place and be with a certain person; and nightmares. Symptoms vary, since they are reflective of the child's unique coping ability.

Authorities agree that any child who demonstrates explicit sexual knowledge is in fact a victim. Children don't learn that kind of information in appropriate settings and can't make it up. When we hear of such behavior, the tendency is to resist the thought that the unthinkable might have happened. Believe it! Then communicate that belief clearly to the child, because victims struggle with the fear of being punished for being bad or for disclosing the secret they were supposed to keep. Not being believed by parents or people the child cares about will magnify the damage done to the child.

The child victim and the parents are both in crisis. The child has the crisis of admitting what happened, while the parents have the crisis of dealing with social responses in addition to their own personal anguish. Parents frequently feel blamed by society for not protecting their child. Many report that when someone is told of the child's being sexually assaulted, the first questions imply that the parents knew and didn't do anything. We must be clear in our communication that we believe an assault does not necessarily indicate a failure in parenting, or that the child is at fault. Responsibility for the assault lies with the offender.

Ministry to the Parents

The areas mentioned in the earlier section on ministry to the physically and emotionally abused child also apply here. Additionally, some particular areas need attention when you minister to the family that has experienced a sexual assault on one of its children.

The first thing to remember is to support the parents, since parents who have adequate support are in a good position to help the child. Some ways to express that support follow.

1. Express faith in the parents' ability to care for the child and make decisions about what must be done.

2. The sexual assault of a child often leaves the parents overwhelmed with feelings of guilt at not having been able to prevent it. In dealing with the guilt of the parents, you as a ministering person are in a good position to be nonjudgmental and to assure them that it was not their fault. If an element of neglect or unconcern was present, or if the parents were too caught up in their respective careers, that guilt may be more realistic. You can begin to help them examine the ways they want to change their values and life-style as a result of this trauma. This kind of examination usually comes later in the process, after the immediate crisis is past.

3. The parents may be filled with rage at the assailant and at God for allowing it to happen. Again, your presence and nonjudgmental listening can be very important. The parents will need to do a lot of talking. They need caring people to listen.

4. Later, they may begin to ask why God let this happen. You can struggle with them around the age-old mystery of suffering and its meaning. They may identify with some of Job's complaints and struggles with God. Another couple who has gone through and survived a similar experience or a local support group of parents of abused children can be very helpful in the healing process.

5. Assist the parents in the task of differentiating their concerns from those of the child. For example, the parents are concerned about safeguarding their child, but restricting play activities may be perceived as punishment. You may be able to provide some perspective and clarification, if that occurs.

6. Help the parents in their dealings with the criminal justice system. In cases where prosecution is possible, the process is filled with confusion, delays, and frustrations. A major stumbling block is certification of a minor as a witness. The parents are likely to be working with police, prosecuting attorneys, victim advocates, and the person providing treatment to the child. Although important and necessary, the legal process adds stress on top of the enormous anxiety of the original crisis. If the offender is apprehended and sentenced, the parents can feel some relief, in addition to the satisfaction of knowing that they did all they could.

Ministry to the Child

Both parents and concerned adults must provide constant and consistent reassurance to the child victim. The communication needs to include "We believe what you have told us," "We know it was not your fault," "We are glad you said something," "We are sorry about what happened," and "We will do our best to protect and support you."

Any child who has been sexually assaulted needs professional help. If the abuse was ongoing yet kept secret by the child, the duration of the therapy will be longer than for the child who told after the first offense. Treatment needs to be provided by an objective professional who has been specially trained. The therapy will help the child integrate the abuse into a total life experience and become a survivor.

The child who was assaulted will need to work through many unpleasant thoughts, feelings, and memories. This process is likely to spill over into relationships outside of home and the therapy room. When a child, in your presence or in the church, is behaving in an inappropriate way (e.g. hitting, masturbating), try distraction rather than prohibiting the behavior. Negative messages from adults are powerful, and the child already feels at fault. It will be better to provide the child with external structure and more interesting activities to assist in controlling the inappropriate behavior. Eventually the child will be able to talk about the conflicts, and then you can listen.

All members of the victim's family need sensitive support and caring from the religious community. In addition, the religious community can provide educational opportunities to members at large, which may result in collective efforts to address inadequate laws, unsafe conditions, and areas of wider community concern. Above all, it is our hope that the religious community can be the center of healing and hope for the abused child, the family, the congregation, and society.

NOTES

1. Lloyd DeMause, ed., *The History of Childhood,* in Alfred Kadushin and Judith Martin, *Child Abuse: An Interactional Event* (New York: Columbia University Press, 1981), p. 1.
2. Charles J. Hanley, "43 Countries Fighting Wars This Year," *Cincinnati Enquirer,* Oct. 19, 1986, sec. E, p. 1.
3. Cheryl McCall, "The Cruelest Crime," *Life,* December 1984, p. 58.
4. Blair and Rita Justice, *The Abusing Family,* pp. 61–66.
5. Ibid., p. 59.
6. Lenore Walker, *The Battered Woman* (New York: Harper & Row, 1979), p. 55.
7. E.g., P. E. Quinn, *Cry Out! Inside the Terrifying World of an Abused Child.*
8. Justice, *The Abusing Family,* p. 99.
9. James W. Fowler, *Stages of Faith: The Psychology of Human Development and the Quest for Meaning* (San Francisco: Harper & Row, 1981), pp. 135–150.
10. Ibid., pp. 136–137.
11. Ibid., pp. 144–149.
12. Justice, *The Abusing Family,* p. 207.

FURTHER READING

Brady, Katherine. *Father's Days: A True Story of Incest.* New York: Seaview Books, 1979.

Fortune, Marie, and Denise Hormann. *Family Violence: A Workshop Manual for Clergy and Other Service Providers.* Seattle: Center for the Prevention of Sexual and Domestic Violence, 1980.

Justice, Blair and Rita. *The Abusing Family.* New York: Human Sciences Press, 1976.

Loontjens, Lois. *Talking to Children/Talking to Parents About Sexual Assault.* Santa Cruz, Calif.: Network Publications, 1984.

Magnuson, Ed. "Child Abuse: The Ultimate Betrayal," *Time,* Sept. 5, 1983, pp. 20–22.

McCall, Cheryl. "The Cruelest Crime," *Life,* December 1984, pp. 35–42, 47–52, 57–62.

Quinn, P. E. *Cry Out! Inside the Terrifying World of an Abused Child.* Nashville: Abingdon Press, 1984.

12

Disabled Children
Sue H. Enoch

Society establishes certain standards for the appropriate behavior of children at any given chronological age or stage of development. The child who cannot perform these expected "normal" behaviors soon becomes labeled as "exceptional," "disabled," or "special." The differences may be lack of language, inability to read standard print, lack of movement, or uncontrolled activity. For these children every action presents a new challenge. Each disabled child is unique and the limiting variables are many. We will discuss both the general effects of disability and the specific implications for several disability groups.

The Impact of Disability

Because the disabilities seen in most school-age children were present at birth, the major impact of the child's disability is on the parents or family unit. Generally, the children do not begin to recognize real differences between themselves and other children until the intermediate grades. Because they have always been as they are (blind, deaf, physically disabled, etc.) they are initially accepting of the disability as a matter of fact. The parents, however, are acutely aware of the uniqueness of their child. They are constantly confronting long-range educational planning, ongoing medical evaluations and interventions, and the questions, spoken and unspoken, of people they meet daily. At the same time parents are coping with all of the practical mechanics of living with a disabled child, they are also struggling with their own emotional responses. Guilt, anger, and fear are often near the surface. They experience grief, real and long-lived, as the dream of what their child might become is replaced with the reality of the limits the disability imposes.

Sue H. Enoch is Minister of Childhood Education, Crescent Hill Baptist Church, and Elementary Program Supervisor, Kentucky School for the Blind, Louisville.

The death of that dream brings real grief with its anger, denial, and (it is hoped) finally acceptance. These feelings, which begin at the initial diagnosis of the disability, intensify as the child enters and passes through the educational process and our church programs. We cannot minister to a disabled child without understanding this chronic sorrow and ministering to the family.

The disabled child is limited most by range and variety of experiences. The parents may limit experience because of fear for the safety of the child. A child who has been ill for long periods of time often remains at risk in the mind of the family. The child who has been teased by other children may be unnecessarily protected from similar threatening experiences. Because most of a young child's learning takes place through experience, the impact is great. Disability is a crisis that causes the child not to function within the expected norm. It is long-term and ongoing.

Society tends to impose the greatest number of restrictions upon the child. Everything we do is designed for able-bodied persons. Whether in building design, entertainment, or transportation, accommodation for disability is a low priority. When we are confronted with a child who is not able to function within those guidelines we quickly become frustrated and confused. Our reaction is to retreat so that maybe it will go away. Our first question is, "Can't something be done?" Our deep need is to heal the disability, to make things whole and right again. When we can't fix it, we leave it alone. In this case "it" is a person, a child of God. Our own helplessness defeats us at the very point where ministry should begin—acceptance.

The first impact of disability is isolation. The child is often left to play alone or to sit in the company of adults. Other children, or their parents, are afraid to come near. Uninformed parents refuse to allow "normal" children to be near disabled children for fear they will "catch" the disability. The children and their parents are forced to withdraw from public places to avoid pain.

Disabled children have great difficulty developing peer relationships. Parents trying to compensate become so child-centered they have no adult relationships. The cycle perpetuates itself and no one can maintain healthy socialization. Anger, frustration, and overdependence, on the part of both the child and the parent, become a major problem.

The disabled child must constantly struggle for the right to participate in society. Even though legislation now mandates access to public services and institutions, these regulations are often inadequate, poorly enforced, or totally ignored. It then becomes the role of parents, friends, and the minister to be the child's advocate.

It is frequently assumed that disabled children always function below normal expectations mentally. This is not true. Children who are visually impaired, hearing impaired, or physically disabled function well within normal intellectual limits. Communication may be limited due to the particular disability, requiring additional effort to share the child's thoughts, but the reward is frequently a bright, alert mind. No generalizations are adequate about the level of intellectual functioning possible for any disabled child.

Initially, the psychological impact of disability is evidenced in the family, not in the child. By the time a child enters the intermediate grades (3, 4, 5), the differences become more apparent. At whatever age the child understands the differences, several things may occur. Isolation may begin to cause loneliness. "Normal" children, who once tolerated the difference, suddenly become impatient with doing things with someone who can't do them well. Outwardly visible indications of the disability become targets for teasing and name-calling. Children can be very cruel to each other, and the disabled child may respond with withdrawal, self-pity, or anger.

As disabled children recognize differences, these differences are often experienced and interpreted as negatives, things that can't happen: places they can't go, things they can't do, schools they can't attend. Often this results in a very low self-esteem. "If I can't do all the things the other kids can do, I must not be any good." Their feelings of worthlessness are exacerbated when other persons refuse to let them try. Disabled children may soon believe they really can't do anything and give up.

Being different may also create strong feelings of anger. The children begin to ask why they are different, why others don't want to be with them, why they can't become what they want to become. The anger may be manifest in withdrawal and a refusal to attempt any activity, or in defiance, resulting in unrealistic goal setting and refusal to accept any limitation of the disability.

A major focus of any child's life is the educational process. Public Law 94-142, the "Right to an Education for All Handicapped Children Act," guarantees a free, appropriate public education for every disabled child. The law is an excellent one, but its implementation is often flawed. It requires appropriate evaluation and parental involvement for placement in any educational program. Writing an individual educational plan with specific goals and objectives for the child to meet is necessary, in addition to ongoing monitoring of the child's progress. The parents are placed again in the role of advocate. Even though professionals provide information, the final decisions about programs, services, and schools are ultimately the parents'. They must decide what to fight for, how far to appeal, and what compromises to make. One mother told me, "It's so frightening to think that if I make a mistake I will, at the least, waste a year of my child's life, and at the worst, ruin his chances for a productive adulthood." The quality of the educational program for a disabled child may well make the difference between some level of productive independence and complete dependence.

Disabled children and their parents tend to spend a great deal of time dealing with the medical community. They may see a variety of specialists (one fourth-grader I know has seventeen) who may give conflicting advice. They may spend hours each month waiting in clinics for doctors who spend five minutes with each child. Medical science has learned to save the lives of many young disabled children, but they are unsure of the long-term implications. The frequent tests, probes, and appointments demand tolerance and patience.

Disabled children may require corrective surgery for physical impairments, ear infections, eye surgery, or monitoring of medication levels, resulting in a higher incidence of hospitalizations. They frequently have early and intimate awareness of hospital care, causing fears and angers based on real experiences. The link with the medical community will exact a great deal of time and energy from both the disabled child and the family

Types of Disability

The impact of disabilities on children, as discussed, has many general characteristics. Any specific disability adds certain unique problems to the crisis.

Hearing Impairment

Two kinds of hearing loss affect children, conductive and sensorineural. The type of loss affects both the prognosis and treatment of the impairment. A sensorineural loss is one in which the nerve cells in the ear or the nerve pathway to the brain are impaired. This type of loss often cannot be helped through use of a hearing aid and rarely responds to any form of medical intervention. Because the nerves are damaged, the condition will remain as it is. A conductive hearing loss is one in which abnormalities in the external or middle ear prevent sound from getting through the pathway to the inner ear. This type of loss may be helped by use of a hearing aid and frequently responds to medical intervention. Some types of conductive losses are not stable, so the reaction of the child to auditory cues may vary from day to day.

Because of the variety of hearing losses and the variety of educational techniques available, good communication with a hearing-impaired child's family is critical. An age-old controversy between educating a child orally (using only amplification, speech reading, and speech training), manually (using only sign language), or through total communication (using a combination of amplification, speech reading and training, and sign language) still continues. It is necessary that we understand the specific educational technique being used and follow it when dealing with a hearing-impaired child.

Visual Impairment

Visual impairment occurs when a part of the eye's mechanism or the nerve pathway from the eye to the brain is impaired or fails to develop properly. The impact of that impairment will vary depending upon the amount and degree of vision remaining. The child may read Large Print, learn Braille, or use recorded materials. Children may travel using specialized mobility techniques or little adaptation. They may attend a school for the blind or a public school.

It is important that good communication with the visually impaired child's family be maintained in order to choose the most appropriate and effective methods to be used. The child will help you understand his or her vision if you are honest and unembarrassed in your questions.

Physical Impairment

Physical disability is the most diverse of all the groups we have discussed. A physical disability may limit coordination, movement of one limb, or total range of body movement. It may be stable or progressive. The cause may be accidental, birth related, or hereditary. Some of the most common causes of physical disability are cerebral palsy, muscular dystrophy, and spina bifida.

Cerebral palsy is caused by damage to the motor area of the brain. It is permanent and stable. It results in varying degrees of impairment, from slight weakness in one limb to total involvement of all motor ability.

Muscular dystrophy is a neurological disorder that is progressive. It results in weakness of muscles and will ultimately result in death. There is no specific treatment, although physical therapy and medication are often used to alleviate the symptoms.

Spina bifida is a condition present at birth in which a portion of nerve tissue is found in a sac outside of the spine, often in the lower back area. It usually results in impaired use of lower extremities, limiting mobility and bodily functions to varying degrees. Medical complications are common with spina bifida.

As with every disability group, talking with the child and the family is the best source of information.

Needs of the Disabled Child

The needs of a disabled child will vary according to the severity of the disability, the amount of early intervention provided, and whether the disability is present in isolation or in combination with other disabilities. Some general characteristics are the same for all disabled children.

The need to be treated as a child, not a disability. Disabled children are more like other children than they are different from other children. It is important that we remember and emphasize their childhood rather than focusing our energies and efforts on the disability. They are children who need to be loved, want to have fun, and are eager to learn and try new things.

Disabled children are not necessarily intellectually limited. They must be allowed opportunities to use their abilities in as many ways as possible. They should be respected as capable individuals, emphasizing the things they can do rather than the things they cannot do.

The need to be accepted. Whatever the disability, these children need to be affirmed for who they are—members of the family of God on earth. Their pain, sorrow, joy, and success are a part of our own. They are people of worth, with gifts to share with us all. Disabled children should be included in all the activities available for their peers. This may mean adaptation of the activity, but it will be worth the extra effort required.

The need for community and communication. It is easy for disabled children and their families to become isolated. Hearing impairment establishes barriers to the community due to lack of expected communication modes. Both the natural family and the church family should participate in whatever language teaching model is used to encourage language development.

Materials must be provided that are appropriate to the child, whether they be amplified for the hearing impaired, enlarged for the visually impaired, or made accessible for the physically impaired. The important thing is to consider the child's needs and adapt the materials to meet that need.

The need for independence. Disabled children need to develop as much independence as possible. They need to try things and fail, as well as succeed. They need to be disciplined. They need to be left alone sometimes. They need limits established and goals set. They need to be expected to do their best. In other words, they need to be treated like any other child of the same age in terms of behavior and development. The adaptations for their specific disabilities must not impede the growth of independent persons with socially appropriate behaviors and self-care skills.

Visually impaired children must be able to travel safely and feel secure in their surroundings. Their independence is increased when a sighted person learns proper sighted guide techniques.

Faith Issues

The faith issues for disabled children will vary according to the amount of reasoning ability and language they possess. The issues are going to be much more advanced for a visually impaired child of normal intelligence than for a multihandicapped child with limited ability. However, the issues seem to group themselves into three categories.

The first issue for disabled children may very well come when they notice they are different. They begin to ask, "Why me? Why can't I hear? Why did God make me this way?" The question most often finds us without an answer. I cannot reconcile the God who loves and cares for me with the image of God choosing to make a particular child disabled. It is too presumptuous, too uncaring. The presence of disability in the world and in the life of a particular child is as inexplicable as the presence of any suffering in the world. It simply exists; it is a part of life. Disability is a reality of the child's life. What is most important for children is to know that their disability does not separate them from the love and care of God.

The child may ask, "What have I done wrong? What did my parents do wrong?" Jesus answered that question clearly in his interaction with the blind man in John 9:1–34. When his disciples asked whether the man's sin or his parents' had caused him to be blind, Jesus answered, "His blindness has nothing to do with his sins or his parents' sins" (John 9:3, TEV). The disability is clearly not a punishment for wrongdoing. I do not know why children are disabled, or why they must endure pain and frequent medical treatment. I do accept Jesus' word that the disability is not a punishment, and I do know God loves those children.

The New Testament is rich with stories that illustrate Jesus' acceptance and care for people who were different. He healed the slave of a Roman soldier (Luke 7:1–10), he accepted the despised tax collector (Luke 19:1–9), and he forgave the Samaritan woman (John 4:5–30). When Jesus visited the synagogue in Nazareth to preach his first sermon he named himself an advocate for disabled persons (Luke 4:18–20). The encounter with the Gerasene demoniac illustrates his willingness to cross barriers that isolate in order to heal (Mark 5:1–20). Each encounter demonstrates inclusion of people in the family of God who were not the norm for their society. It is this acceptance that is important.

Disabled children may also question the image of God as a good God. They may become confused as the stories of God the Creator and their own disability seem contradictory in their mind. The Genesis account repeatedly tells us God was pleased with what was made (Gen. 1:25, 31). The goodness of the world, the beauty around us, and the love of family and friends are all good creations of God. Disabled children are loved and cared-for creations of God with gifts and abilities to share with all of us. It is in helping the children to recognize the goodness and love within themselves that we can lead them to recognize the goodness of a God who loves them. Daniel Day Williams helps us understand God's image not as physical form or intellectual capacity but our capacity to be in communion with another, or our capacity to love and be loved.

The third confusing faith issue for children may come in the stories of the miracles of healing. Jesus healed a paralyzed man (Matt. 9:1–7), two blind men (vs. 27–31), a dumb man (vs. 32–34), and many others during his earthly ministry. The children may ask why Jesus doesn't heal them now. We teach them to pray for what they need, and they may feel they need to be healed. An honest discussion of seeking God's comfort can be based on Matthew 7:7–12. All of us must ask, in faith, for the strength to live with or change those things we feel are wrong with our lives. God knows how to give us the good gifts we need. They are not always the gifts we want, just as parents and teachers don't always give us what we want. Children should be led to develop trust in a loving God who is faithful to care for all of us.

The issues of faith for disabled children have no easy answers. The questions offer opportunities for caring adults to admit that simple answers do not exist. We can continue to demonstrate our own trust in God despite suffering and imperfection. Helping children understand that they are not separated from but loved by God, as people of worth, is critical to the development of a strong, healthy relationship with God and the church family.

Suggestions for Ministry

The discussion of the impact of disability and the needs of specific disability groups provides some guidance for ministry with disabled children. These can be summarized in the following areas.

Family support. Living with a disabled child is living in chronic sorrow. The constant challenges, both medically and educationally, can easily deplete the resources of the most stable family. Support can be given in a number of ways.

Take time to listen and share the concerns of parents and siblings. Just having a safe person with whom to talk will decrease the stress level. Accept, in a nonjudgmental way, whatever anger, grief, and confusion you may hear. Listen carefully for ways to intervene.

Become a referral source. Learn who does what in your community and learn about the referral agency. It can be frustrating and frightening trying to locate needed services. Help the family through this maze.

Establish a network of respite. Parents of disabled children are often reluctant to leave the child. Find, or become, someone they can trust with care of the child so they can get away from the constant caregiving and supervision. Provide special activities for siblings so they can have extra attention and feel special.

Friendship. Disabled children need the accepting, loving friendship of other adults. Become that significant adult who can be depended upon for support and counsel.

Guided integration. As a minister, you set the tone for the church's acceptance of disabled children. Education of the church family about the needs of disabled children, and ways they can help, is vital. Help the church family develop Jesus' attitudes toward disability. He was not frightened by them, he took time for them, he accepted them as they were, and he affirmed their ability to care for themselves. Help the church implement acceptance in all educational, recreational, and social programs.

Specialized training and materials are available for use by most denominations. Lead children's workers to become knowledgeable of, and sensitive to, the adaptations necessary for disabled children to become fully participating members of the church family. Remember that ministry should be *with* disabled children, not *to* or *for* them. They should be accepted as equally participating members of the ministry.

Pastoral care through medical crises. Because they have more medical crises than others, disabled children are sometimes forgotten when in the hospital. Your understanding and support through each hospitalization is important.

Guidance in faith issues. As you develop a relationship with both the family and the child you will become approachable for both. In addition to the faith issues of the child, the family is also dealing with guilt, anger, and rejection. Your presence and acceptance can bring those issues into focus. It is typical for parents of disabled children to carry a great deal of guilt about their children. "Surely there was something I could have done to prevent this. Why didn't I_____?" If the cause for the disability is hereditary, the guilt is even stronger. The guilt leads to compensation through overprotection and doing everything for the child. As the child remains dependent, anger surfaces, directed at the child because of lack of independence. Then guilt arises for being angry because, after all, the parent caused the disability. This cycle can continue for years unless your gentle intervention helps parents deal with the guilt.

The family needs assistance in dealing with their grief over the death of a dream and in learning to live with reality. The intervention is not unlike that needed for any grieving family, except that their grief does not end.

Advocacy. In social, educational, and religious settings, disabled children need persons who will speak up for them and seek to lead the institutions to change. As minister to a disabled child, you can with knowledge lead to wider acceptance and positive action.

Ministry to disabled children is ministry that seeks to include all persons within the family of God. Its motive must be genuine love for, and acceptance of, children with disabilities. They are first of all children, much loved by God.

FURTHER READING

Hearing Impairment

Benderly, Beryl Lief. *Dancing Without Music: Deafness in America.* Garden City, N.Y.: Doubleday & Co., Anchor Books, 1980.
Mendel, Eugene D., and McCay Vernon. *They Grow in Silence.* Silver Spring, Md.: National Association of the Deaf, 1971.
Yount, William R. *Be Opened!* Nashville: Broadman Press, 1976. An excellent overview of Christian education for the hearing impaired.

Visually Impaired

Crim, Lottie R. *Come Care with Me.* Nashville: Broadman Press, 1983. Discusses issues in providing emotional support for parents of disabled children.
Frailberg, Selma, and Louis B. Frailberg. *Insights from the Blind.* New York: Basic Books, 1977.
Lowenfeld, Berthold. *Our Blind Children: Growing and Learning with Them.* 3rd ed. Springfield, Ill.: Charles C Thomas, 1977. Deals more with developmental issues.
Lowenfeld, Bethold, ed. *The Visually Handicapped Child in the School.* New York: John Day Co., 1973. The classic overview of techniques for teaching and implications of eye conditions.

Pastoral Care

Hartbauer, Roy E., ed. *Pastoral Care of the Handicapped.* Berrien Springs, Mich.: Andrews University Press, 1983.

Hauerwas, Stanley. *Suffering Presence: Theological Reflections on Medicine, the Mentally Handicapped and the Church.* Notre Dame, Ind.: University of Notre Dame Press, 1986.

Hogan, Griff, ed. *The Church and Disabled Persons.* Springfield, Ill.: Templegate Publishers, 1983.

Stewart, Jack C. *Counseling Parents of Exceptional Children.* Columbus, Ohio: Charles E. Merrill Publishing Co., 1978.

Williams, Daniel Day. *The Spirit and the Forms of Love.* New York: Harper & Row, 1968.

13

Children with Learning Disabilities
Allen R. Gilmore

Everybody in church knew him. He looked like a ten-year-old version of the all-American boy. Reddish-brown hair, bright-blue eyes, freckles, a flashing smile—he was a film director's dream come true, a cute, budding Tom Sawyer awaiting discovery. But that's not why everyone knew him. They knew him because he was a "bad boy."

Church school teachers quaked at the mention of his name. Directors of music groaned when his parents brought him to choir practice. The minister of youth and the director of education both looked weary at the mention of his name. Billy could charm adults, all right, but fifteen minutes in any activity with him could change that. Adults became exasperated at his behavior. In a very short time span he could reduce otherwise loving and level-headed adult church workers to fuming, anxious persons struggling to contain their frustration.

Billy, it was claimed, had the shortest attention span in the world. Then when his attention wandered, he would go into action. He would talk during quiet times. He could not sit still very long. He rarely left his classmates alone. With chatter and physical contact he would disrupt any activity. Many times he was quarrelsome and belligerent with peers, sassy to adults. He read poorly. He was impulsive and emotional at times.

Billy's parents often looked tired and were obviously embarrassed by his behavior. They blamed themselves and, it was rumored, sometimes blamed each other. His older sister clearly loved him but increasingly perceived him as a pest to be avoided. He seemed bright enough, but it was reported that he struggled in school and was barely promoted each year.

Every church has a Billy or two. Adults usually feel frustrated and

Allen R. Gilmore is Executive Director, The Pastoral Counseling and Consultation Centers of Greater Washington, Washington, D.C.

guilty when they try to meet the needs of these youngsters. Ideals of loving and helping children to grow and develop give way to hoping one can survive the time Billy is in your activity until he can be passed on to someone else. Concepts of an open, growth-oriented environment give way to thoughts of restraints, corporal punishment, and harsh judgment. Sophisticated theologies can be reduced to thoughts about evil and possession by the demonic!

But Billy isn't bad. He isn't evil or possessed. He is a child in crisis. Billy is one of a large group of children increasingly being recognized as *learning disabled.* He suffers from a group of problems or disorders often referred to by behavioral scientists as a "syndrome." This syndrome affects approximately half of all children who are brought to the office of child psychotherapists before the age of thirteen, and an astonishing four out of five of them are boys. Educators and clinicians are making strides in identifying and helping these children. Religious institutions need to learn from these professionals but are also ahead of them and can be instructive to them in some ways.

Learning disability is one term used to refer to children who may suffer from one or several problems. Other common terms that refer to all or part of the same difficulties are: minimal brain dysfunction (MBD) and attention deficit disorders (ADD). Children who suffer from learning disabilities are relatively easily recognized by their behavior traits, but the syndrome can only be diagnosed definitively by competent professionals using objective measures. Children who are described as hyperactive, inattentive, and impulsive may also be suffering from some physical (organic) problem or illness or may be emotionally disturbed in a general sense, rather than being learning disabled. Therefore, those in ministry need to ascertain what assessments physicians and school personnel have made about the child. Usually by the time a child is in the third or fourth grade, much of the data necessary for such an evaluation is in hand.

As church workers we need to recognize this disorder, not merely to equip ourselves to survive the antics of difficult children in our parishes but because these children suffer serious emotional consequences, including poor self-image, low self-esteem, and feelings of self-loathing, guilt, and depression. Socially, such children are often lonely and isolated. They embody all those human difficulties to which a gospel of grace and love speak. In order to be the personification of such a gospel, we need to understand their difficulties.

Understanding Learning Disabilities

The etiology of learning disabilities is thought to be neurological. Although exact details of how these nervous system deficiencies cause various aspects of the syndrome are not known, central nervous system problems play a part in each of the observable characteristics of the child.

A common characteristic is hyperactivity. Billy can't sit still. Many people equate hyperactivity with learning disabilities. It is almost always present and thought by some to be the basis for the entire syndrome. One theory proposed is that learning-disabled children have a neurologically caused inability to concentrate on anything for as long as the average child. Apparently the neurological centers of the brain that enable most children to screen out distractions are not developed to the same degree in learning-disabled children of the same age. They are labeled "immature" or "underdeveloped." Because of an underdeveloped or underactive control center, the child cannot concentrate on one thing at a time and is easily distracted.

This neurological dysfunction most often leads to impulsivity on the part of the learning-disabled child. Impulsivity takes the form of unacceptable social behavior which drives family and adults who work with children to distraction and away from close relationships with these children. The children blurt out whatever comes to mind, whenever it comes to mind. They interrupt church school classes and choir practice. They may inadvertently reveal intimate family business to strangers. Such behavior is upsetting to adults and is compounded by a seeming lack of regard to verbal instruction—the kind most often used in church settings.

Billy may have to be told repeatedly what is expected of him and what behavior is acceptable and what is not. Often this "stubbornness" is due to impairments in auditory processing. Simply put, Billy may hear what is said, but his central nervous system processes the information differently because he hears it differently. Words that sound alike are often confusing (close, clothes; bed, bread; sew, so), and directions become distorted. If directions are given more than two at a time ("Come in, hang up your coat, and take your seat"), someone like Billy may miss one of the instructions because of a combination of neurologically based difficulties. First, his attention span is short. Second, he is struggling not to be hyperactive. Third, he is struggling to concentrate. Fourth, he is trying to listen rather than blurt out the thoughts in his own mind. Fifth, he is trying to concentrate enough to follow not one direction but maintain attention long enough to hear three. Sixth, he is trying to process like-sounding words. Seventh, he is trying to distinguish subtle tones in voice inflection or body posture on the part of the adult that give clues about the priorities placed on the several instructions by the adult.

That's quite a list (and actually incomplete)! Other children do it without thinking. Billy would be very surprised to find that Albert

Einstein, Thomas A. Edison, Woodrow Wilson, and Cher had the same problems. Many people of great intelligence and talent have struggled with learning disabilities.

Some learning-disabled children also have visual processing impairments. Dyslexia is the term used to describe one such visual processing problem, where persons see letters or numbers in a reversed order. Again, neurological difficulties play an important role in causing this phenomenon.

Many writers expand the list of disorders in the syndrome to include impairments in tactile processing (the ability to distinguish size, shape, texture, and the like by touch), intersensory integration (repetition of unhelpful patterns of behavior in new situations or perseveration), intellectual deficits (lower general IQ scores), motor impairments (hand-eye coordination problems, such as batting a ball), and inability to project oneself into another person's situation (lack of empathy). The list is long. The behaviors are common, everyday ones necessary for fitting in easily and perceiving oneself as acceptable and successful.

The impact of struggling with these problems is enormous, pervasive, and often determines the direction a child's life may take. Many writers report that children with learning disabilities are perceived as "difficult children" from birth. A large percentage are described as having difficult births, being premature or being born with the cord wrapped around their necks. Many had colic or were food sensitive. Often they were anything but cuddly as infants, rejecting both holding by parents and the mother's breast. From the beginning, they were treated as "difficult" rather than "easy" children. These reactions often trigger guilt, fear, and resentment on the part of adult family members and older siblings. The child not only has neurological deficits but has struggled from the beginning with the negative reactions of those persons who provide primary care.

Learning language and following verbal direction are also great problems for many of these children. The "terrible twos" often last eighteen months longer than for the average child. Possession disputes with playmates and siblings are often very intense. These children frustrate and tire parents because of their extreme reactions and the fact that their motor activity rarely ceases. They are the last to fall asleep at night and are up before the rest of the family in the morning. All these behaviors are observable before school age. Before Billy ever gets to class, he has already begun to think of himself as different—"bad."

A chief problem that these children have from early in life—eighteen months and younger—is frustration. Frustration is the term psychologists use to describe the negative feelings an individual experiences when a goal is blocked. If these children cannot communicate their ideas and feelings effectively, they feel frustrated. For most children, the anger associated with frustration gives way to novel experiments in trying to solve the problem. For learning-disabled children, new behaviors are difficult to achieve for reasons already cited, and the frustration and anger intensify. This may lead to belligerent behavior as these children give vent to their feelings, or it may lead to depression if these negative feelings are turned inward in self-punishing ways. Learning-disabled children are never easygoing or happy-go-lucky.

Matriculation at school exacerbates the crisis. In most educational settings, conformity and self-control are essential. Inability to concentrate and follow directions, and the other symptoms mentioned earlier, are not well tolerated. The larger the pupil-teacher ratio, the worse the problem. The term "learning disability" was coined by educators, rather than clinicians, because the syndrome inevitably leads to easily observable deficits in the classroom situation. Language arts and mathematics are difficult areas for these children even in the first and second grades. The reasons are clear. It is difficult to read, or write, or do mathematical functions with the types of difficulties associated with learning-disabled children. An attention deficit alone would cause trouble. Problems in other areas of the syndrome spell disaster. By fourth grade, these children are usually labeled "slow learners" in need of "resource help." The labels are useful and necessary in securing admission to federally funded special education programs. However, they also bring more problems to these children. The labels single them out as special in a negative sense, making them easy targets for other children's ridicule.

Ministry to the Family

Church communities need to be aware of the families of these children. If parents understand the nature of learning disabilities, they often do well with their children and their feelings about themselves as parents. Regardless of the level of understanding, they often struggle with feelings of guilt about their deficiencies as parents or the fact that the neurological characteristics of their children may have been inherited. This problem can be compounded if a parent believes himself or herself to be also learning disabled.

If the parents do not understand the nature of learning disabilities, the family stress can be unmanageable. Parents naturally look for someone to blame. They start with the child. They blame each other. They often blame physicians or school personnel. They may blame God for visiting them with this affliction, or they may see the child as a punishment sent by God for transgressions they think of having committed themselves. Theologically, the problem of evil becomes paramount.

Since Sigmund Freud made his discoveries, parental influence (nurture) has been emphasized in the shaping of children's personalities. Hereditary characteristics and injuries suffered in utero or at birth have largely been ignored (nature) as areas of study in personality development. The pendulum has started to swing back, but parents who are largely unaware of the etiology and process of a learning-disability syndrome will not realize that they are not to blame for the child's difficulty. As we will see shortly, no institution is so well equipped as the church to speak to these issues.

One final word is necessary about families of children with learning disabilities. We have been writing as though the family is intact and functional: that is to say, the parents are in a stable marriage, family financial resources are adequate, siblings don't have special problems of their own, and everyone is physically healthy. Change any of these variables, or other related ones (a seriously ill grandparent in a distant city, for instance), and the stress on the learning-disabled child can become greatly intensified. Whenever one observes that a learning-disabled child has begun behaving in suddenly more distressing ways, a check with the family about recent changes in family circumstances is always a good idea.

What Children with Learning Disabilities Need

Children who are in crisis because of learning disabilities have very specific needs. Obviously, they need close personal attention. Churches are institutions. Institutions have a difficult time providing close personal attention. The church may be the one institution in society that attracts persons who are dedicated, committed, concerned, and idealistic enough to want to provide the close personal attention these children need. Some of these persons may even have special skills in providing such a relationship because of their vocations. They may be teachers, therapists, or clinicians. The church must be careful not to contribute to professional burnout by working such people outside of regular work hours after they have been on similar jobs all day. Even if they don't provide direct contact with children, they could provide useful consultation to those who do.

In any event, the church as caring community can model such attention in a society where individual attention is often lost. Personal attention will enable the child to break the cycle of guilt and low self-esteem, thus overcoming the alienating distance between the child and others that such unacceptable behavior will have created.

The church may be able to provide such workers because the church has always understood that love means commitment. Commitment is not solely dependent on feeling; commitment fosters patience. Patient adults can help meet two very specific needs that every learning disabled child has: the need to learn to compensate and the need to find a niche. All of us compensate for certain deficiencies and accept this process as normal. For instance, we write ourselves notes or make lists to compensate for imperfect memories. Learning-disabled children need to be taught such compensating behaviors repeatedly. Ultimately, compensating behaviors will enable these children to function well, often by the time they reach adolescence.

Finding a niche is closely related to compensating. The average child finds niches easily by gravitating naturally to areas of competence or interest. The person with the good speaking voice becomes an actress or preacher. The well-coordinated child becomes an athlete. Learning-disabled children often have such terrible feelings about their abilities that they can't discover a niche. Compensating techniques will enable the child to develop enough self-confidence to find the right niche. Again, committed persons working closely with children can enable each child to develop compensating behavior and begin to find a niche.

Finally, all children, but especially learning-disabled children, need to find peers who are accepting. Learning-disabled children are not easily accepted by peers. The church has encouraged group formation based on ideals of openness and equality for all persons, regardless of how difficult it may be to relate to a person. Adults who are youth leaders and model such "unconditional positive regard" become models for children and are "doing theology." They have *become* the love of God rather than only *talking* about God's love. Such modeling encourages children to begin to accept the learning-disabled child and to distinguish between the child's behavior (which must be corrected) and the essence of the person (who is being loved).

Faith Issues

Both learning-disabled children and their families usually have a real struggle with religious faith. The children imagine that other persons don't have such struggles. They ask why God made them this way. Parents ask if God is punishing them for something they did or failed to do. Brothers and sisters ask why their sibling has this difficulty and is so hard on the family. They think that perhaps God is punishing them for things they have done or failed to do.

It is difficult to believe that God would allow life to be such a struggle for some and not for others. It is difficult to believe and become a person with faith in a God of love and justice. It is easy for these children to identify with Job in their travail. One thing after another going wrong, one painful experience after another every day, one loved one after another saying hurtful things "with your best interests at heart"—all these experiences speak to the learning-disabled person.

It is also easy for a learning-disabled person to identify with Moses. Every learning-disabled child knows what it is to be asked to do something, to perform, to lead, and to feel a sickening fear of inadequacy. When Moses told God that leadership of Israel was impossible for him because he was not a public speaker, he expressed the self-doubt and performance anxiety that every learning-disabled person experiences daily. In the classroom these thoughts take the form of, "I know the right answer, but I just can't get the words right." That's how Moses felt. God gave Aaron to Moses to help him speak, overcome his fear, and break his isolation.

Isolation becomes a key factor in the lives of learning-disabled persons. Living in isolation means that one cannot live in relationship to others. The inability to experience living in close relationships to others on a human level makes it virtually impossible for a person to conceive of a personal or right relationship with God. It becomes difficult for these children not to blame themselves, or God, or someone else and continue living in isolation.

Isolation simply reinforces the frustration. These children often sense that they are bright and creative, but can't express themselves well either verbally or in writing. After the frustration mounts, impulsive behavior and displays of temper increase. This pattern leads inevitably to guilt. Guilt becomes the most serious religious problem for learning-disabled children. God, they think, loves bright, well-behaved children, not "dumb" or "bad" ones. How can God love a bad child?

Well-meaning adults often try to help by pointing to the biblical formula for forgiveness: confess, ask forgiveness, and repent. This formula, perfect for most situations, only leaves the learning-disabled child feeling worse. Neurologically based hyperactive, impulsive behavior makes repentance very difficult to achieve. With Paul, the learning-disabled child can state, "I do not do the good I want." Despite vows never again to engage in a particular behavior, keeping such a vow is virtually impossible through no fault of the child's.

What can break the cycle of feeling abandoned or punished by God, the cycle of loneliness and guilt leading to isolation and more frustration? As we have seen, the cycle is broken by learning to compensate and find a niche that fits well. When these things occur, the child becomes open to hearing that God loves persons and seeks to be with them in all sorts of difficulties.

A story was told to me about Jimmy when he was ten years old and played boys' soccer. Jimmy was a chunky, fairly well coordinated boy with average speed. He quickly developed a reputation as a loner who wouldn't pay attention at practice. His coach was a school principal who knew Jimmy's family well and found out that Jimmy was in a resource program for learning-disabled children in public school. The family and the coach were Roman Catholic and members of the same parish where Jimmy attended religious instruction classes (CCD). He had a bad reputation. Jimmy had played a couple of seasons of soccer without distinguishing himself as an offensive player. Coaches kept him busy by telling him to keep trying to score. Much of the time he was bored when he didn't have the ball, and his attention wandered when he had little to do. The coach noticed that Jimmy had one outstanding characteristic compared to the other boys. He seemed fearless on the field. No situation or person intimidated him. The coach decided to make him a "sweeper"—the key to the team's defense, along with the goalkeeper, in young boys' leagues. With a lot of patience and Jimmy's hard work, the team defense became the best in the league.

Jimmy consolidated the gains by playing several more seasons of good soccer. He was never a great athlete, but he found his niche as a defensive player. He learned to concentrate on doing a few things well. He managed to keep being promoted in school, largely because he settled in as a key member of his team. They became his friends. He completed CCD classes successfully and was confirmed. Jimmy got the personal attention he needed to help him compensate for some deficiencies (this is different from emphasizing strengths). He found his niche in an area important to him, and the boost in self-esteem helped him to settle down in school and church.

The problem with this account is that it sounds farfetched, dramatic, rare. Actually, it is quite typical. Educators and therapists who work with such children are amazed at the dramatic results achieved when adequate resources are directed at compensating for learning disabilities.

Ministry to Learning-Disabled Children

Religious institutions have a unique opportunity to minister to children with learning disabilities. Ministers and other professional staff in ministry must take the lead in working with these children and their families, but this is one crisis where a community of faith can be mobilized effectively to meet needs. Professional and lay leadership are both necessary to develop an effective ministry to such children. You need to think about a three-pronged approach to this crisis: ministry to the child, to the family, and to the community. Specifically, the minister who wants to work with such children needs to understand the problem as much as possible. The reading list at the end of this chapter will help. A conversation with elementary school personnel will help even more. Consultations with psychologists and social workers who specialize in working with learning disabled children will add to your understanding immeasurably.

When you are reasonably well acquainted with the subject intellectually, think about the children in your congregation who might fit the description. Observe each child in church activities. Talk to adult workers, including the teacher and other professional staff. Perhaps you will be told that your assumptions are correct. If so, try to get to know that child. If there is doubt about the nature of the problem, reserve judgment. In either case, pay a pastoral call on the family.

Be prepared to find parents who are defensive or apologetic. They may fear you will be critical of the child's behavior or object to his or her participation in religious activities. If the child has definitely been identified as learning disabled, your new knowledge of the subject should make you a welcome resource for the family. Coming to bring a word of grace and love to a family that struggles to rear a child in turmoil can cement a pastoral relationship. If the child has not yet been identified as learning disabled, you can make gentle mention about learning disabilities as a possible source for behavior problems. This also gives you a chance to refer the family to one of the professional resources you may have already discovered in the school system or in the therapeutic community. Be careful not to make a diagnosis of your own, but suggest to the family that this impression may be something they would like to investigate. Sound a note of hope! If the impression is correct, positive, effective action can be taken.

Let me amplify the suggestion to get to know a learning-disabled child. Elementary-school children are best. Third-graders or early fourth-graders are ideal. By this age, school problems are being noticed and the child has begun to suffer the effects of deficiencies. An understanding, nonjudgmental adult may be a rarity in the child's life. In most religious settings, a child of this age will soon be part of a confirmation class (or similar class, depending on the religious tradition). You can begin to make preparations for teaching this child yourself, or for other professional staff to do so, if you know the child's special needs. For instance, children with auditory discrimination problems need not be always lectured. Children who don't read well aloud might do better acting in a drama that depicts a Bible story or theme. Getting to know the child at age nine or ten gives you a head start for an experience with a twelve-year-old. The family may be able to tell you exactly how the child learns best. They will certainly be able to tell you from painful personal experience how the child fails to learn. Hearing what a child can't do will give you a clue as to the specific nature of the deficit. These specifics will help you avoid creating those situations in your own relationship with the child.

Getting to know a learning-disabled child is not much more difficult than forming a friendship with any child. A few suggestions may help. Speak about something that interests the child. Admiring clothing or appearance or noticing a favorite toy or activity is a good conversation starter. Don't expect a long conversation. Carry on the conversation while engaging in some activity if possible. A walk around the block is perfect. Don't discuss school unless the child brings up the topic. Always inquire about pets and learn the names of favorite ones. Seeing the child in church and asking about Fido is a great way to reestabish the conversation. Let the child bring up "faith concerns," but a simple prayer at the end of the walk will help establish your role and cement the relationship. "O God, we thank you for this day and for Tommy and our friendship."

Developing a ministry to the community on behalf of learning-disabled children will take great commitment and can bring you a lot of personal satisfaction. Two communities are involved: the religious community and the secular community in which the religious community exists.

Within the congregation, consider developing a training program for all lay educators and professional staff. You may want to do this as part of a denominational or judicatory program. The program should concentrate on identifying children with learning disabilities, educational and other professional resources available to them in the community, and specific suggestions for developing a personal or teaching relationship with these children.

Out of such a program, a local congregation might develop a group of adults who can train others in the congregation to work with learning-disabled children. This group could become a resource group for other adult workers and might include professionals in the community who would volunteer to provide leadership.

Another way to approach the topic is to make learning disabilities one aspect of a congregational program dealing with "specific children." You could present programs around a number of the topics dealt with in this book and develop adult leadership in several areas.

Once your own congregation is informed, you may want to consider the community at large. If you get this far, you have already developed a good inventory of the educational and therapeutic resources available for such children in the community. Where there are gaps, you and your congregation can take the lead in seeing that they are filled. Some educational programs require public funding. Other programs that can be very helpful require committed volunteers. The religious institutions may want to sponsor communitywide educational experiences for adults to help them become more aware of the problem and its solutions. Juvenile justice systems may also be in need of more information. In any event, you can speak out and provide leadership in the community on behalf of learning-disabled children.

Finally, if you really want to understand the problems of learning-disabled children, take a personal inventory of your own intellectual capabilities and learning patterns. Most of us quickly discern a pattern of strengths and weaknesses. Our "weaknesses" often turn out to be disabilities for which we have learned to compensate and find a niche. Many clergy did well at languages but struggled to learn mathematics. We have learned to compensate for these deficiencies and found our niches in a profession demanding good verbal skills. If you can remember how difficult some basic intellectual skills were for you to develop, you already have an understanding of what the learning-disabled child is going through. Give thanks that you have found a niche. Help find the niche for a child.

FURTHER READING

Fried, Hilda, ed. *"Plain Talk" About Children with Learning Disabilities.* Pamphlet. Rockville, Md.: National Institute of Mental Health, U.S. Department of Health and Human Services, 1979.
Gardner, Richard A. *Dr. Gardner Talks to Children with Minimal Brain Dysfunction.* One-hour cassette tape. New York: Jason Aronson, 1975.
————. *Dr. Gardner Talks to Parents of Children with Minimal Brain Dysfunction.* One-hour cassette tape. New York: Jason Aronson, 1975.
————. *MBD: The Family Book About Minimal Brain Dysfunction.* New York: Jason Aronson, 1974.

14

Children Suffering
from Stress and Anxiety
John L. Florell

This chapter focuses on giving pastoral care to children who are in crisis because of stress and anxiety. Pastors have a number of ways to be helpful to these children. One of the first and foremost is referring parents, children, or the whole family to a pastoral counselor, psychiatrist, social worker, or psychologist. Even after referral, however, the need to provide pastoral care to the family, parents and children, is great. At times referral isn't available or the parents are not cooperative. The emphasis here will be on (1) using different methods to relate to children and support them through crisis and (2) developing preventive programs that help children cope better with problems in their families, or any other crisis that leaves them feeling stressed or rejected.

Identifying the Crisis

Children often reflect the particular life-style of their families. Because children are extremely concrete, they rely more on experience than words to deal with their world. When children experience a crisis that threatens their social network and reflects on their sense of self-esteem, as when their parents have conflict, they reflect the stress in their relationships with their parents, siblings, other children, and adults. They act out their stress in the way they play, the stories they tell, their school behavior, peer relations, and almost every other aspect of their lives.

Spotting problems in children is usually a matter of keeping your eyes and ears open to see and hear how children express their frustration. Listen to their stories. Though it would be a mistake to take literally a story told by a child six to twelve years of age, listening to feelings of

John L. Florell is Executive Director, Illinois Pastoral Services Institute, Bloomington, Ill.

anger, sadness, and fear will help you know what the child is experiencing emotionally.

The combination of a literal, concrete worldview experienced in an emotional, experiential way is a paradox of which pastoral people must be aware. Children do not think abstractly, even in the upper level of the preteen age group. They believe what they see, not what they hear, and they take it literally. When children react, they are quite emotional. They do not think things through in the sense adults do; they want adults to experience what they are feeling rather than fix the problem. A frequent mistake adults make is trying to placate or give children what they want, or trying to understand what they are doing, when the most successful reaction is to let them know we feel the feelings they are trying to get across to us.

Often a child's anxiety is precipitated by parental or family conflict. Children become very empathetic to a parent who is experiencing a crisis. The way they express this empathy is in concrete behavior. Therefore, children's behavior mirrors the turmoil of their parents' life. The following case study illustrates a typical example of an empathetic child mirroring his parents' conflict.

The Richardses were a moderately well-to-do family, members of a large urban church. Mr. Richards was a middle management person in a large publishing house. Mrs. Richards, who did not work outside the home, raised the two children, Betty, age fourteen, and Bob, age ten. She was a devout Christian who served on the governing board of her church, taught Sunday school, and served on the Christian Education Committee. Betty was a good student, a cheerleader and volleyball star at her middle school. She was friendly and active in youth fellowship. Bob was athletic, popular, and an academically average student who participated in the church choir program and Sunday school. Both parents were strong Christians and attended church regularly.

Mrs. Richards contacted the head pastor, almost casually, about their concern over the son, Bob. Bob was rebelling in several ways: not wanting to go to Sunday school, letting his grades slip at school, telling obvious lies, and, the family suspected, taking money and personal items from around the house. All this behavior was unusual for Bob, according to his mother.

The minister, who knew Bob, dropped into the Richards house on a family visit and invited Bob to his office to play checkers, one of Bob's favorite games. During the checker game, the pastor tried to empathize with Bob as Bob talked about his school, his soccer team, and, finally, his family. At one point, the pastor reflected what Bob was saying about his father being gone so much. "You really feel terrible when your dad is gone so much." Bob responded, "Yeah, we just don't feel like a family anymore."

Later, the minister was able to share with Bob's parents what Bob was feeling. Mr. Richards revealed that he was feeling estranged from his wife and didn't enjoy the time he spent at home. When asked whether he was thinking of getting a divorce or separating, both parents denied any such thoughts and Mr. Richards said, "That would be sinful. I would never do that to my kids! In fact, we don't want them to know anything about our trouble." The minister shared his impression that Bob already knew at some level and that Bob's problems reflected what was going on between his parents. The minister was able to refer the parents for marriage counseling, and as their relationship improved, Bob's behavior also improved.

This typically is how children are affected by their family's interaction. Even though parents may feel that their children are not perceptive enough to know what is happening, children pick up the tones and attitudes within relationships extremely well, even though they may not be able to articulate what they experience.

Methods for Ministry

Pastors must be able to play, have a sense of humor, use symbols such as toys, and facilitate communication through playing games and putting the child at ease. To be able to deliver effective pastoral care to children, pastors and church professionals need to be genuinely interested in working with them. Children sense feelings and attitudes quite well and can see through insincerity.

Often it isn't so much what children say as how they use symbols like toys. The following case study shows how one young child used symbols to express the stress and internal conflict caused by her parents' problems.

The Michaelses were a young family. Mr. Michaels was a schoolteacher and an active deacon in the suburban church to which his family belonged. Mrs. Michaels was a nurse at the local hospital. Their daughter Joyce was eight years old. The pastor was called to the Michaels home after a fire had broken out. The fire had started in Joyce's room, and it appeared she had set the fire intentionally. Joyce would not talk about the fire to anyone.

The pastor took a small playhouse and family dolls to the Michaels house and started playing with Joyce. In her play, Joyce continually showed the child doll isolated from the parent dolls. The parent dolls were also able to fly and perform superhuman feats. Mr. and Mrs. Michaels, who were watching the pastor and Joyce play, were surprised at her perception of them. Both parents admitted they were so involved in their careers and community responsibilities that they weren't paying much attention to Joyce or each other.

As Joyce felt more openness from her parents, she was able to talk to them about her anger and sadness. She also wondered if her parents were going to get a divorce. The Michaelses assured Joyce they weren't going to get a divorce and were able to talk about things they had done and said that caused Joyce to be anxious about their relationship.

Joyce's situation is like many others which pastors encounter. She interpreted behavior she saw and acted out how she felt. Her actions included setting fire in her wastebasket and silence when questioned or playing with the minister. Pastoral care was expressed in playing with Joyce; it was her way of communicating to the pastor and her parents.

Playing is just one method of providing pastoral care to children who are stressed or having difficulty adjusting to a family crisis. With children who have developed fine motor skills (usually six years and above), pencil and paper exercises—like drawing pictures of their families, themselves, their feelings, their dreams, or their wishes—can be an excellent outlet for what they are feeling and experiencing.

Stories are another excellent way to provide care to children who are stressed. Children are often reassured by the stories adults tell. When telling stories of their own, children often draw on the experiences and feelings of adults. Richard Gardner, a noted child psychiatrist, uses a therapy method called "counter story," which can be adapted nicely for doing pastoral care with children.[1] After a child tells a story with a negative or unrealistic ending, the minister takes the same story and tells it in a way that reassures the child that he or she can cope with the situation. The story as told by the minister will have a more realistic or optimistic ending, modeling for the child a different way of perceiving the situation. This subtle communication helps the child feel the empathetic response of the caregiver while suggesting that other, more positive feelings are possible.

Many children are quite active in their expression of emotions, making quiet play or storytelling too passive for them. Large-muscle activity like running, doing a karate routine, throwing a ball, playing tennis or paddleball, throwing horseshoes, wrestling, or playing tag can also give children a feeling of rapport with someone providing pastoral care. Physical touch or contact along with parallel play often gives a reassuring feeling to active children.

Parents can be taught how to deal with their children by observing pastor-child interaction. The pastor's responsibility is to show parents a child's concrete thought processes and how the child relates emotionally to what is happening in the family. Though the main interaction is with the child, the pastor is modeling for the parents.

Ministry Related to Age and Stage

Interaction with children, of course, depends on their age and rate of development. Though children have developed their intellectual abilities considerably by ages six to eight, they are still very concrete and oriented around activity and behavior rather than language. As children enter school, relationships become important and they spend more time outside the home. Speech can translate action, and children start to talk in a way that parallels their behavior. Play is structured, as in games, and interpretations and instruction are the best ways to communicate at this age.

As children reach nine or ten years of age, they are more independent and rebellious in passive ways. This is a time when school problems may develop and sibling rivalry intensifies. Children continue to parallel action with speech. Children can also use their imagination and lie convincingly if it serves their purpose. Play is more complex, games with sophisticated rules are more popular, as are large-muscle organized sports like basketball, soccer, baseball, volleyball, or other team sports. Noncompetitive games are best for the pastoral caregiver with children of this age, along with activities that are not competitive, like throwing a ball or playing around without keeping score. Several noncompetitive board games emphasize sharing feelings, communicating, and learning to cope. The Ungame[2] and the Talking, Feeling, Doing[3] game are two examples. A structured approach that encourages talking is to throw a Nerf ball back and forth with the understanding that only the person with the ball can talk. In a family setting this game structures conversation and makes sure each person gets a turn to talk.

When children become preteens, eleven to twelve years of age, they start to take on adolescent characteristics such as spending more time with peers, being more concerned about how they look, feeling anxious about making physical/sexual transitions, and moving into a society that will take them more away from their family. Children at this age enter an age of anxiety where they fear the unknown: conflicts about changing schools, growing up, being given more responsibility, maturing sexually, and developing their own individuality. Though the emphasis at this age is still on being the dependent child, children bounce behaviorally between being a child and being an adolescent.

It is important to remember that these preteens are still quite concrete and, despite being able to articulate well, should still be approached as emotional beings who experience life behaviorally rather than abstractly. Preteens respond well to structure, genuine compliments, reciprocal relationships, and being understood verbally and emotionally. Pastoral care should focus on building positive images. Group activities become more popular with this group. Methods that help children deal with their anxieties (for example, the stop-thought technique where the child takes a deep breath, says "Stop, stop, stop," and thinks of something pleasant) can be very helpful in relieving anxiety.

Children develop at different rates, so these guidelines are not meant to be hard and fast in terms of chronological age. Any developmental crisis can be magnified by a crisis with a friend, a dating situation, a school crisis, parental conflict, or trouble in a peer group. At almost any age a child can be taught to relax and focus on a reassuring religious or everyday image. Breathing deeply, relaxing muscles, and focusing on a soft woolly lamb can put the most anxious child at ease.

Preventive Pastoral Ministry

No matter what method is used, children who are under stress or suffering from anxiety may not respond to any pastoral care initiative. For this reason, preventive group activities can be helpful and informative to both the child and the child's family.

Some groups are specifically aimed at helping parents with parenting skills. A number of prepackaged programs are intended to enable parents to help their children have better self-esteem, communicate effectively, develop internal values, and cooperate with peers and parents. Such programs as STEP (Systematic Training for Effective Parenting) from the American Guidance Service[4] and Acting Parenting from Active Parenting,[5] provide leadership training and support material to educate parents to help their children. Churches can provide help for parents by sponsoring such workshops to strengthen parent-child cooperation.

Another group approach is to focus on the children who are in crisis or who have high potential to develop problems. When family life, school activities, peer relationships, or body changes cause anxiety, a group activity through which children gain a sense of belonging and learn the support of fellowship and positive peer pressure can help build good self-esteem and a feeling of security. This method is particularly effective with preteens. When working with children from six to twelve, it is best to keep them separated in boys or girls groups.

A church can sponsor a group for children from different kinds of family backgrounds. The children may come from intact families, stepfamilies, or single-parent families and from any background or socioeconomic class. The idea is to work on the children's self-esteem in ways that are appropriate for each age level. Children should be selected so they are developmentally compatible with the other children in the group with regard to personal issues and the ability to communicate and cooperate within group activity. A commitment should be made by parents to review the material their children will be using in the group activity.

The younger the children, the shorter and more concrete the sessions should be. Six- to eight-year-olds can be taught to give themselves positive messages like "I'm a child of God. I'm important, and those around me are important too." Self-reliance can be learned by mastering basic tasks and doing simple household chores such as preparing an easy meal, running the washing machine and clothes dryer, making beds, cleaning the bathroom, and purchasing food or groceries while parents watch. When parents praise the completion of these small jobs, and children learn to compliment themselves, mastering these tasks provides the foundation for positive self-esteem. Strong self-esteem is one of the most potent elements in enabling children at any age to handle stress.

For groups of nine- to ten-year-olds, the positive message can become something that can be passed on to others. "I like [child's name]" can be followed by having children say something they like about each other. More complex home responsibilities such as preparing a complete meal in a regular rotation with other family members, leading family discussion, and organizing the cleaning of the house will give children a sense of mastery over their environment. At this age, mastery of self-care tasks gives children confidence to go outside the home and take care of themselves. Self-esteem is enhanced by mastery. Children must also learn to deal with the anxiety of being more independent. Teaching children simple relaxation exercises can help them begin to handle anxiety-producing situations. Role play, with emphasis on polite self-expression and religious values, helps provide a foundation for children to take more responsibility in life.

The preteen group is the age where group activity can have its strongest impact in terms of pastoral care. Mary Zimmerman, a pastoral counselor in Corvallis, Oregon, has conducted self-esteem groups for preteens that are based on better communication, improving self-image, and stress reduction. These methods can be readily adapted to a church's pastoral care of children. The interviewing of children is very important at this age. Parents must agree to come to a parents' group once a month to review the material to which their children will be exposed. One family party will be held at the church during these sessions.

The ideal is for a group of ten- to twelve-year-old boys or girls to explore their physical, emotional, and sexual changes and their feelings about puberty. The parents are asked to preview material, explore their own feelings, and plan ways to encourage communication with their sons or daughters. Written assignments such as "Everything I would like my parents to know about me, my feelings, my fears, and my questions" are designed to stimulate discussion both in the peer group and with preteens and their parents. The children are taught how to listen, solve problems, diet, exercise, and reduce stress.

Recognition by the parents that their preteens are growing up is the ultimate goal for building self-esteem at this age. Parallel to this recognition by parents is peer recognition and having positive role models from older teens. One of the important techniques developed by Mary Zimmerman to help accomplish this task was to have preteens put together a panel discussion where they questioned older teens about growing up. Though parents do not participate directly in the panel discussions, the leader and their children inform them of the results.

In a group of preteen girls, one of the issues that came up was "What do I do when my parents try to involve me in their fights?" The others suggested confronting the parents and telling them she didn't want to be involved. Another girl wondered how you become popular. Peers and older teens suggested, Be yourself, go with people who have interests similar to your own, be friendly but don't sacrifice things that are important just to be liked. Several girls were anxious about starting their periods while they were at school, particularly if they had a male teacher. The pastoral care leader invited a gynecologist to one of the meetings, who reassured the girls that their first period would probably be light and that they would have some warning it was coming. She also suggested how to get help from the school nurse. This emphasis on knowing your body was carried through in further sessions with a physician so the girls learned more about maturation, good health practices, proper nutrition, exercise, and relaxation. The culmination of this emphasis on the body was a health picnic.

The girls also had regular sharing sessions which they would start by sharing the good news and the bad news for the week. They found an outlet for their feelings and support. They discussed the concepts of death, dying, heaven, hell, and whether their parents would be punished for bad behavior.

These talks were supplemented with sessions that taught problem-solving techniques. The children were taught to define their problem, to look at alternative ways to handle their problem, to ask what the consequence of each alternative would be, to put their solution into practice, and to evaluate how well their solution worked.

Listening and other communication skills were also taught. The children learned to listen better by learning to paraphrase, by putting what they heard into their own words and saying it back to the parents. The parents then confirmed the children's understanding of what they had said. The children also learned to communicate effectively through the use of "I" messages. Here the children took ownership of their own feelings and thoughts rather than giving "you" messages that would give credit for their thoughts and feelings to others.

Children completing self-esteem groups appeared to be better prepared to make the difficult transition from preteen to adolescent. These skills also helped them deal with their anxieties about personal and family crises. They came to identify the church and the giver of pastoral care as a place and person from whom they could get help with problems. This is one example of preventive programs the church can provide for its members and the community at large. Coalitions of churches can provide programs in communities where an individual church may not have the resources to provide such programs. Programs that focus on family communication, spiritual sharing, leaving the family, grief, and being your own person in the midst of your family are other themes that make good preventive programs.

Pastoral care of stressed children focuses on meeting them where they are in their own crisis of development. The more concrete and emotionally aware the giver of pastoral care, the better the chances of getting through and making an impact on the children to whom he or she is ministering. Programs that help children handle their anxieties and enhance their self-esteem are positive expressions of pastoral care.

NOTES

1. Richard A. Gardner, *The Psychotherapeutic Techniques of Richard A. Gardner* (Cresskill, N.J.: Creative Therapeutics, 1986).

2. Ungame (Anaheim, Calif.: Ungame Co. 1975).

3. Richard A. Gardner, The Talking, Feeling, Doing Game (Cresskill, N.J.: Creative Therapeutics, 1973).

4. Effective Parenting, Publishers' Building, Circle Pines, MN 55014-1796.

5. Active Parenting, 4669 Roswell Road, N.E., Atlanta, GA 30342.

FURTHER READING

Gardner, Richard A. *Dr. Gardner's Fairytales for Today's Children.* Cresskill, N.J.: Creative Therapeutics, 1974.

———. *Separation Anxiety Disorder: Psychodynamics and Psychotherapy.* Cresskill, N.J.: Creative Therapeutics, 1985.

———. *Therapeutic Communication with Children: The Mutual Storytelling Technique.* 2nd ed. Northvale, N.J.: Jason Aronson, 1986.

———. *Understanding Children: A Parent's Guide to Child Rearing.* Cresskill, N.J.: Creative Therapeutics, 1979. Reprint of 1973.

Kvols-Riedler, Bill, and Kathy Kvols-Riedler. *Redirecting Children's Misbehavior.* Boulder, Colo.: RDIC Publications, 1979.
Schaefer, Charles E., and Kevin J. O'Conner, eds. *The Handbook of Play Therapy.* New York: John Wiley & Sons, 1983.

PART III

Resources for Ministry with Children in Crisis

15

Talking About Faith with Children
George F. Handzo

How do we talk about faith issues with children? Aren't they too young to really know about God? If children do know something, they may think about God in very strange or idiosyncratic ways. On top of that, we cannot persuade them to talk about things they do not want to talk about. These questions and statements are all true to a greater or lesser extent. Regardless of these difficulties, however, we are called to minister to children, which includes talking with them about God and their faith. Where should we begin?

Respect and Acceptance

We need to begin this exploration by overcoming our myths and prejudices about children's thinking and feeling processes. We must accept the children in our care as equal partners with us in the journey of faith. It is often much harder to act out this effort than to believe in it. We are trained from our childhood to value clear and rational thinking, to believe right and wrong answers exist, and to assume that most of the right answers and important knowledge reside with adults. We often talk about "mature" faith as if it is the only kind that matters. Those of us who consider ourselves theologically astute may have special difficulty tolerating and valuing faith statements and struggles that are obviously unsophisticated.

Children are exquisitely sensitive to this kind of condescension and paternalism. They guard against exposing themselves in situations where their questions or comments might be rejected or considered silly. They generally want to please adults and are afraid that their questions might be considered unworthy of respect. Their fears are

George F. Handzo is Director of Protestant Chaplaincy and Pediatric Chaplain, Memorial Sloan-Kettering Cancer Center, New York.

confirmed by adults who are clearly more interested in talking than in listening, or by adults in authority who jump to correct them without exploring their thoughts and feelings. They quickly back off when their statements are challenged rather than responded to and reflected upon. For the most part, children will talk to us only if they feel they are fully accepted children of God with a faith system that may be different from that of most adults, but one that is no less important.

Thinking About Faith

Children do think a lot about faith and have more ability than most adults give them credit for in the area of theological reflection. They may not talk about faith in the same way as adults, but their insights can be quite complete. Sofia Cavalletti, in *The Religious Potential of the Child,* has shown that even preschoolers can appreciate the mystery of baptism and the basic lesson of the parable of the good shepherd. In *The Bible—A Child's Playground,* Roger and Gertrude Gobbel have dealt extensively with how children can and do use the scriptures for their own reflection. The depth of this thinking does not seem to be related to any experience with Sunday school or other forms of organized religion. It seems simply to be one of the things children think about as they grow up in the world. We should not confuse children's inability to talk about God with an inability to think about or appreciate God.

Even when we understand that children do think and talk about faith questions, it can still be difficult to understand their individual faith systems. The basic principle to remember is that children mix logical, concrete thinking with fantasy.

School-age children are learning to use logical thinking. In this mode, children may have an unending and sometimes irritating assortment of specific questions to ask: Is this specific Bible story really true? Where does God live in heaven? What is heaven like? They will tend to focus on any apparent inconsistencies in our story. They latch on to a specific train of thought and want to follow it to what they think is its logical conclusion. Children are not trying to trip us up or antagonize us with these lines of questioning and reasoning. They are trying out a new way of thinking that has opened up new vistas for them, much as they would examine all the facets of a new toy.

The problem is compounded by the concreteness of their thinking. A classic example is the child who approaches a priest on the street and asks him to "cross" her. The priest obliges by making the sign of the cross over the child's head. The child responds, "No, Father, I want you to help me cross the street." This example points up both the specific and concrete nature of children's thinking at this age and the necessity for being clear with children about what they are saying or asking. Clarity of communication is important in talking to children because they can think so differently.

Additionally, children have very individual faith systems. We can never assume that any specific child will be thinking or feeling at the level indicated by the system of cognitive or faith development. These systems are generally helpful guides and categories but may not predict a certain child's level.

As logical as children's thought patterns may be, we also need to take into account their still active fantasy life. This feature may sound like a liability because it offends our belief in theology as a logical, rational discipline. However, it turns out to be an advantage for both the minister and the children. Children are often more willing than adults to deal with reality in terms of stories, analogies, and parables. Therefore, they can readily appreciate the message in a Bible story, whereas adults may need to have it spelled out for them. Children are able to see themselves in Bible stories and parables in a way that is often difficult for adults. They are more willing to speculate and use their imaginations as they explore their faith. As Sofia Cavalletti has shown, children have very little trouble appreciating the mystery of faith and those elements in it that are fantastic. Dying children are helped by their fantasy lives to accept the promises of heaven. The fact that heaven is not like anything we know in our reality is not as much of a problem for them as it is for adults. Adults often want concrete proof while children can often accept the unreal.

Theological Issues for Children

Faith needs in times of crisis are much the same for children as for adults. The differences are not in the questions but in the language used to ask and answer them. We should not be totally disoriented because we are talking to a six-year-old instead of a sixty-year-old. The faith needs of the two are virtually identical. Their feelings toward and about God are of paramount importance. Both children and adults need and want to be in a loving, caring relationship with a benevolent and forgiving God. They both need to know that, whatever their situation, God offers forgiveness and continued presence. They need help in resolving guilt about their part in any tragic events and dealing with any anger they may feel toward a God who did not change things. Most of all they need the hope that comes from knowing that God has not abandoned them. Any other issues should be passed over so that attention can be focused on the relationship to God.

We must be clear about what basic message we want to bring to this child at this time. We want to avoid trying to reorient the child's whole theology. We must always remember in crisis situations that we are there for the purpose of dealing with some specific issue or situation. We should not be giving general lessons in Bible study, theology, or catechesis. We are present to heal a specific hurt. It is not the time to worry about problems with the child's doctrine. It is the time to worry about the child's relationship with God. If we can preserve the child's loving relationship with God through this crisis, we will have plenty of opportunities to teach doctrine later. If that relationship cannot be preserved, no amount of doctrine will help.

Given this focus, what is the goal for our ministry with this child? The answer will vary considerably depending on our own theology. However, my experience is that the child's conception of God needs to include some sense of God as supporter and caregiver, as opposed to a God who simply does things for or against people. Understanding God's actions on a cognitive level is often not emotionally satisfying. It does not make us feel better. The goal of our pastoral care is to help the children relate to God as one who loves and cares for them and always will do so.

We must try hard to avoid clouding our discussions with theological problems which may be important but are not central to the moment. For instance, a child may say, "Is my mommy in heaven?" Suppose you believe that the resurrection will truly come at the return of the Messiah and only at that point will we be united with God in heaven. Technically, your answer to the child's question should be no. However, this answer would not be helpful to the child. The child really wants to know if Mommy is in God's hands, is at peace, and is being taken care of. The child asks this long question in shorthand form. It is only confusing to correct the literal statement or question. The important point is to provide reassurance.

Because of their concreteness, school-age children may want to focus on the mechanics of how God does or does not act. If this is where the child wants to be, then we hope the child can come to see God's actions or lack of them as benevolent. It is also important to affirm the child's right to be angry or resentful at God when the child does not like or agree with what God has done or allowed. Arriving at the conception of a benevolent God may be difficult if the child is angry. We need to acknowledge this anger and let the child know that it is acceptable, so the child can appreciate that anger and love are not mutually exclusive feelings.

Preparation for Ministry

If we are going to talk to a child about a situation in which faith issues might be involved, how can we prepare? One important way is to

gather information from others who know this child well. What does the
Sunday school teacher say about the child? Does the child have a real
interest in faith questions and Bible stories? Which ones? Who are the
child's favorite Bible characters and why does the child identify with
these particular people? Does the child relate to the doubting Thomas
or the petulant Peter? What Bible characters and stories are we reminded of by the child and the child's situation? These questions may
help us understand the child's general self-image, relationship to God,
and vision of God. They will give us hints about stories and faith resources we might productively use to connect with the child in our visit.

Next we must bear in mind that our central task in these situations
is not to talk *to* children but to have children talk *with* us. Our goal is
not to preach at them but to work with their faith systems as the
children present them to us. If we tell children something that does not
connect to where they are in their faith pilgrimage, it cannot be received. We cannot put the fifth floor on a building before the fourth
floor is built. In order to know where we can begin to make connections
with children, we have to know where the children are in their own
thinking. To find this out, the children have to tell us.

We must be prepared to encounter two possible traps in dealing with
children's thought patterns. First, it is very easy implicitly or explicitly
to dismiss children's concreteness or logical lines of thought as being
irrelevant to the theological point we think is at issue. Indeed, children's questions may not be germane to the issue. However, they will
have some importance to the particular child even if the child cannot
conceptualize its significance. Children may also ask a lot of questions
to which we do not have concrete answers. The temptation is strong to
dismiss these questions rather than admit that we do not have answers.
This strategy will result in losing contact with the particular child and
going on to issues that will not make an impression.

The second temptation is to answer all questions concretely. Questions about heaven are in this category. We can easily fall into the
children's mind-set and try to provide answers on their level. This
strategy will ultimately fail because children have more questions than
we have answers. The process will wind up being unsatisfactory for both
the child and ourselves.

We must prepare to find a middle ground between these two traps.
First, we need to take children's questions seriously and explicitly acknowledge them as important. Second, we need to be ready to admit
when we do not know an answer, yet without closing off discussion and
appearing disinterested. Last, we need to help children move on to a
more fruitful line of inquiry. A typical conversation might look like this.
(Although this conversation and the ones to follow are not verbatim
accounts of specific visits and are somewhat simplified to make a point,

they are typical of what I have heard and expect to hear from children I visit.)

CHILD: What does God look like?
MINISTER: Gee, that's a pretty important question. Have you thought a lot about it?
CHILD: Yeah, some. What do you think?
MINISTER: Well, I haven't really come up with a good answer. I guess I'm just not smart enough to pull it all together.
CHILD: I've had that feeling too. I keep thinking I should be able to know what God looks like, but I can't figure it out.
MINISTER: I think it's not that we're dumb. I think it's that God is so much more than anything we can picture that we can't get a handle on it. How does that sound?
CHILD: I hadn't thought about that. I guess that might be true.

The child's question is taken seriously, and the child's views are solicited at every step to make sure a connection is maintained. This conversation might go on to discuss Jesus as the revelation of God or who we think God is.

Beginning the Visit

In beginning a visit with a child, it is important to enter the relationship slowly. The amount of introductory time needed will obviously vary with the depth of your prior relationship with the child. Children are sensitive to encroachment or interrogation until they feel comfortable. Children need to feel as if they are in control, or at least not being controlled. If you are open, and wait for them to come to you, they will probably do so quickly. This waiting may be a frustrating experience when you have a "mission" to accomplish, not to mention many other tasks waiting.

It is easiest to begin with what the child is doing at the moment, whether that is a game, a toy, or a television program. Fairly soon, you should let the child know why you are there. Children know enough about adults to guess you have an agenda. It is important to announce this agenda in terms of your concern for the child and your desire to be there with him or her. Then you can begin to introduce the issues of the particular crisis or situation involved. Again, you need to raise questions and indicate that having feelings about the crisis is normal. Do not be afraid of silences. Give the child a chance to size you up and make a response.

Introducing faith issues into the discussion requires patience and gentleness. First, you need to be open to the possibility that children may not be interested in faith issues. Their sense of loss, physical pain, or any number of other concerns may be so pressing that the place of God in their suffering may be too much to think about. However, you should at least raise the issue of faith. The timing will be influenced by your previous relationship with the children, their openness to discussion up to that point in the visit, and what you know about their interest in faith issues. The place to start (and end) is with the place of God in their lives at the moment. You might ask, "Have you thought about God during this time?" or "Do you think God has been a part of all this?" or "Has God had anything to do with all of this?" Another strategy is to make reference to Bible stories or Bible characters, as mentioned earlier. Job is a helpful story in times of physical illness. You can even tell the story if the child is not familiar with it.

In order to have any discussion of faith issues, you must first understand how the child thinks God operates in the world generally. This basic understanding of God's overriding purpose and intent in the world is essential before any discussion can take place about the role of God in a life crisis. It is important to ask children how they see God acting or not acting. However, this discussion should not begin out of the blue. It might proceed in the following way.

CHILD: Why did God make my mommy die?
MINISTER: Do you believe that God causes people to die?
CHILD: Well, I guess so. Doesn't God make everything happen?
MINISTER: Well, some people believe that. I believe that some things happen because people make mistakes [in the case of an accident] or because our bodies don't work right and can't be fixed [in the case of illness].

You might also begin with something like the following:

MINISTER: Do you see God working in your illness?
CHILD: I don't know. It's hard to feel him.
MINISTER: Have you felt him at all?
CHILD: I guess he helps me.
MINISTER: How?
CHILD: He watched over me when I was in surgery.
MINISTER: Yes, I believe he did.

Obviously, the answers you provide to these questions will depend on your own theology. The goal is to come to an understanding about God's role in the world which is helpful to the child and will serve as a context within which to interpret the child's current situation. The importance of coming to this understanding cannot be overemphasized. You cannot assume that because the child is a steady, lifelong member of your Sunday school that the child shares the normative theology of your denomination. Children tend to form and try out their own conceptions of God.

What Does the Child Really Mean?

An important skill to develop is the ability to discern what the child really means. We must keep asking ourselves, "What is the child really saying?" or "What is the true meaning of the question?" Part of our skill as pastoral caregivers is to determine what the child is really asking. We may have to determine this on our own since children may not be consciously aware of all they are asking. A good rule of thumb is to follow our instincts, yet keeping all the options in mind so they may be followed up later.

First, the true intent of the question may be emotional rather than factual. We may be tempted to answer the question about Mommy being in heaven purely on a logical, concrete level as if we were answering the question, "Where is my mommy physically at this time?" In reality the child is not concerned about *where* Mommy is but about *how* Mommy is. The question "Why me?" falls into this same category. It is an expression of anguish and hurt that needs to be named and accepted, not a request for information. One response is to name the underlying feeling by saying, "It must hurt a great deal to have had this happen to you."

However, sometimes the questions are requests for facts. School-age children have learned to use facts to control and master a situation. Therefore, they are seeking to understand the facts of the situation and are helped by that understanding. The question "Where is my mommy?", for example, initially demands a factual answer. As has been pointed out, however, that answer must be given with an eye toward the emotional consequences for the child. The child would seem to want a fact to hang on to but also wants reassurance that Mommy is being taken care of. One might deal with these possibilities as follows:

CHILD: Where is my mommy?
MINISTER: I believe she is in heaven.
CHILD: Is she with God?
MINISTER: Yes, I believe she is, and I believe God is taking good care of her. Have you been worrying about her?
CHILD: Yes.
MINISTER: What do you worry about?
CHILD: I worry that something bad will happen to her and then I won't get to see her when I go to heaven.
MINISTER: That really is a worry. It's hard not to worry when it's something we can't see. But I believe that God will always take care of us for ever and ever. Does thinking about that help you worry less?
CHILD: Yes, it helps, but I still worry some.
MINISTER: Of course, but maybe when you start to worry you can remember really hard about how God promises to take care of us.

In compressed form, this example shows the interplay of the child's need for facts, the need to address the underlying feeling, and the possibility of sharing our own belief in a way that may be helpful.

Another possible trap is seeing a child's question as theological when it is something more obvious. Unlike adults, children will not confine their questions to our realm of expertise. We might be tempted to interpret as philosophical or theological a question such as, "Why did my mother die?" when the child simply wants a reaffirmation of the medical facts. The most obvious response is "Your mother died because she was very sick, and sometimes when people are very sick they die." The child may or may not go on to ask about the involvement of God in the event.

Dealing with concrete questions is one of the biggest differences between children and adults. Again, the basic problem is to determine how detailed an answer the child can digest. Generally, children look for much shorter and more succinct answers than adults provide. Giving too much of an answer is a danger when we are dealing with an area about which we know a great deal. The best strategy is to give a minimal answer to any question and allow the child to ask for more. If too much is given, the child may become lost in all the words and abandon the dialogue altogether. We have to resist the temptation to explain the point fully and, instead, give children pieces of information they can handle. For example:

CHILD: Why did God let Jesus die?
MINISTER: Because God wanted to make it so we could live in heaven.

One might be tempted to talk about God's love, grace, and eternal salvation. However, we are challenged here to pick one point we feel is central to this child's circumstance.

Another way to deal with tough questions is to reflect them back to the child and let the child provide answers. This strategy allows us to connect children with more certainty and to work with their own faith systems. We need to affirm their thoughts and feelings but also challenge them to grow in their faith.

CHILD: Why didn't Jesus come down from the cross?
MINISTER: That's a difficult question. Have you thought about it?
CHILD: Some.
MINISTER: What have you been thinking about?
CHILD: Well, I wondered if God didn't forget about him for a little while.
MINISTER: Do you think that really happened?
CHILD: I guess not.
MINISTER: Does it feel as if God forgets about you sometimes?
CHILD: I guess so.
MINISTER: I think there are times in our lives when we all feel that God has

forgotten about us. It feels lonely. But we believe God is always
here. God promises never to leave us alone. We have to keep
remembering that and reminding ourselves. Can you do that?
CHILD: I can try.
MINISTER: Do you want to think of some other reasons why Jesus didn't come
down from the cross?

In this example, the child's feelings are solicited and validated. No
matter what we think, we always want to be specially careful not to
suggest that the child's feelings are wrong. At the same time, we want
to challenge beliefs that are not helpful to the child in coping with the
situation. The above example also points to the tendency of children to
impute to Bible characters what they or people around them are feeling. In this case, the child's own sense of abandonment was projected
onto Jesus. Therefore, the faith question was more helpful in revealing
the child's feelings than in teaching us about the child's beliefs.

Sharing Our Faith

With all the emphasis on dealing with children as they are and valuing their own feelings and beliefs, where can we share our own faith?
Certainly, we should not hide our own beliefs. They can be valuable
support to children who are struggling with their own faith. The basic
principle is to avoid sharing in a way that devalues children's beliefs or
implies that we are right and they are wrong. The construction "I
believe" is often helpful, because it can be said without implying a value
judgment. Children need to hear alternatives to their belief systems,
especially when their system is not working for them. They will be more
accepting, however, of new ideas that are offered to them rather than
imposed on them.

As part of sharing our own faith, we should not neglect prayer. Many
people underestimate children's interest in and use of prayer. School-
age children take comfort from familiar prayers and prayer forms. We
should use prayer with children in much the same way that we use it
with adults. It is often helpful to allow children to set the agenda for the
prayer by asking, "What should we pray about?" Children should be
encouraged to view prayer as something they can do rather than simply
something that adults can do for them. They need to know that their
language is as appropriate for prayer as stilted adult language. Prayer
can also be a mechanism for sharing our own faith. Along with prayer,
we should always think about using the sacraments that are within our
traditions, just as we would with adults in crisis.

Summary

Talking to children about faith issues is extremely important in times of crisis. It is one of the gifts we as religious adults can give to children in our care. The task needs to be approached, however, with sensitivity, caring, and acceptance of the children, their feelings, and their beliefs. We need to remember to solicit the child's feelings carefully and respect them. We need to listen carefully and follow what the child is asking of us. The basic skill, however, is to listen to what our intuition tells us and listen to the child within each of us. We need to let our concern and love for the child guide what we say and do. If we allow our love to show, children will respond and lead us where they want to go.

FURTHER READING

Cavalletti, Sofia. *The Religious Potential of the Child.* New York: Paulist Press, 1983.

Claypool, John. *Tracks of a Fellow Struggler: How to Handle Grief.* Waco, Texas: Word Books, 1974.

Gobbel, A. Roger, and Gertrude G. Gobbel. *The Bible—A Child's Playground.* Philadelphia: Fortress Press, 1986.

Simundson, Daniel J. *Where Is God in My Suffering?* Minneapolis: Augsburg Publishing House, 1983.

16

Pastoral Assessment of the Child and the Family

Carolyn W. Treadway and John L. Florell

When ministering to children in crisis, we must be aware of the child's strengths, resources, problems, and needs. The child may be our primary unit of focus, so it is important to understand children individually and intervene directly with them. We must remember, however, that the child is part of a family system that includes not only parents and siblings but also extended family members, the present family situation, and the family's history. It is important to understand the child *in the context of* the family! Because family pain is often revealed through symptoms in the child, we need to understand what the child's behavior is expressing for the family as a whole.

In this chapter we will explore ways of looking at the child's world from a systemic pastoral perspective. Through this lens we view an individual *as part of* an operative family system. This provides new understandings and methods of intervention for our ministry with children. If we can think systemically, we can utilize the wider family system as our focus for intervention and change.

Systemic thinking is based on circular, not linear, cause and effect. Simultaneously, everything influences everything else. In families, each person is connected to and has an effect on everyone else. All persons operate as part of the larger family, functioning not according to their "own nature" but according to their position in the family. Both individual and family problems originate not in the nature of individuals but in the way the family system is functioning. To remove a child from the family for independent observation will give incomplete information, because the child will function differently outside the family system. In fact, the child's functioning even within the family will differ depending upon changing relationships with others. Therefore, even in assess-

Carolyn W. Treadway is Pastoral Counselor, Illinois Pastoral Services Institute, Bloomington, Ill. John L. Florell is the institute's Executive Director.

ing "individual" problems, we focus on the process of family interaction.

Sometimes the relationship between a child's problems and family functioning is clear, as when Johnny starts failing in school just after his parents separate and announce their impending divorce. At other times, the interactive links between symptoms and family functioning are much harder to discern.

Jeannie, age nine, was referred for counseling by her pediatrician because she was able to raise her temperature to 104 degrees without medical cause. As the family story unfolded, three tragic deaths of important family members had occurred in the past few years, including two in separate accidents at an intersection near Jeannie's house. Because the family used this intersection every day, Jeannie worried that "if we leave home, we will be killed." Having a high temperature kept Jeannie *and* her family at home (caring for her) and also provided the whole family with a focus for the diffuse anxiety left over from their unresolved grief. As counseling provided a different outlet for these feelings, Jeannie's temperature stayed normal without further problems.

Systemic focusing on the child in the context of the family does not mean using parents or siblings to address the child's problem. Instead, it means viewing the interaction of all family members to discover how the "presenting problems" are co-created and maintained (and can be changed or modified) by all family members.

In our ministry with children, we need to be aware that common childhood problems (such as phobias, depression, bed-wetting, soiling, and drug use and abuse) are typically symptoms of *family* distress. Pastoral persons are often called upon by parents, relatives, and Christian educators to help with problem children. We can be careful not to take sides in family tensions, yet in the church we may know and have some leverage with the entire family. We also have the advantage of seeing the child in interaction with other church children. Problems may become noticeable in comparing an individual child's behavior with that of peers.

Most children, for example, go to church or school without any expression of fear. When fear interrupts a child's normal developmental task of attending school, it usually indicates some trauma within the child or the child's family life. Any childhood phobia regarding school, food, sleep, relationships, places, or play should be treated quickly. The longer phobias persist, the more difficult they are to change. Children who are quiet, compliant, and doing reasonably well in school may not appear to have problems even though they may not relate well with their peers. Parents are usually the first to express fears about their child's social isolation. A pastor can encourage discussion about children that usually frees parents to share their anxieties.

Jenny was a quiet ten-year-old fifth-grader. An average student and the middle child in a family of three, she was exceptionally well behaved, shy, and somewhat withdrawn. During a pastoral visit Jenny refused to talk to the pastor. Her parents started expressing their concerns about her social isolation and general sadness. The pastor referred them to a pastoral counselor, who found Jenny was suffering from childhood depression.

Though bed-wetting is usually not a problem after age seven, some children do continue. For some this is a problem of maturation, but if there has been a significant dry period and bed-wetting reappears, it could be a symptom of family distress. For example, a nine-year-old girl started bed-wetting after two years of nighttime bladder control. Her parents had just had another child, and this was her response to the changed family situation.

The problem of soiling has more ramifications than bed-wetting. After bowel control has been established, bowel problems not caused by disease or diet are often the result of control issues between parents and the child. Having fecal accidents in their pants, or hiding feces in annoying places, represents an expression of anger and frustration that most school-age children do not use.

Mike, a seven-year-old, was having "accidents" in his pants at home and school. These accidents started after the third family move in six years. Mike's mom and dad told the minister making a new member call that Mike was just having problems adjusting to a new home. The minister planned regular visits with the family and arranged to have several boys Mike's age come with him on a couple of visits. Mike expressed his anger at moving but thought he might like his new home. The soiling ended after about a month of pastoral visits.

Alcohol and drug abuse are problems that are affecting children at younger and younger ages. Even grade school children are becoming addicted to alcohol or marijuana. Though drinking at a young age does not necessarily mean a child is addicted, the younger a child begins drinking, the higher the potential to develop a drug or alcohol problem in a short period of time. In homes where both parents work, or in single-parent homes, children may have extra access to alcohol. Change in a child's behavior and deteriorating ability to carry out school or personal responsibilities may indicate problems. Parents often come to pastoral people in the church to seek help in dealing with these problems. Frequently the child's drinking reflects a family problem. Referral to a drug or alcohol dependency unit, so the problem can be adequately assessed, is one of the most responsible suggestions a pastoral person can make.

Detecting physical or emotional abuse is a difficult task. Because the pastor can go into the home on pastoral visits, he or she may notice indications of abuse when other professionals cannot. Obvious physical bruises, scrapes, and broken bones can be seen outside the home, but emotional abuse may be revealed through family interaction (such as constant parental belittling or lack of attention) or a child's emotional distress (extreme anxiety, difficulty in relationships, or poor self-esteem). If parents are overly neglectful, demanding, or punitive, this could signal potential abuse. When asked by her Sunday school teacher to describe herself as a part of the church body, one ten-year-old defined herself as an appendix, "good for nothing but being taken out." At a subsequent pastoral home visit, the girl's father commented in striking parallel: "She's always causing trouble; we'd be better off without her."

Pastoral persons seeking to minister to children in difficulty must minister to their families as well. One of the most practical ways to become acquainted with families is to make a pastoral call in the home. Usually this should be informal, of short duration, and oriented around getting to know the family. Families volunteer a great deal about their style of life by how they act when you visit. Children's behavior also reveals much about what is happening in their family. You can observe how parents and children interact regarding communication, authority, discipline, and family values. It is helpful to take notes on each family visit to refresh your memory.

Pastoral visits can indicate whether a family is spiritually illiterate. Parents may want their children to be brought up in the church but may themselves have little insight about spiritual matters such as prayer, Bible-reading, or God's activity in their lives. They may teach one way while they act entirely differently, even though children learn from their parents' actions much more than by what they say. Pastoral family visits also provide opportunity to note some warning signs of a family in difficulty, such as lack of appreciation between family members, poor communication, difficulty in dealing with problems, and little quality family time together.

While ministering to children and families, whether in the church or home or any other setting, we need to learn to see the family as an interactive whole and to understand how the child fits into the family interaction. Keeping certain key questions in mind as we relate to family members can be very helpful in keeping our systemic view.

First, *what is the overall picture of this family?* What is the family's basic style of interaction? Is this an open family rooted in encouragement, acceptance, and love, in which all members are treated with respect as persons and given both security and freedom to grow? Is it a closed family rooted in fear, judgment, and old habits, where authoritarian rules make it hard to grow? Is it a directionless family, whose roots have come loose and where each person fends for herself or himself?

Virginia Satir, a noted family therapist, says that in vital, nurturing families self-worth is high, communication is clear and direct, rules are flexible, and linking to society is open and hopeful. The pastor can evaluate whether these characteristics are part of this family. What is the general appearance and feeling tone in the family? What would it be like to live in this family? Does the family spend quality time together? Do they have activities in which the whole family participates, such as sharing meals, story times, or games? Or is there a low priority given to family commitments, an avoidance of shared time, lack of responsibility to other family members, and resistance to using the family as a resource to solve problems?

During a family visit, Tina, age nine, told the pastor of her activities outside the home. Her parents were surprised and said the young girl never participated in family activities. Tina reported that she was never given a chance to do anything with her family because her parents were "always doing their own thing."

Second, *how can we describe (or map) this particular family and the way it interacts?* We can draw mental pictures as we gather information. Who are the members (names, ages, descriptive data)? Who is close to whom, who is distant from whom? What are the subgroups or coalitions in the family and how do they operate? For example, are the parents linked more to each other or to a child or children? Who comes in to relieve the stress if there is tension between any two persons? Are the boundaries in this family (between persons, between subgroups, between family and society) clear, diffuse, or rigid? Who is in conflict with, or overinvolved with, or not connected to whom? Can persons in this family be both separate from and together with the others? Can persons be different and spend time apart without producing anxiety? What are the roles and who carries them? For example, which child is "mother's protector," which child is "scapegoat," and which child is "heir apparent"? Who carries the family's feeling state? Who has the power? What are the family's spoken and unspoken rules, and how do they influence family interaction? What are some of the family's predictable patterns of behavior, so that if "this" happens, then "this" will follow, and then "this"? (If Dad gets angry, then Mom cries, then Joey comforts her, and then Dad gets madder.) What repetitive, nonproductive behavior sequences are noticeable? These "stuck" sequences may lead the family to ask for help.

Third, *how effectively can this family communicate?* We know that the style and effectiveness of communication either helps keep the family together or drives it apart. Communication also greatly influences the self-esteem of members of the family. We watch both verbal and nonverbal communications, looking for that which leads to mutual understanding and that which is nonproductive. Virginia Satir has named four basic communication styles used by most persons when under stress: blaming, placating, distracting, or computing (being super-reasonable). We watch to see who uses which style, then try to help all family members communicate more effectively or congruently, so that what they say is what they feel. We help them speak in a manner that can be heard by others in the family.

Pastoral persons can readily observe the styles of communication and the quality of listening in a family. When a family is in trouble and members lack appreciation for one another, communication is often harsh and constantly critical, by children as well as parents. If communications are blocked by silence, accusation, authoritarian tactics, or other poor techniques, the family is probably having problems that produce frustration between parents and children. These problems may well be ignored or left unresolved because the family cannot talk about the real issues in their interaction.

> In the Jackson family, the father was consistently the "blamer" in family communication and the mother the "placator," keeping the peace at any cost. When the parents argued, the two sons, age nine and eleven, would jump in as "distractors." The boys would argue fiercely with each other until the parents would stop fighting in order to reprimand the boys, and the arguments would remain unresolved. Repeatedly, the boys hid partially eaten food under the playroom couch. The father responded angrily whenever more food was discovered. The pastor described the boys' food stashing as a metaphoric communication for all the feelings in the family that were swept under the rug and could not be spoken about. This helped open a doorway for family members to express more directly and verbally what their feelings really were and to work them out.

Fourth, *what is the life-cycle stage of this family and is its functioning developmentally appropriate?* Families go through life-cycle stages just as do individuals, and each stage has its own developmental tasks. For families with young and preteen children, a key task is to accept new members into the family system. To do this, the couple must adjust the marital system to make increasing space for the children, take on parenthood, and change relationships with the extended family to include parenting and grandparenting roles. Many times, families experience difficulty at transition points in the family life cycle, such as when the first or last child enters school. When something goes wrong in a family's expected sense of motion through developmental time, and something that is supposed to happen does not (or vice versa), a symptom may develop in a child or children. Understanding the current symptom requires understanding where the family is trying to go in relation to where it has already been.

Fifth, *what influences from past time are affecting the family's interaction at this time?* Events from *past* time can greatly influence problems seen *now* in family members. If a ten-year-old is having difficulty, we can inquire about each parent at ten to learn if there is a connection between the issues of the parent at ten and the problem of the child today. All families pass down their history, perceptions, expectations, rules for functioning, and so forth. Problematic themes and issues can also be passed from generation to generation. Family trees can be marked by use of alcohol, divorce, or certain health problems, for example. Sometimes certain children are "selected" as primary bearers of family problems. When problematic issues or events from the past converge with similar issues or events in the present, watch out! Stress at such a juncture takes a quantum leap, which may place the family in crisis and cause them to seek or be referred for help. Understanding the current crisis requires an awareness of not only the present situation but what has gone before.

When the Brown family's young son, Ted, was critically injured in an accident, the family was plunged into an abrupt crisis. During the weeks of uncertainty about Ted's future, both immediate and extended families were in a state of high anxiety. As Ted gradually recovered, his father's anxiety only increased, for Ted's injury tapped into his vast reservoir of feeling about his own brother's sudden death two decades before. Ted's father needed to address his *own* parents about his brother's death before he could help his son on the road to recovery from his injury.

Our own reactions to a child and a family provide associations and information that can be useful in understanding and helping the family. Our own family experiences and accustomed family roles will influence how we understand what we observe and how we define our roles in helping. It is important, therefore, for us to know our own family system and our part in it in order to help others with theirs.

How can we help a family to change? What functions do the current presenting problems serve for the whole family system, and what will happen to the family if these problems change or disappear? A full answer to these questions could easily take an extended study of family therapy. For interested readers, several references are listed at the end of the chapter. Pastoral persons need to remember that change can occur by modifying the functioning of the whole family, instead of trying to solve the child's problem directly. The child's symptom, per se, does not have to be changed if *other* persons in the family can be helped to change their relationships with one another. New input can be added to cancel out what has gone wrong.

> The parents of Sue, age eleven, brought her to the pastor asking for help because Sue had become frightened by "seeing a man in her room." For three months Sue had grown increasingly fearful. She was unable to be alone day or night. The whole family was keyed up about this behavior, and Sue's schoolwork and school relationships had suffered as well. The pastor, who knew the family well, was aware that the elder brother was the high achiever and preferred sibling. She also knew that Dad was very busy with farm work, which involved his son but not his daughter, and that the mother had a job which took her from the home many afternoons. Observing the family interaction systemically, the pastor hypothesized that Sue's puzzling symptoms of terror served to get her attention she was missing. She prescribed specific ways for each parent to give Sue constructive attention. As the interaction between child and parents slowly changed, Sue's fears dissolved and she resumed more independent behavior at home and school.

Understanding how a person in the family is likely to function, or to be able to change, comes from observing his or her interactive position in the family. Change in any part of the family changes the interaction of the whole family. Choosing with whom to intervene is based *not* on who has the presenting symptom but on who has the greatest capacity to bring change to the family. The pastor, therefore, asked Sue's parents to change (by paying more attention to Sue) so that Sue's behavior in the family system could change.

Summary

When ministering to children with problems and in helping families to change, pastors must consistently focus their vision on the wider family context and realize that this entire system helps create and maintain the presenting problems. Mary Jane's problems with schoolwork, Bobby's asthma, Jennifer's bed-wetting, and Jeff's depression may have their roots and their solutions in the relationship not only between parent and child but between parent and parent, or between parents and their own parents. When the child is the family's problem focus, our first task is to "defocus" the child. With systemic understanding of how all parts of a family interact, we can ask about other component parts of the system and help the family realize that all are linked. As pastors help families address not only their children's current presenting symptoms but underlying family interactive issues, we are advocates for children and for the family in a fundamental, life-changing way.

FURTHER READING

Family Therapy

Carter, Elizabeth A., and Monica McGoldrick. *The Family Life Cycle: A Framework for Family Therapy.* New York: Gardner Press, 1980.

Friedman, Edwin H. *Generation to Generation: Family Process in Church and Synagogue.* New York: Guilford Press, 1985.

Minuchin, Salvador. *Families and Family Therapy.* Cambridge, Mass.: Harvard University Press, 1974.

Napier, Augustus Y., with Carl A. Whitaker. *The Family Crucible.* New York: Harper & Row, 1978.

Satir, Virginia. *Conjoint Family Therapy.* 3rd ed. Palo Alto, Calif.: Science & Behavior Books, 1983.

———. *Peoplemaking.* Palo Alto, Calif.: Science & Behavior Books, 1972.

Child Therapy

Gardner, Richard A. *Therapeutic Communication with Children: The Mutual Storytelling Technique.* 2nd ed. Northvale, N.J.: Jason Aronson, 1986.

Polson, Beth, and Miller Newton. *Not My Kid: A Parent's Guide to Kids and Drugs.* New York: Arbor House, 1984.

17

The Extended Family
Wayne E. Oates

As pastors, we can be overwhelmed by the needs of the children to whom we minister. The extended family offers us a significant resource for ministering to the child. We pastors, with our personal and professional contacts, are also an important part of a young parishioner's extended family, as is the local Christian community in our church. The extended family also offers new relationships of caring friendships with grandparents, neighbors, teachers, physicians, social workers, lawyers, and many others. They form the network or system of nurturance for this child. They offer a resource for sharing the care of a child. In fellowship with them, we can discover a more profound Christian interpretation of the meaning of the word "family."

What Is Meant by "Extended Family"?

The term "extended family" has both a long history and a contemporary meaning. The term "family" occurs about 270 times in the Old Testament. "The house," or *bayith,* referred to the smallest unit or "nuclear" family occupying one dwelling. It normally consisted of parents and their unmarried children, although occasionally it included household servants. One of the major tensions in families today is the "return to the nest" syndrome in which adult sons or daughters leave home for marriage or work but suffer separation, divorce, or unemployment and come back to their parental home to live for economic or emotional reasons. In wartime this is a common happening for young wives and mothers when husbands are away in military combat. In today's epidemic of drug use, young parents may abandon their chil-

Wayne E. Oates is Professor of Psychiatry and Behavioral Sciences and Director of the Program in Ethics and Pastoral Counseling, University of Louisville School of Medicine, Louisville, Ky.

dren, so grandparents or aunts and uncles take them into their home. When a parent dies, leaving a widowed spouse with children, what is spoken of ordinarily as the extended family becomes a nuclear family if grandparents become part of a son or daughter's household. The child for whom you are caring may live in such a house.

In the Old Testament, the family is often referred to as "father's house" *(beth 'ab)*. This is something like what we think of today as the extended family. It refers to a cluster of houses in which live two or more nuclear families claiming descent from the same ancestor. They were bound together by ancestry and by a common form of work. The "family business" of today, which provides a topic for a separate study in its own right, is a contemporary example. In my own city, both major newspapers, a television, and a radio station have been owned and operated for three generations by one such "father's house." Recently the whole family received local and national attention when they sold these assets to a national conglomerate company.

The Old Testament also refers to the "clan" *(mishpahah)*. This was the linking together of several extended families. They often claimed a single ancestry, although intermarriage also took place. In small-town culture, in ethnic neighborhoods of Old World immigrants, and in such religious groups as the Amish and the Mennonites, we have contemporary examples of the clan. Sometimes geographic isolation of mountain and desert communities contributes to the development of clans. As in the Old Testament, security against outside violence still prompts the formation of clans. That the feuds of mountain communities and the Mafia of urban communities revolve around "families" reflects clan culture in America.

The New Testament contrasts with Old Testament perceptions of both nuclear and extended families. The "clan" disappears linguistically. It is severely challenged in Jesus' confrontation of those who were obsessed about the family inheritance in Mark 10:17–22, Luke 9:61–62, and Luke 12:13–21. The nuclear family of parents and sons (or daughters) is affirmed when Jesus and Paul both approvingly quote the Old Testament commandment to honor father and mother (Mark 7:9–12; Matt. 19:19; Luke 18:20; Eph. 6:1–3). Luke 1:17 speaks of John the Baptist's ministry as "turning the hearts of the fathers to the children." In 1 Timothy 5:8 an adult person who will not provide for relatives is looked upon as having "disowned the faith and as being worse than a heretic."

A most vivid contrast, however, comes when Jesus says, "Whoever does the will of God is my brother, and sister, and mother" (Mark 3:35) and, "Every one who has left houses or brothers or sisters or father or mother or children or lands, for my name's sake, will receive a hundredfold, and inherit eternal life" (Matt. 19:29). The nature of the family has been redefined, and the inheritance is a lasting and not a perishing one. In Acts 3:25 and in Paul's prayer in Ephesians 3:14–21, the word for "family" is *patria* and refers to the family of humanity under the parenthood of God. Every family on earth and in heaven is named after this progenitor. The family is given a name that scales every barrier and transcends all identities which do not include full participation with the whole human community.

One of the common meanings of the verb *episkopeō* is "see to it." Getting the "overview" of Jesus' and Paul's perception of the family enables you and me to see to it that the component parts of the whole human community as a living system of face-to-face relationships are mobilized around the nurture and the enlargement of children's life. They are not shut up to the suffocation of an unventilated nuclear family. God has other faces and forms in addition to those of mother, father, brother, and sister. Basic trust and sources of hope are not shut up to these significant persons alone. Children can love them without becoming an idolater of them. With the minister, children continue to enlarge their bases of comparison of the nuclear family members' representation of God with their knowledge of grandparents, uncles, aunts, cousins, neighbors, Sunday school and public school teachers, 4-H club and scout leaders, pediatricians, nurses, childhood and youth peer groups, and all the "other" strangers beyond the narrow confines of the nuclear family. In turn, these persons become resources with whom we ministers become acquainted, to whom we may introduce both the child and the parents. They, in turn, can become your allies as you distribute your feeling of concern and encourage them to invest themselves in this particular child.

Learning the Family Tree

One of the most reliable and accessible ways of pastorally activating the extended family in the care of the child in crisis is to know, and know how to call upon, all the generations of family members related to the child as well as the parents. In a particular child's instance, it should be standard practice to ask about the whereabouts and the accessibility of the grandparents. The child may have a very "special" devotion to one or more of these grandparents. The role of grandparents in child-rearing is becoming increasingly more vital. According to the July 29, 1986, U.S. Census Report, 770,355 births, or about 21 percent of the 3,669,141 live births in the United States in 1984, were to unwed mothers. If these mothers become working mothers, the grandmother often becomes the one who spends the most time with the child. For this and many other vital reasons it should be routine for a pastor to be as positively related to the grandparents of the child as possible.

In fact, a basic principle of getting to know a congregation well and remembering their names is to learn them as members of "family trees." As Edwin Friedman says:

> When family members are able to see beyond the horizons of their own nuclear family area of trouble and observe the transmission of such issues from generation to generation, they often can obtain distance from their immediate problems, and as a result become free to make changes. . . . Family trees are always trees of knowledge and often they are trees of life.[1]

The church includes persons of all generations in a way that is unique among institutions in our age-graded society. If we, as pastors, were to try to *avoid* dealing with a given child's crisis apart from a multigenerational approach, we would have great difficulty doing so. Therefore, to do so consciously and systematically *before* crises occur is the essence of wisdom.

The Interprofessional Extended Family

Not only the blood kin family composes the available resources for the pastor in caring for the child in crisis. The wide range of persons in other professions can help the Christian minister provide an interprofessional extended family for both the child and the parents. They can also serve as an extended family for the pastor. Here is a brief case in point.

> A former student of mine in a nearby community looked upon me, his former professor, as a meaningful part of his own extended family. (The good news for you and me is that we would hardly be pastors at all if we ourselves did not also have such "extended families.") This pastor friend of mine was ministering to Jethro, a mentally retarded five-year-old boy in his church. The nuclear family included the father, the mother, and a two-year-old brother. Jethro couldn't talk very well and didn't catch on to what you were saying as quickly as his little two-year-old brother. The two-year-old brother could understand what Jethro wanted better than his parents could and took up for him. The mother and father thought it was just the five-year-old's stubborn streak and used a belt on him, sometimes breaking the skin. They were afraid to go to a doctor with Jethro, though they felt there was something wrong with him. They were afraid the doctor would turn them in to the police for beating their child.

I asked the pastor to have them call me and to assure them I would not call the police. I interviewed the mother by telephone. I first told her of my deep interest in her little boy, and then I asked her to describe his actions for me. He was of kindergarten age and they wanted him to go to kindergarten like other children, but they knew he couldn't make it as he is. They had become so put out with him that they punished him severely, but it did no good. Then they decided to quit whipping and try loving him into doing what he should. I told her that a man who worked with me, a psychologist, was an expert on figuring out what is wrong with little children and making a plan for their parents' care of them and for their schooling. This was a poverty-level family. The father made barely enough to hide the children's nakedness and feed them. I told her that the psychologist worked with a United Way program in our department of pediatrics and could see them even though they had little money.

The mother gave me permission to call him and explain the child's needs and the parents' fear of being reported to the police for child abuse. I called him. He told me to have them call him immediately and to assure them that if they decided to stop punishing the child he would not report them to the authorities.

He saw the family as a group, tested the child's mental and behavioral abilities, and diagnosed him as educably retarded. He designed a program for the child in the public school kindergarten and gave much encouragement, appreciation, and guidance to the parents. Now the pastor of the family can confer with the psychologist and help the church school teachers to care for the child with a love that "abounds more and more with knowledge and discernment," as the apostle Paul prayed.

The road ahead for the little boy and his family will be difficult. We hope that they will not be putting unnecessary hardships in their own way. They certainly will not walk that road alone. A faithful and wise pastor saw to it that the whole extended family of the "larger family" of the church and community was mobilized around the hurting necessities of one little five-year-old boy.

The contemporary practice of marriage and family therapy in the context of the spiritual community of faith is based upon such a systems approach. Two exceptionally helpful books on the subject are J. C. Wynn, *Family Therapy in Pastoral Ministry*, and Edwin H. Friedman, *Generation to Generation: Family Process in Church and Synagogue*. The former is written by a Protestant minister and the latter by a Jewish rabbi. Both authors bring wide experience and deep understanding to the working pastor in the Hebrew-Christian community.

Pastoral Friendship: A Cohesive Force
in the Extended Family Network

Help for Jethro and his parents was quickly mobilized. It looks easy, but it does not happen by chance. It took place because the two professional helpers involved knew each other personally and were friends.

"The first zone of sociality beyond the family, then, is the bond between friends, or what we call the circles of friends," as Martin Marty has said.[2] Through our capacity, initiative, and energy in making friends, we *extend* the extended family of the families that make up our church. The church itself is an extended family that pushes each nuclear family into relation with other nuclear families. As a church, they can be an ingrown family of families. Six, eight, or ten "family names" may comprise 90 percent of the church membership. Through insecurity, suspiciousness of outsiders and strangers, they may actually function to keep it this way. As pastors, we can become comfortable and restrict all our friendships to this closed-in group, but we need not do so.

Our task as pastors is to reach out beyond these walled-in fellowships. These are friends, but they are friends *by necessity* of family origin, geographical location, and church tradition. We are called as undershepherds of Jesus Christ to make friends *by choice* of strangers beyond the confines of our local church, personal biases, and parochial interests. For example, the psychologist who had the unique resources for Jethro's care is a Jewish person who holds faithfully to his religious community. We *chose* him because we have a long-standing friendship with him, trust him, and highly value his knowledge and expertise. One of our main bases of fellowship with him is our common devotion to the well-being of little children. *Choosing* him as a part of the extended family makes concrete the meaning of *haireō*, that New Testament word used to describe Moses choosing to "break out" of Pharaoh's family "when he was grown up" and to associate himself with the enslaved Hebrews instead (Heb. 11:25).

Remarkable enough, *haireō* is the word from which we get our English word "heretic." It was heretical for Jesus to speak to a Samaritan woman, "for Jews have no dealings with Samaritans." Even though it was heretical to make friends with the Jewish psychologist on behalf of our one little boy, Jethro was helped and our world as two Christian pastors was enlarged. In the closed-in world of the ingrown family, the abuse of Jethro was the secret to be kept. Now this is no longer necessary. The nuclear family, cut off from an extended family, is at great risk of abusing each other verbally, incestuously, and violently.

Considerable research has accumulated both in the history of the emergence of Christianity out of Judaism and in the study of family violence to dramatize the revolutionary character of Jesus' teaching about the "larger family" of the human species. In the watering down of these teachings of Jesus, however, contemporary church life is a repetition of the situation of the closed-in, unventilated nuclear family he confronted in the Palestine of his day. I often illustrate this in counseling with parents by asking them what would happen if they did not put a vent pipe on their clothes dryer. They say, "It might catch on fire." Then I tell them the same hazard occurs when a family shuts off contact with other people who can enable all of them to grow and to learn. The heat of anger and sexual passion can turn in on the family members themselves and cause their relationships to "catch on fire." After a short time, the burning secret of brutality or incestuous sex becomes a secret that cannot be kept. The irony of it is that we as pastors are the firefighters! Fire prevention is a better way to go.

The minister, therefore, who lays hold of the resources of the extended family of the individual families of his or her parish must at the same time choose friends beyond the walls of the parish. This outreaching friendship extends to public school teachers, doctors and nurses, employers, law enforcement officials, college and university communities, ministers and parishioners of other faith groups, government officials, and anyone else whom you trust, respect, and can establish dialogue with as a friend.

Such friendships are best formed in your shared commitment to one child and one family who are in crisis. Children in crisis the world over provide a common language that supersedes the barriers of family, ethnic, theological, and geographic differences. They are your open sesame to the closed doors of relationship throughout your community.

To form friendships that grow into an extensive, well-rooted larger "family" of resource persons helping children does not just happen. It takes living and working in the same community over a considerable length of time. Those who have very short pastorates will be limited. When we go to a church and its larger community, people wonder if we are going to stay very long. They have seen pastors come and go, and some of them have been the cause of the departures! This keeps them from investing themselves too readily in friendship with new persons. If they think you are "on your way up and out" of their church, they will remain superficial with you. But as you put down roots and stay longer, the network of friends who can be resources to you in helping people in crisis widens and deepens.

Of course, this is only half the truth. The apostle Paul did not stay in one geographical area very long either. He specialized in transcending the borders of a tight-knit Jewish enclave of persons. He introduced people to each other and taught them to look out for each other's well-being. He extended his network of caring persons over much of the known world of the time. He did so by writing letters and sending messages by one of them to others of them. In Romans 16:1–2, he says, "I commend to you our sister Phoebe, a deaconess of the church at Cenchreae, that you may receive her in the Lord as befits the saints, and help her in whatever she may require from you, for she has been a helper of many and of myself as well." Paul chose to cross over barriers between Jew and Gentile, bond and free, male and female, young and old, weak and strong in forming this extended family he called "the saints." When he mentioned "the family" in his prayers, he prayed "before the Father, from whom every family in heaven and on earth is named" (Eph. 3:14–15).

The Function of the Christian Faith
and the Formation of the Largest Extended Family

By the grace of Christ, we have had one little boy in crisis set among us to teach us through his struggle about the function of faith in God in the formation of the largest extended family. When you and I as ministers, moved by compassion for one child in crisis, climb over the walls that separate us from those who can help us help that child, three very important works of the Spirit of God happen.

First, the power of God in Christ works through you and the family of the child in crisis to lower the importance of that nuclear family. It lowers the intensity and isolation of that family and that child. God sets the solitary isolated family into the context of the larger community of care. The importance of the family is lowered but not denigrated or obliterated, as in the case of totalitarian state control of the family. Instead, the bond of honor and dignity, freedom and responsibility of father and mother for each other and the child is sustained and ennobled. The intensity of that family is lowered, however, just as a heat vent lowers the heat in the family clothes dryer. Thus the family can do its rightful works of love toward one another without the buildup of rage, possessiveness, and violent abuse.

In the second place, as the child grows into maturity the ethical teachings of Jesus come into action to provide a safe ethical structure for the child's aggressions and sexuality. The extended family does more "in the field" demonstration of the ethical heart of the gospel than we dare expect. The aggressions of a child are seen best on the playground with neighborhood peers and the parenting patterns of other parents. The processes of love, courtship, and marriage take the values of two sets of ancestors and blend them into a new nuclear family. When families of widowed and divorced parents blend, a "suprasystem" of at least four and sometimes six family traditions comes into being. The remarried family with two sets of children from two other marriages tests the mettle of character. The church in turn, with us pastors and our associates as coaches, can actualize their learning of the ethical teaching of the gospel by forming life support groups of parents and children within the life of the church. Without the moorings of ethical guidelines for treatment of one another, the chaos that ensues makes casualties of the children. The younger they are, the more at risk they seem to be.

Two vignettes illustrate the power of the extended family of caregivers to heal, sustain, and communicate the whole counsel of God in Jesus Christ. In both cases, the church and its ministry was their main source of good news in a world of rage and fear.

An eleven-year-old girl called her pastor and said that her mother and father were in a fistfight. Could he talk with them on the phone if she could get them to do so? The pastor and the parents consented to her appeal. He asked their permission to visit them. By the time he got there, they had made peace with each other and were very contrite. They wanted to confess this in church (they were not members although their daughter was). The pastor said this would be possible, but they needed first to get some professional help to prevent later outbursts of rage and losses of control. They agreed and the pastor arranged an appointment for both of them with an internist. It was discovered on diagnosis that the father not only had sudden rages but also whole days of amnesia and occasional seizures. These symptoms were caused by the effects of a chemical cleaner he used all day in his work. Therapy and preventive measures, including a job change, followed. The rages and the amnesia were eliminated and the seizures controlled by medication. Several weeks of peace were celebrated by their profession of faith and baptism.

A ten-year-old had the habit of running away from home when she came to an impasse with her stepmother. The stepmother in turn did not want her to return. Each time the child ran away, she went either to the church or to a friend's house and called the minister of youth. The minister of youth made visits to the home and persuaded the whole family to go to a therapist. The stepmother felt at the outset that the daughter was demon possessed. A pastoral counselor dealt with this concern and was able to take some of the religious "curse" off the child. A long process of therapy with many crises has followed. The family has stayed together, learned more about handling their angers, and with one voice say that the church is their refuge, God is their strength, and without the church and God's patient care they could not make it.

Finally, the Christian gospel we communicate to families with children in crisis gives them access to the largest possible family of humankind. Strange people with even stranger skills of caring become neighbors in the deepest sense of the word. Their God no longer remains too small; nothing less than a God after whom every family on earth and in heaven is named will suffice. In God we are given access to the truly extended family of the father and mother of two little boys, ages five and two. As ministers, we have the awesome and adventurous privilege of gently leading them into that expanded world of God's family that has no outer boundaries, only inner barriers. The love of God in Jesus Christ breaks every barrier down.

NOTES

1. Edwin H. Friedman, *Generation to Generation: Family Process in Church and Synagogue*, pp. 31–32.
2. Martin E. Marty, *Friendship* (Argus Communications, 1980), p. 61.

FURTHER READING

Friedman, Edwin H. *Generation to Generation: Family Process in Church and Synagogue.* New York: Guilford Press, 1985.
Wynn, J. C. *Family Therapy in Pastoral Ministry.* New York: Harper & Row, 1982.

18

Referral: When, Where, How
Charles R. Koch, Regina Andrews-Collette, and Virginia W. Hammond

You do not have to be a trained specialist to minister to children in crisis. The basic needs of children experiencing a crisis can be met by a caring, sensitive, alert pastor. Your presence and willingness to listen, your offer of adult friendship and understanding conversation, and your representation of faith, hope, and love, will all be of help to the children as they make their way through the maze of a crisis. Most will come through the experience unscathed.

It is a reality, however, that some of the children to whom you minister will get stuck in their crises and will need further professional help if they are to survive the experience emotionally. Choosing to minister to children in crisis calls for knowing when and how to refer the child and the family. You must know the referral sources in your geographical area. This chapter is a brief discussion of when and how to refer, plus a description of the persons to whom you might refer and the places that offer therapeutic services for children.

When to Refer

When you are in conversation with children, particularly those closer to the teen years, it is important to pay attention to the emotions they

Charles R. Koch is Clinical Assistant Professor, Division of Child Psychiatry, School of Medicine, University of Pennsylvania, Philadelphia, and Director, Child and Family Mental Health Component, Hall-Mercer Community Mental Health/Mental Retardation Center, Philadelphia.
Regina Andrews-Collette is Staff Therapist, Child and Family Outpatient Service, Hall-Mercer Community Mental Health/Mental Retardation Center, Philadelphia.
Virginia W. Hammond is Director, Child and Family Mental Health Services, Hall-Mercer Community Mental Health/Mental Retardation Center, Philadelphia.

express, the behaviors they imagine, and the actions they take. The following is a list of thoughts, behaviors, and actions that should elicit concern on your part. Any of the situations mentioned below probably call for referral, certainly for professional consultation.

Suicidal Thoughts

Suicidal thoughts per se will rarely, if ever, merit referral. Although suicide in the latency age group rarely occurs, suicidal thoughts are quite common. The mere presence of such thoughts does not predict suicidal behavior. Indeed, the minister can see this as a measure of the trust the child places in the relationship; it provides an excellent opportunity to explore this sensitive area with the child. Once satisfied that both are speaking of thoughts only, the minister is in a sound position to reassure the child. "All boys and girls have felt this way at some time in their lives; indeed, grown-ups have these troublesome thoughts also." One may continue, "These thoughts and ideas tell us we are feeling 'really' bad. Talking about what makes you feel so bad will help you to feel much better."

Suicide Threats and Attempts

Suicidal threats are the most worrisome to the minister. These assessments are risky and are best left to the professionals. Fortunately, they rarely occur and, when they do, are usually in the context of severe chronic family dysfunction, which is usually known to the minister. The child's parents ought to be informed and impressed with the seriousness of their child's despair. If there are no parents available, the minister should help the child to get an evaluation at a community mental health facility. Suicide prevention hotlines are a resource in many areas.

Suicide attempts are medical and psychiatric emergencies and must be assessed in a setting where medical intervention is readily available. This is typically in the emergency department of most hospitals. One must assess all *attempts* as serious, no matter how naive. Aspirin and other medicines found in all households can be lethal in large doses. Minor scratches from razor blades are as serious as the ingestions and must be treated similarly.

Homicidal Thoughts

Homicidal thoughts may represent only the expression of intense anger and do not predict homicidal behaviors. If these thoughts are expressed in the first meeting with the child, however, and you do not know the child well enough to make an assessment about his or her capacity for violence, the child should be referred to the community mental health facility. Should there be homicidal thoughts in a child whom the minister knows well, they should be assessed in much the same manner as suicidal thoughts are assessed.

Homicidal Threats

Homicidal threats must be assessed by a mental health professional at the nearest mental health center on an urgent basis. The child's parents must be notified of the seriousness of the problem and must be prepared to take part in the evaluation. In some states, threats may be enough for the mental health facility to commit the person for involuntary psychiatric examination, possibly hospitalization.

Consequences of Sexual Acting Out

This is a difficult category of complication for those who minister to children. It is included, however, because venereal diseases, and even pregnancy, can occur in ten- to twelve-year-old children. (We have seen venereal disease in a six-year-old boy contracted from a much older sister.) When the counselor suspects that a venereal disease may be present, the pediatrician is the professional to whom referral should be made. Different states have various laws about the pediatrician's legal status in the treatment of minor children for infectious diseases. Some states may require that the parents be notified.

Intoxications

It may sound strange to indicate intoxications among the reasons for referral when one is dealing with latency-age children, but it is not. The incidence of drug abuse among this population has increased remarkably in the past decade. The problem is further complicated by the fact that these children may have been supplied by older children (or pushers) and may not know what the substance is.

Suffice it to say that any intoxication must be referred for medical evaluation at the emergency room of a hospital. Laboratory testing can identify most drugs in urine or blood serum in a matter of hours. Alcohol remains the most common drug abused by children (and adolescents), but other psychoactive substances are increasingly being abused by this age group.

Mental Illness

Depression is the most common mental illness found in this age group. Schizophrenic disorders are rare. The depressive syndromes in children do not necessarily mimic those seen in adults. The depression may manifest itself in hyperactive, behavioral, or conduct disorders. Anorexia, insomnia, and early morning awakening are frequent symptoms of depression in adults but are rarely seen in children. The depressions of childhood are sustained over weeks and even months. Sadness for a period of hours or even an entire day may be a reaction to specific events. In and of itself, such sadness is not an indication for referral. However, a depression of several weeks' duration would suggest that consultation is indicated. Suicidal attempts would merit referral as previously described.

How to Prepare the Child and Family for Mental Health Referral

Often the decision to refer concludes a difficult and agonizing process for both the minister and the family. Questions about one's competence and skills may surface, as well as concerns about the abilities of the other professionals to handle effectively the problem at hand. First, it is very important to acknowledge the existence of these feelings and, second, to accept the fact that no failure is inherent or implied in acknowledging that the child is in need of a different intervention and should be referred to a mental health practitioner in the community. Moreover, such a decision to refer does not denote defeat or failure but reflects professionalism, personal maturity, and self-knowledge. To paraphrase a sage of yesteryear, "When in doubt, seek guidance"—consult the expert.

A prudent and resourceful minister must be able to recognize and heed the signs that a professional intervention is necessary. Some of the indications that referral may be necessary are (1) no significant progress within a reasonable length of time, (2) emotional problems requiring medical attention, and (3) strong personal feelings (anger, blame, inadequacy) overwhelming the minister concerning the child or parent.

Once the decision to refer has been made, both child and parents need to be prepared to understand and accept the referral. The goal at this stage is to find a point of common agreement with the parents as a way to help the family accept the need for the recommended course of action. In this phase the minister will also need to help the parent resolve guilt feelings relative to the problem. Once these basic issues have been attended to, supporting or shepherding the parent through the implementation stage can be addressed. This process is facilitated when a thorough explanation ıs provided to the parents, to include:

Assessment of the situation and the child's specific mental health needs
Description of the parents' options concerning appropriate services, providers, and probable cost
The minister's investment in, and support of, a successful resolution to the problem
Guidelines for the implementation of the referral process
Mechanisms for follow-up contact

The realities involved in working with children and adults make one acutely aware of the need to distinguish between acute and chronic psychological problems. Some situations require immediate attention and intervention, while other conditions or situations are not immediately life threatening and would not be adversely affected by the wait involved in the typical referral process.

An effective referral process provides not only the rationale for the recommendation but also relevant information about the provider. The mental health needs of the latency-age child could be attended by several practitioners in the field of child psychiatry.

It is usually helpful to the parents and child if they are provided with specific information regarding the professional to whom they are being referred. For example, it is not difficult to detect parental anxiety in such questions as "How long will it take? Will they say it's our fault? Isn't therapy very expensive? Who will see our record?" Specific information can do much to alleviate and abate these anxieties.

Often, parents are concerned that their children's behavioral or emotional maladjustment is a reflection of their own parental inadequacies. It is the role of the person who engages the parent to explain that there are many parents who feel the same way. However, the important thing to do at this point is help the parent accept a referral to one of the agencies that deal with children's problems in order to begin the intake assessment and remediation process.

Resources

Mental Health Professionals

It is important that the pastor know the available resources for referral. A variety of professional persons work with children in crisis. Information regarding these various professional services can be obtained from pediatricians, medical societies, mental health or child guidance clinics, psychological associations, psychology departments of large colleges or universities, or the directories for a particular type of disability (such as the National Association of Retarded Children and the Mental Health Associations in your area).

Psychiatric social worker. This social worker has additional psychiatric training at a master's or doctoral level and is trained in human behavior, human psychology, and the use of community resources.

Clinical psychologist. A clinical psychologist is trained in mental processes and human behavior and holds an advanced degree from an accredited graduate program in psychology. Clinical psychologists provide a wide breadth of services ranging from evaluation to therapy in a variety of settings. Some states require licensing.

School psychologist. A school psychologist is specially trained in the area of identifying and remedying educational, learning, and emotional problems in children.

Child psychiatrist. A child psychiatrist is a licensed physician who is additionally trained in the area of psychiatric disorders of adults and children and treats emotional disorders in a mental health setting or in private practice. He or she is able to diagnose and treat mental illnesses and emotional disorders and may prescribe medication.

Family therapist. These individuals are trained to treat mental disturbances within the context of the family system. Their goal for intervention is to modify and improve the functioning of the family system as well as the identified individual.

Mental health specialist. A mental health provider with training in mental processes and human behaviors, and with a degree usually at a bachelor's or certificate level, is called a mental health specialist.

Pediatrician. This is a licensed physician additionally trained in the treatment of medical illnesses of children. Pediatricians are also trained in normal and abnormal growth and development of children.

Psychiatric nurse. A trained and licensed RN with specialized training in the care and treatment of psychiatric conditions is called a psychiatric nurse.

Pastoral counselor. A pastoral counselor is a clergyperson trained in theology, personality theory, intrapsychic processes, counseling, and therapeutic techniques.

Programs and Institutions

The programs and institutions in which these mental health professionals work are also programs and places to which either you or the mental health professional may refer a family.

Pastoral counseling centers. These centers provide outpatient services for individuals and families. They usually have a variety of mental health professionals on the staff, some of whom are especially trained to work with children.

Inpatient psychiatric units. These are short-term facilities, available usually to children from ages three to eight. Children are evaluated for a period of approximately thirty days. Referrals for this type of program usually involve these criteria: severe emotional disturbance, severe behavioral disorder, victim of child abuse, unmanageable at home, fire setter, or otherwise dangerous to themselves or others.

Long-term psychiatric hospitals. For stays of more than thirty days (maybe several years), referrals are made, usually after the child has been evaluated in a short-term unit and recommendations are made for certain structures that provide psychiatric intervention in a therapeutic milieu.

Residential programs. These facilities provide mental health services to children and are similar to long-term psychiatric units. Children at such a facility may use psychiatric services located on the grounds or may be seen at another setting. This program is usually for children whose emotional needs are not as severe as children in a long-term psychiatric unit (hospital).

Community mental health centers. Community mental health centers were established to provide outpatient mental health services to children and their families. Referrals can be made to children from birth to age eighteen. They may have different units: (1) a developmental disability unit, which serves that population which has been diagnosed as mentally retarded or developmentally delayed, and (2) a child and family unit, which provides outpatient therapy to children and their families. These therapies may include individual, play, group, and family psychotherapies. Psychiatric and psychological evaluations are also performed.

Occasionally, psychopharmacology is indicated and is combined with another treatment modality. Community mental health centers are mandated to provide therapeutic services to all individuals who live within their mental health service areas, subject to a financial interview.

Family service agencies. This type of agency provides counseling by social workers in family relationships and for individual social adjustment problems. Psychiatric consultation and psychological evaluations are performed here also.

Court system. The court (juvenile division) usually becomes involved when jurisdiction is needed over cases of delinquency, neglect, or dependency (if there is a contest of custody). The population targeted is eighteen years or under.

It is sometimes necessary to hold certain types of children in a detention or youth study facility while awaiting juvenile court hearings in delinquency cases.

Self-Help Groups

Al-Anon/Alateen. The mission of Al-Anon/Alateen is to offer a support system to relatives and families of individuals with an alcohol problem. Alateen is a support group for children and youth.

Child abuse prevention programs. The objective of this type of agency is to help parents understand and cope effectively with the pressures of parenthood. It seeks to prevent and treat all forms of child abuse by providing community education, counseling for individuals, families crisis intervention, family life education, and self-help groups. With regard to child abuse, it is extremely important that suspected abuse be reported even if it is not conclusively proved. It is not necessary for the person who is making the referral actually to have witnessed an incident. It may be a matter of reporting information that has been learned from the child or suspected by the counselor. Child abuse statutes in most states require that each complaint be investigated within 24 to 48 hours of the reported incident. It is best to err on the side of good judgment and make the referral.

FURTHER READING

Oglesby, William B., Jr. *Referral in Pastoral Counseling.* Rev. ed. Nashville: Abingdon Press, 1978.